The
Romance
of
Reunion

CIVIL WAR AMERICA

GARY W. GALLAGHER,

EDITOR

NORTHERNERS
AND THE SOUTH,
1865-1900

THE

ROMANCE

OF REUNION

NINA SILBER

THE UNIVERSITY OF NORTH CAROLINA PRESS   CHAPEL HILL & LONDON

The paper in this book meets the guidelines

for permanence and durability of the

Committee on Production Guidelines for

Book Longevity of the Council on Library

Resources.

Library of Congress Cataloging-in-

Publication Data

Silber, Nina.

The romance of reunion : northerners and

the South, 1865–1900 / by Nina Silber.

p. cm. — (Civil War America)

Includes bibliographical references and

index.

ISBN-13: 978-0-8078-2116-9 (cloth: alk. paper)

ISBN-10: 0-8078-2116-0 (cloth: alk. paper)

ISBN-13: 978-0-8078-4685-8 (pbk.: alk. paper)

ISBN-10: 0-8078-4685-6 (pbk.: alk. paper)

1. Reconstruction. 2. Sectionalism (United

States)—History—19th century.

3. Northeastern States—Civilization.

4. Southern States—Civilization—Public

opinion—History—19th century. 5. Public

opinion—Northeastern States—History—

19th century. I. Title. II. Series.

E668.S57 1994   93-18626

973.8—dc20   CIP

06 05 04 03 02   7 6 5 4 3

To my parents,

Irwin and Sylvia,

and to the memory of

Frances Hutchins

CONTENTS

ILLUSTRATIONS

ACKNOWLEDGMENTS

This manuscript, first in the form of a dissertation and then in its present incarnation, has been a touchstone in my life for several years. It has often been the focus of all my energy; it has occasionally been a distraction; it has frequently opened up intellectual horizons and new lines of communication. Most happily, it has brought me into contact with many people who, I believe, have enriched this work.

The ideas for this study first took shape during my graduate student years at the University of California at Berkeley. Here, several professors helped to awaken my curiosity about the mysteries of cultural history, southern history, and issues of race and gender, including Lawrence Levine, Barbara Christian, Mary Ryan, Carolyn Porter, and James Gregory. As my adviser on this project, Leon Litwack not only offered me his knowledge and expertise in southern history and the history of race relations but also communicated to me a method and approach for understanding history and the people who make it.

In many ways I may have learned the most from my fellow graduate students at Berkeley, a truly outstanding group of scholars whose goodwill never ceases to amaze me. I will always appreciate the advice and encouragement I received from Jeffrey Lena, Michael O'Malley, Elizabeth Reis, and Anita Tien. Thanks are also due to Steve Aron, who introduced me to the wonders of the thesaurus, and to Sharon Ullman, who ultimately impressed upon me the crucial importance of gender in all historical analysis. I am grateful to the History Department at the University of California at Berkeley for the fellowship support I received while working on my dissertation, and to the Western Association of Women Historians, who honored me with their graduate student fellowship in 1987.

In the summer of 1987 this manuscript, which was then only a glimmer of an idea, led me on a transcontinental journey from the fragrant eucalyptus groves and cappuccino dives of Berkeley to the muggy swamp that is Washington, D.C. Thanks to a Smithsonian Fellowship and the modern miracle of central air-conditioning, a dissertation finally took shape. In Washington I was again lucky to stumble upon an exceptionally warm and forthcoming group of scholars who, through weekly seminars, afternoon volleyball games, and Tuesday night revelries, made researching and writing extremely bearable. Nancy Bercaw, Pete Daniel, Christine Hoepfner, Karen Linn, and Mary Panzer all made a difference in terms of my work and my appreciation of the nuances of history.

As I began to present and polish my initial ideas in the form of papers and articles, I again came in contact with many generous scholars who gave me valuable insights and ideas about various parts of this manuscript. Henry Abelove, Edward Ayers, Gail Bederman, Anne Boylan, Catherine Clinton, Drew Faust, Gaines Foster, Richard Fox, Gary Kulik, and Jeffrey Sammons stand out in this group of supportive individuals. I am also grateful to the Boston University Humanities Foundation for the generous support I received which allowed me to complete this manuscript in the spring of 1992.

It has been a rare pleasure to work with the folks at the University of North Carolina Press. It would be hard to assemble a more helpful and considerate group of people. No young scholar could have a better editor, able to steer one through the mysteries of the publishing process with intelligence and compassion, than Lewis Bateman.

My husband, Louis Hutchins, whom I first met at the microfiche table in the Berkeley library, was not my toughest critic nor my sharpest editor, nor even my most proficient typist (although he did offer some tough criticisms and sharp editorial remarks). He was, however, my rock of support and gave me the confidence and encouragement which convinced me that I could see this project through to its conclusion.

In light of all this manuscript has taken me through, it is, perhaps, fitting that the final revision was sent to the Press only two weeks before my son, Benjamin Silber Hutchins, was born. In some strange and unexplainable way, he has actually lightened my load in these past hectic months. His joy has given my life and my work a new perspective.

I am sorry that my mother-in-law, Frances Hutchins, did not live to see this work completed. Her sparkling curiosity always challenged me; her deep and abiding compassion always warmed my soul. I dedicate this book, in part, to her memory.

I also dedicate this work to my parents, Irwin and Sylvia Silber. Early on, they instilled in me an intellectual curiosity and a commitment to understanding the social and cultural forces which have shaped the lives of ordinary people. I will always be grateful.

THE
ROMANCE
OF
REUNION

INTRODUCTION

"The war," proclaimed the New England author Charles Dudley Warner, twenty years after Appomattox, "is over in spirit as well as in deed." Modern readers might well be skeptical of Warner's excessive optimism, yet in the late nineteenth century such enthusiastic forecasts became something of a mind-numbing mantra in American society. One could find evidence in both North and South, among Civil War veterans, journalists, novelists, and countless other Americans, of an intensifying plea for sectional accord. On this occasion, Charles Warner's remarks were prompted by that writer's 1885 visit to the southern states and, more specifically, by his stop at the Cotton Exposition in New Orleans. Here, at this enormous showcase for the industrial opportunities of the New South and for feelings of sectional accord, Warner added his voice to the swelling refrain for harmonious reunion.[1]

Ten years later a group of southerners reversed the direction of Warner's travels, but not of his sentiments. A number of southern politicians, former soldiers, and business leaders traveled to Chicago in 1895 in order to attend the unveiling of a Confederate memorial. Dedicated to the Rebel prisoners of war who were buried in that city, the memorial and the event attracted a considerable amount of local and national attention and offered a pivotal symbolic moment for once again measuring the progress toward national unity. Even more, it became a moment when reunion prompted the possibility of patriotic reflection, when orators declared that America's greatness was revealed in this uniting of former enemies. "The scene presented here to-day," declared former Confederate and South Carolina politician Wade Hampton, "is one that could not be witnessed in any country but our own."[2]

On one level, of course, there is nothing all that remarkable in either Charles Warner's or Wade Hampton's pronouncements. Both, after all, were made in the context of celebratory events which sought to broadcast precisely these types of conciliatory statements. Yet, when one recalls the intensity of the sectional conflict and the four years of war that caused more loss of life and property than all previous American wars combined, it is noteworthy that, in only two decades since Robert E. Lee's surrender, the context for uttering these ideas had been created. It is also noteworthy just how little the remarks of Warner and Hampton tell us about actual events. Indeed, in both cases there is a subtext that is left unstated, for what both men were witnessing, to a great extent, was less an emotional bonding of northern and southern people and more a financial bonding between investors and business leaders in both regions. The New Orleans exhibition, like other world's fairs held in the South, was organized precisely as a vehicle for showing off southern economic potential to northern investors. The Chicago event, financed primarily by men like Philip Armour and Cyrus McCormick, offered a prime opportunity for Chicago business leaders to develop a commercial relationship with the South. But, in the climate of reconciliation that had emerged in the late nineteenth century, few chose to stress these types of crass, commercial links. Politicians, journalists, and even financial leaders usually raised the bridge of sentiment and emotion in elaborating on the ties that now bound the people of the sections together. They all, in effect, paid homage to a romantic and sentimental culture of conciliation that characterized the North-South relationship in the Gilded Age years.[3]

This book is about that conciliatory culture that blossomed in the late nineteenth century. More specifically, it is about the idea of reunion as it was imagined, and occasionally acted upon, mostly by northerners and especially by those of the middle and upper classes. This work gives particular emphasis to the metaphors and cultural images of reconciliation, and to northern images of the South, attempting to locate those images in the context of the political, social, and economic transformations that swept over American society in the Gilded Age. Consequently, it has less to say about the real-life South and more to say about the ideal and desired South. At the same time, it is not an examination of ethereal images and rarefied myths. Rather, this study works to understand those images as tangible products and powerful mechanisms in late-nineteenth-century culture, to see how the northern vision of reunion and of the South was both a reflection of and a factor in the political and social realities of the northern people. I have sought, in other words, to understand why a sentimental rubric took hold of the reunion process, indeed, within ten years of the war's conclusion, and to understand how and why that romantic framework shaped the thoughts and actions of a good number of Yankees while it was strenuously dismissed by others.

Surprisingly, there is little in the historical literature that speaks directly to the reconciliation question. Paul Buck offered the first, and in many ways the last, synthesized and scholarly consideration of postwar reunion over fifty years ago in his seminal study, *The Road to Reunion.* Since Buck's writing, numerous historians of the South have pondered the postwar posture of that region, thus drawing out one side of the reunion question. Like many, they have been fascinated by the experience of white southerners who were forced to come to terms with the extremely un-American experience of defeat, and by how that sense of defeat did or did not hinder their conciliatory feelings.[4]

In contrast, the northern view of the reunion process has received considerably less scrutiny. My own research interests have been prompted by a desire to round out the study of the reunion process, extending the consideration which scholars have given to the South to the northern side of the equation as well. Thus, whereas southern historians have focused their scholarship on the southern experience of defeat, I have tried to understand the northern experience of victory, specifically, how the northern people interpreted the significance of their triumph and how they came to terms with a victory that necessarily entailed the defeat of fellow Americans. Unlike Buck, who accepted all compromise as a sign of progress and emerging nationalism, my own objective has been to look for the meaning which northerners gave to their victory, to the idea of reconciliation, and, by extension, to the South. My goal, in part, has been to understand the crucial historical transformation in which, as some have said, "the North won the war, but the South won the peace."

In many ways, this has turned out to be a study about remembering, especially of how northerners remembered the Civil War and the southern past. Aside from reexamining the work of Buck, I have also turned to a number of scholars who have recently begun to consider the question of historical memory. These scholars have made the point that a historical study of memory should not emphasize the accuracy of individual recollections but should "explore how people together searched for common memories to meet present needs, how they first recognized such a memory and then agreed, disagreed, or negotiated over its meaning, and finally how they preserved and absorbed that meaning into their ongoing concerns." I have tried to understand northern memories of the Civil War in terms of what they tell us about the social and cultural realities of the northern people in late-nineteenth-century America, especially in terms of who did the negotiating and how that negotiation process unfolded.[5]

Yet any student of northern ideology in the late nineteenth century quickly realizes that forgetfulness, not memory, appears to be the dominant theme in the reunion culture. "The past is dead," explained the editor of the Trenton *State Gazette* in 1882. "Let us live in the present and act the part of men." Here, indeed, was a telling yet typical observation that was voiced by many northerners in the postwar years. Nonetheless, as scholars have noted, forgetfulness, just as much as memory, requires an analytical and contextual approach. Historian David Blight finds, for example, that black activist Frederick Douglass placed himself at the center of the national debate over Civil War amnesia and struggled courageously to make Americans remember the causes and the lessons of the Civil War while so much of the country had apparently embarked down the path of neglecting and forgetting. As Blight shows, the struggle over memory, or lack of it, greatly contributed to the northern relationship with the South and the entire process of reunion.[6]

Indeed, in many ways the late nineteenth century was one of those notorious "twilight zones," periods, as C. Vann Woodward has said, "between living memory and written history" which became "favorite breeding places of mythology." As the Civil War faded from the collective memory of Americans, a vast array of myths, especially about the South, seized the popular imagination. These were not, as David Thelen explains, "disembodied values," but rather "creations of people with real needs." Among white southerners the myths were inextricably linked with the psychological repercussions of defeat. In the post–Civil War period, former Confederates learned to accept their loss by turning the old South into a land of idyllic plantation settings, heroic men, and elegant women. They transformed the system of slavery into a happy and mutually beneficial arrangement which offered enjoyment and contentment to all of its participants. In short, an army of southern novelists, journalists, and dramatists assumed command of a far-reaching campaign which resuscitated many antebellum stereotypes and deployed a romantic image of the white and wealthy antebellum South throughout the cultural landscape. In creating this "lost cause" ideology, they provided white southerners with an emotional vehicle that had profound religious, psychological, and social functions—functions that were especially suited for a society that suffered from defeat, humiliation, and internal dissension.[7]

Northerners, too, were caught up in the creation of this regional iconography in the post–Civil War period and used this romanticized image to reinforce the mawkish and sentimental view of reunion. But it would be misleading to suggest that northerners completely accepted the South's lost cause ideology. A number of different northern constituencies—veterans, blacks, former abolitionists—opposed the "forget and forgive" mentality and continued to keep questions of black oppression and the South's infringement of civil and political rights at the forefront of their concerns. Even those who joined the reunion bandwagon and accepted the myths did so with certain qualifications. In short, northerners used the southern image not in the way that southerners did, but to soothe their own specific set of social and psychological needs.

Not unlike the southern proponents of the New South revolution described by C. Vann Woodward, northerners, too, often possessed a "divided mind" about building up a new South while longing for the old. Northern elites longed to travel to the old, patriarchal retreats of the plantation class even as they effaced the plantation landscape with the new railroads and factories of the industrial society. Of course, as Woodward has pointed out, the New South movement failed to make the complete and total transformation that its advocates had promised. Consequently, throughout the late nineteenth century, northerners could still see just enough of that old southern lifestyle—the ruins of old plantation estates, the gray-haired veterans of the Confederate army, and the old-time servants who had lived in the days "befo' the wah"—to reflect mournfully on its passing away. In this regard, the ambivalence of southern society was perfectly suited to the ambivalence of the northern mind-set. Confronted with the haunting specters of class conflict, ethnic strife, and alienation that their own industrialized society had produced, many northerners remained unconvinced about the benefits of industrial progress and about obliterating whatever remained of the old southern legacy; in many ways, they were unconvinced as to the unqualified benefits of the Union victory.

Sectional union thus could offer a bridge for northern ambivalence, between a modern and premodern world.[8]

When northerners looked at the South in the postwar years, they cultivated specific types of images and promoted a specific version of reunion that was best suited to Yankee needs. They transformed their anger against the southern aristocracy into feelings of pity and respect, ultimately sentimentalizing the unhurried and leisurely lifestyles of the planter class. Moreover, in light of the social turbulence of the Gilded Age, northerners were not unmindful of the type of class and racial authority which southern planters had apparently exercised over their subordinates; they learned to respect the southern elite for what they saw as an authoritative yet harmonious relationship with their slaves. Not surprisingly, northerners also replaced their wartime concerns for southern blacks with a less political and more sentimental interest in the African American as a picturesque element on the southern landscape or as a pathetic and entertaining performer. Northerners eventually cast southern blacks outside their reunion framework altogether, portraying them as strangers and as foreigners, as a people who were best placed under the supervision of those southern whites who knew them best.

Nor were class and race the only considerations in the North's reunion ideology. In the symbolic and iconographic representations of reconciliation, gender served as a central metaphor which shaped northern society's understanding of the relations between the sections in the postwar period. Indeed, it has become almost commonplace to talk of the northern "rape of the South" during the Civil War, of how the northern army ravaged and ruined that willful feminine entity of Dixie. In fact, the South's feminine identity appeared and reappeared in many different contexts—in the antagonistic discourse of the immediate postwar years as well as in the softer and more sentimental rhetoric of reconciliation. In the 1860s, for example, northerners connected the very essence of the Confederacy with southern women and assaulted the spiteful southern woman as the ultimate object of their anger and retribution. By the 1870s, however, the southern female had become the tempestuous and romantic belle, the object of the northern man's desires, and, ultimately, the feminine partner in a symbolic marital alliance which became the principal representation of sectional reunion. This image of marriage between northern men and southern women stood at the foundation of the late-nineteenth-century culture of conciliation and became a symbol which defined and justified the northern view of the power relations in the reunified nation.

Gender, in other words, was not just another factor in the reunion ideology. Images of gender have frequently appeared in various forms of political discourse, and they have been, according to historian Joan Scott, "a primary way of signifying relationships of power." Because of its association with "natural" and immutable functions, gender has offered a potent metaphor for legitimizing political relationships, for making power arrangements seem basic and fundamental. Moreover, notions about gender have also frequently served as a gauge for such subjective concepts as "culture" and "civilization," as a way to measure one's own and one's enemy's society. Thus, as several scholars have noted, gender not only emerged in the postwar dialogue between the sections, it also figured prominently in the pre–Civil War discourse as well. Because women were assumed to be the moral caretakers of the age, southern female characters in antebellum fiction often embodied the antimaterialist sensibilities of the region and the prewar era. But in other contexts, especially as the sectional dialogue became increasingly bitter, the feminine metaphor was not always meant to be so flattering. Indeed, northern antislavery literature frequently cast the South in the role of "other," transforming the entire region into a land of women and blacks. Abolitionist discourse isolated the South through a variety of metaphors which indicted all southerners, whether white or black, male or female, as weak, feminine, and out of control. Finally, some scholars have suggested that the feminine image of the South loomed large not only in abolitionist ideology but also in the political thinking of antebellum southerners. Relying on female iconography to suggest powerlessness and alienation, southerners used the image to underscore their increasing marginalization from the political process.[9]

Yet, when abolitionists compared the antebellum South to a brothel or when postwar cartoonists lampooned the spiteful attitude of plantation belles, they had not simply chosen a common and convenient metaphor. Rather, in shaping their discourse in this way, they had drawn on the very different notions of gender which characterized the North and the South in the mid-nineteenth century. The symbolic, regional representations of gender reflected the contrasting sexual conventions of the North and the South, conventions which were rooted in distinctive antebellum social structures. In her recent study of antebellum southern womanhood, Elizabeth Fox-Genovese explains how the divergent social systems of the antebellum North and South gave rise to distinctive views of men's and women's roles. Caught in an expanding industrial economy, northern middle-class society participated in the formation of a system which increasingly separated work and home and made a corresponding split between men's and women's spheres. The southern plantation economy, in contrast, never made such sharp distinctions and never relegated southern women to their own, autonomous sphere. Instead, elite southern white men ruled supreme over house and field, over black men and women as well as white women. Because the southern system rested on the labor of slaves, southern gender conventions, whether for upper-class men or for upper-class women, did not demand the commitment to labor which infused the northern code of economic responsibility in both the home and the workplace. Southern white women, explains Fox-Genovese, "to be ladies, had to have servants."[10]

And, according to historian Bertram Wyatt-Brown, southern white men, to be men, needed not only slaves but also their code of honor. As lords and masters of all that they surveyed, as the protectors of women and as the possessors of slaves, southern white men relied on a code which counseled both chivalry and violence, both deferential respect to white womanhood and the forceful passions and energies that shaped their social power. They were men who constantly had to demonstrate their superior strength and force to the surrounding community, whether through dueling, drinking, or gambling. Northern middle-class men, in contrast, lived in what Edward Ayers has called a "culture of dignity," in which institutions figured more prominently than notions of honor and community. These men abhorred many of the vices of southern men and committed themselves to individual self-improvement, to economic responsibility, and, most of all, to self-control. Certainly, this is not to suggest that all northerners and southerners always adhered to these distinct conventions. Still, as many northerners and southerners understood their positions on the eve of the Civil War, the two societies rested on two completely different patterns of behavior and codes of morality, all of which was filtered through opposing forms of gender behavior.[11]

During the 1850s and 1860s northerners berated southern manhood and southern womanhood from the standpoint of these opposing notions of gender. Northern antislavery advocates assaulted the "brute force" and "pugnaciousness" of southern men, indicting them for their worship of seemingly "masculine," but extremely distasteful, vices. They also attacked white southern men and women for their apparent disregard for any and every form of honorable labor, for their devotion to a system which rested on idleness and slothfulness. This awareness of contrasting gender conventions continued to influence northerners in their choice of metaphors in the postwar period. During the 1860s their depiction of the southern woman as the Union's prime enemy offered not only a metaphoric assault on the Confederacy, but also an explicit condemnation of southern womanhood, a critique of the weak moral fiber and poor work habits northerners connected to the southern female. At the same time, northerners demonstrated their opposition to southern manliness through their images of an emasculated and feminized Jefferson Davis and, later, through their depictions of weak and effeminate southern men who were mired in their impotent devotion to the lost cause. Amidst the heat of the postwar sectional debate, such metaphors encapsulated both northerners' overall critique of the South and their specific condemnation of the unrestrained vices and habits associated with the southern aristocracy.

Northerners gradually transformed their understanding of southern gender in the context of the emerging reunion culture and developed new metaphors which reflected their changing views of the South and which were, once again, indicative of the social tensions and anxieties that pervaded northern society in the Gilded Age. In effect, northerners began to view the South, and the reunion process more generally, from the perspective of Victorian nostalgia, from a standpoint of growing concern regarding their own society's declining Victorian standards. Indeed, in the 1880s and 1890s middle-class northerners constantly fretted over the waning of proper gender etiquette, voicing their fear that men had lost the independence and authority that had previously been a hallmark of their manhood and that women had moved beyond their proper feminine "sphere." To many, previous gender distinctions had apparently collapsed as men and women seemed no longer to occupy their separate roles and spaces. Northerners also expressed concern over an apparent loss of sexual mores, noting a tendency toward a more open and public display of sexuality, especially among the less well-to-do. Ultimately, Yankees sought to re-create the Victorian ideal through the reconciliation process. Their image of the South conformed to their image of the idealized feminine sphere; in northern eyes, the South became a region of refined domestic comfort, and the union of North and South restored the sense of domestic harmony that northern society no longer possessed. Southern women, who seemed to have discovered the joys of domesticity precisely when northern women had grown weary of them, became the feminine ideal of many northern men. Finally, the specific pairing of a Yankee husband with a southern wife offered the northern man a symbolic vehicle for reasserting authority, for recapturing the sense of manly accomplishment which the Union soldier or the independent businessman had once known. He was once again victorious, not only over the South, but also over womankind.[12]

This gendered view of reunion and of the South had several noteworthy ramifications. On one level, it offered a comfortable and familiar rubric, emphasizing as it did traditional notions of domestic harmony, through which northerners could reunite with former enemies. Yet it was a rubric which clearly placed the South in the position of junior partner, as a submissive woman who had been conquered by northern will. Northerners enshrined the image of their victory in this metaphor, using it to reflect the political and economic leverage they hoped to exercise over Dixie. Even as they relinquished some of their economic and political control, they continued to pay homage to this gendered metaphor of power. But while it clearly implied a relationship of power, this sentimental image of marriage and romance also provided a vehicle through which northerners could depoliticize the sectional relationship. Many apparently felt that the emotional attachment of northerners and southerners was of much greater importance than sectional politics; in this way, it became that much easier to forget the history and the lessons of the Civil War. It also became easier to overlook the South's present-day problems, especially the poverty of many southern whites and the social and economic oppression suffered by southern blacks. These, in effect, became lesser concerns which the South, as junior partner, had won the right to manage on its own.

The focus on gender and on gendered metaphors has allowed me to understand the intersection of culture and politics, to see cultural images in terms of existing power relations and as a force encouraging certain types of political thinking. My study, then, is concerned with the political dimensions of the reunion culture, an objective which has led me to examine a wide variety of sources which fit both conventional and nonconventional definitions of "culture." On the traditional side, this study considers popular magazines, novels, songs, travel accounts, and theater productions of the late nineteenth century, paying close attention to the recurrent symbols of the reunion culture. Other sources examined might be considered, in a strict and narrow interpretation, "political." These include the political rituals of the reunion process, such as Memorial Day exercises and veterans' gatherings, as well as the ideas and actions of late-nineteenth-century reformers and activists, such as Populists and temperance leaders, all of whom were conscious of playing up some version of the reunion motif. I have also tried, especially in terms of the latter, to take a fairly broad view of "northern" society, looking at more than just a handful of northeastern intellectuals. At various points, I have included the observations of communities and individuals from the Northeast, the Mid-Atlantic, and the Midwest.

One additional, and in some ways obvious, point has become clear from this type of survey: not all northerners held similar views of the South or shared a similar preoccupation with reconciliation. Although I refer to the language and culture of "northerners" throughout this study, many of my conclusions apply primarily to the more well-to-do northerners, to the middle- and upper-class readers of the major magazines of the period and to a similar class who toured the South or who attended the Civil War dramas of the late nineteenth century. With respect to some of the ideas presented, my conclusions apply even more specifically to middle- and upper-class northern men. I have found that these individuals and their cultural offerings increasingly set the dominant tone on the reunion question, that their voices gradually drowned out the protests and alternative visions offered by other groups. Certainly, as late as the 1890s, one could hear the voices of Grand Army of the Republic members who objected to a bonding with former enemies, at least the type of bonding that might deny the Union veteran the chance to reflect on his manly wartime accomplishments. Or one could hear the voices of the Woman's Christian Temperance Union members who understood reunion not in terms of marital ties but as a moral cohesion of sisters across the Mason-Dixon line. Nonetheless, by the time of the Spanish-American War few alternative or dissenting voices could be heard. Concerns about masculinity and virility made the WCTU perspective seem irrelevant, while fears of economic dependence made the GAR man seem little more than a pension-grubber or political charlatan.

Thus, as the twentieth century began, northerners revealed a new respect for the South as an equal and willing partner in imperialist expansion. In this context, most northerners found themselves paying homage to a new and invigorated image of southern white manhood—to the manly, even patriotic, veterans of the Confederacy as well as the heroic veterans of the most recent war with Spain. Novelists likewise paid tribute to southern white men and gave American culture a new set of regional icons. Perhaps none was more enduring than the one personified in Owen Wister's hugely successful novel of the early twentieth century, *The Virginian*. In the form of this virile and chivalrous cowboy, gender once again entered the cultural debate and helped to shape a new relationship between the sections. One has only to reflect on more recent images— Scarlett O'Hara and Ashley Wilkes, Jezebel, even Elvis Presley—to realize that American culture would shape and reshape that relationship over and over again.[13]

1

INTEMPERATE MEN, SPITEFUL WOMEN, AND JEFFERSON DAVIS

NORTHERN VIEWS OF THE DEFEATED SOUTH

In the early morning hours of April 10, 1865, George Templeton Strong, a meticulous diarist of the mid-nineteenth century, was sleeping soundly in his comfortable Manhattan home. But, as Strong soon discovered, this was not to be a morning for sleeping late. The prominent New York lawyer's repose was interrupted by "a series of vehement pulls at the front door bell" when a friend came by "to announce the surrender and that the rebel army of the Peninsula, Antietam, Fredericksburg, Chancellorsville, the Wilderness, Spotsylvania Court House, and other battles, has ceased to exist." In a prophetic, but somewhat overly optimistic, afterthought, Strong reflected on the previous day's events at Appomattox, observing that "it can bother and perplex none but historians henceforth forever."[1]

The news of Robert E. Lee's surrender to Ulysses S. Grant shattered the sleep of countless residents of the northern states on that morning of April 10. Charlotte Holbrooke, another New Yorker, was visiting family in Washington, D.C., when word of the Union victory arrived. "The first thing we heard of Lee's surrender," she wrote in a letter to her father, "was just before daylight yesterday when we were waked up by the thunder of the cannon just behind the house. We knew in a minute [what] the news was and rejoiced accordingly."[2]

Throughout the North on April 10, 1865, and for the next few days thereafter, millions shared Strong's and Holbrooke's optimistic rejoicing. While some of the Confederate armies continued to do battle after Appomattox, Lee's defeat occasioned one of the most joyous and enthusiastic celebrations many Americans had ever experienced. An estimated 100,000 people paraded through the streets of Chicago in celebration of the Union victory, and in cities and villages throughout the North there were festive processions, musical offerings, impromptu speech-making, and candlelight illuminations.[3]

Perhaps nowhere was the excitement more keenly felt than amongst the Union soldiers in the South. Edward Hamilton, the chaplain of the 7th Regiment of the New Jersey Volunteers found himself on the road to Lynchburg when word of the surrender arrived. "There was a scene of wild confusion & delight," Hamilton recalled. "The men fired off their pieces with blank cartridges. Hats were thrown into the air. A battery kept firing a long salute." As another soldier recalled, the scene at Appomattox itself was wildly euphoric and prompted a joint celebration of the blue and the gray. "It was hard to tell which side cheered the loudest, Rebs or Yanks. We were soon all mixed up, shaking hands, giving the johnnies grub & coffee & getting tobacco. It seemed more like meeting of dear old friends after long absence than of men ready to kill or be killed a few hours previously."[4]

Apparently, as this account suggested, the joy of the surrender encouraged some northerners, stay-at-homes as well as soldiers, to view their former enemies with a spirit of fraternity and goodwill. "It is natural," commented the Boston *Post*, "that this final success should . . . beget expressions of true magnanimity and forgiveness toward the people of the rebellious states, which, three or six months ago, would have been thought impossible. It is but a token of that solid and lasting reunion which we have always insisted was so easy of accomplishment, if proposed in the right spirit." Certainly some of the first proponents of reunion were those who had never been ardent supporters of the war in the first place, northern Democrats and "Copperheads" who objected to the Republican party's war policy. Yet even the most strident Unionists voiced sentiments of sympathy and forgiveness in the aftermath of Appomattox. In their eyes, a proper attitude toward the Union victory would reveal the righteousness of their cause and the purity of their devotion. As many explained it, nothing short of heartfelt generosity could be expected of a God-fearing and liberty-loving people. "We should be unworthy of (that) liberty entrusted to our care," declared the North's most famous clergy-man, Henry Ward Beecher, "if, on such a day as this, we sullied our hearts by feelings of aimless vengeance."[5]

Northerners used this moment of the surrender to draw conclusions about the war's meaning and to elaborate on the lessons which they hoped Americans would draw from the experience. For men like Beecher, the lesson was of righteousness and forgiveness. For northern workers, Ap-pomattox offered an occasion to reflect on the dignity of human toil, to urge that the Union struggle for free labor be extended to all who worked. Hence the question of the hour was not reunion or forgiveness, but the commitment to free labor for all—black and white, northern and south-ern. Boston's labor newspaper, while rejoicing at the news of Lee's sur-render, also introduced a note of caution. "It is in vain that all this struggle has been experienced, if human rights and human brotherhood are not henceforth better recognized than ever before."[6]

In a few quarters, a decidedly antireunion posture was adopted. North-ern newspapers which leaned toward a Radical Republican position pre-ferred to prolong the spirit of animosity, choosing this time to remind their readers of the traitorous deeds of the Confederacy. Others expressed their outrage at the slightest gesture of conciliation, believing that this would only give ammunition to a class of still unrepentant rebels. Indiana Radical Republican George Julian strongly objected to Beecher's tone of forgive-ness, suspecting that few could feel truly benevolent at this moment. "This fake magnanimity," Julian reflected, "is to be our ruin after all. . . . The rebel officers in Richmond are strutting round the streets in full uniform looking as impudent as may be."[7]

Julian's remarks pointed to the depth of bitterness and anger that, for many, would not disappear simply with the cessation of the military con-flict. Doubts surfaced in the early days after Appomattox regarding the Confederate leadership's willingness to accept defeat. Nonetheless, the actual conclusion of the war prompted many to adopt a hopeful outlook toward the future and the improved economic and political relations that would follow. Hence, while many were still unwilling to trust the rebels, they were glad that the Union leaders had decisively gained the upper hand and could choose to set a tone of forgiveness. George Templeton

Strong, like many others, had initially been apprehensive about Grant's liberal terms of surrender with Lee and his men. Later, however, he approved of the Union leader's decision to send the Confederate soldiers home, as they "will be a fountain of cold water on whatever pugnacity and chivalry may yet survive" in their own communities.[8]

Any bold expressions of reconciliation or more subtle subsiding of bitterness were shattered on the night of April 14. With the news of Appomattox only five days old, northerners awoke on April 15 to the news of President Lincoln's assassination and the attempted assassination of Secretary of State William Seward. Reeling from the heights of joy to the depths of grief, they struggled to comprehend this first assassination of an American president. Those who lived far from any sources of communication learned of the joyful and the sorrowful all at once. Elizabeth Botume, a northerner living in Beaufort, South Carolina, and teaching school to freed slaves, gave her version of this onslaught of events. "The news of this surrender," she recalled, "and the disbanding of Lee's army, and the breaking up of the Confederacy, came with that of the death of President Lincoln. But the joy of the final victory was swallowed up in the grief of this last disaster." This sudden upheaval inspired many to see a divinely orchestrated plan at work. The assassination confirmed deeply held religious sensibilities and an apocalyptic vision of the Civil War. Northern writer Rebecca Harding Davis believed that during this final month of the war "God was dealing with us as with his chosen people of old—by such great visible judgements that we almost heard his voice and saw his arm." And others, like Davis, relied on their religious faith to comprehend the chaos of the war's concluding moments. "The wisdom of Heaven," explained the Boston *Post*, "is certainly in it all. We cannot see it now, but faith will reveal it to us as we advance."[9]

Despite an abiding trust in God, many experienced this sudden change of circumstances with a sense of panic and uncertainty. Charlotte Holbrooke, still in Washington during the assassination and its aftermath, wrote to her brother two days after Lincoln's death, describing how people gathered spontaneously to stay posted on the news, "for we did not know but that the entire government was to be attacked." And Rachel Cormany, a resident of Chambersburg, Pennsylvania, recorded in her diary a similar sense of horror and anxiety. "What does it all mean," she wrote on the day after the assassination. "Is anarchy and destruction coming upon us?"[10]

Behind the panic of northerners like Holbrooke and Cormany lay a terrifying suspicion that perhaps the Confederates were not prepared to surrender after all. Secretary of War Stanton, indicating his belief in a Confederate conspiracy behind Booth's assault, merely voiced the apprehensions of many in the northern states. Northern resentment of haughty Confederate leaders and the "chivalric" southern aristocracy burst forth wildly and uncontrollably as newspapers, politicians, and other speakers sought to suppress even the dimmest expressions of mercy. The clergy struck an early chord against harmonious reconciliation between the sections. "What shall we say of the hellish power that aimed the blow?" proclaimed Reverend William Studley of Boston in his Easter Sunday sermon, two days after Lincoln's assassination. "We thought we had already seen the depths of barbarism and savagery of which the slave-power is capable." Sidney George Fisher, a scion of Philadelphia society, succinctly captured the altered emotions of April 15. "The national exultation at the prospects of peace & union," he noted, "has been suddenly converted into alarm & grief."[11]

The North concentrated its postassassination venom on the leaders of the Confederacy, the same men who had supposedly orchestrated the "slave power conspiracy" of the prewar years and who had foisted the secession movement on the rest of the South. Despite the fact that four years of war had shown that numerous white southerners had a more than superficial commitment to the Confederacy, many northerners emerged from the war clinging to the belief that the real enemies were not the common people of the South, not the average soldiers, but primarily the slaveholding leadership. Even after the assassination, various soldiers and civilians began to show an inclination to look upon the "misguided" Confederate soldiers with some sympathy and forgiveness. Very few, however, were willing to extend any consideration to the leaders, believing them most responsible for fomenting war and for keeping the mass of southerners in ignorance. The white southern masses may have joined in the rebellion, but, as many northerners saw it, they were partially excused out of their own blindness and stupidity, which had been cultivated over years of living under a tyrannical, slaveholding aristocracy. According to *Harper's Weekly*, "The Southern people, who had grown up in ignorance and prejudice, the extent of which we can hardly comprehend, and who have been deluded into the active support of so enormous a conspiracy, have been deluded because their minds were prepared for delusion." Now, in this final ignominious act, the southern leaders once again received the blame. "It is generally believed," wrote Union soldier Charles Lynch, "there was a conspiracy among the leaders of the rebellion to murder Mr. Lincoln, so the cry is that the leaders must be punished." The New York *Tribune*, while not convinced that Confederate leaders had actually plotted to kill the president, believed they must nonetheless assume the blame for having encouraged "a violence and bitterness of speech" among "the ignorant Southern rank and file."[12]

This diatribe against the Confederate leadership signified more than just a political judgment; it also continued the northern free labor critique of southern slaveholders. In the heated ideological ferment of the prewar years, southerners had claimed superiority in military maneuvers, in economic productivity, in political leadership, and in refined civilization over the crass materialism of the North. As most northerners became convinced of the merits of the free labor system, however, they saw the southern system as one mired in indolence and idleness. In living off the enslaved labor of others, the southern aristocracy proved itself deficient and thereby incapable of honest and genuine leadership. In the pre–Civil War years one Wisconsin resident had described the southern ruling class as "a set of cowards, full of gasconade, and bad liquor, brought up to abuse negroes and despise the north, too lazy to work." Such a class, many had concluded, had proven to be the economic, political, and social antithesis of everything the North represented.[13]

But, as historian Michael Adams has observed, there was also a flip side to this notion of free labor superiority. Many Yankees became convinced, especially in light of the early Confederate victories, that southern planters possessed a martial acumen which northerners lacked. Removed from the Yankee world of capital and commerce, southern men seemed to be closer to a world of violence and military valor, where knightly fortitude mattered more than money. Northerners, Adams notes, became psychologically terrorized by the image of the masterful southern soldier, an image which incapacitated them in many Civil War battles.[14]

The final defeat of these seemingly unstoppable warriors allowed the Yankees to make some much-needed psychological readjustments and to proclaim again their superiority in matters of war, leadership, and culture. With victory now secure, many northerners referred ironically to the southern "chivalry" as a class that had merely been posing at being cultured and refined. Indeed, to a people who viewed honest sentiments as the hallmark of true middle-class respectability, nothing could be more damning than the charge of hypocrisy and ostentation that was flung at the South's aristocracy. "The pomp and pride of Southern chivalry," claimed one Union soldier in New Orleans in the post-Appomattox days, "has no Charms for me." Others sought to expose this "chivalry" as lazy, idle, and generally useless. According to many northerners, it was these pretenders—to both economic and political leadership—who now must suffer the consequences for having led the rebellion and, in an immediate sense, for murdering the nation's beloved leader.[15]

At the heart of this attack on the "chivalry" was an attitude not only about labor and about hypocrisy, but also about gender. Firmly imbued with Victorian notions of gender behavior, and a commitment to firm demarcations between male and female "spheres," middle-class northerners were quick to point out the ways in which southerners deviated from accepted norms. They evaluated southern men as weak and undisciplined parodies of manhood and southern women as aggressive creatures who stepped way beyond the bounds of appropriate femininity. Ultimately, their gendered analysis of the postwar South reflected a broader assessment of the power relations between the two sections in the new, reunified society. Yankees spoke of the need for a northern model of manliness, and perhaps for northern men themselves, to restore order to the defeated South. In short, they constructed a gendered view of postwar Dixie that very much fit with their concerns about subduing the South under northern political and economic authority.

On one level, northerners simply used their victory to declare that the manlier men had won the contest. Those of the middle and upper classes, especially, often focused their attack on the manhood of the southern leaders, chiding the "chivalry" for their dissipate ways and suggesting that southern masculinity lacked the restraint which was one hallmark of northern manliness. For the past several years, northerners had recoiled against the southern "bullies" and "braggarts" who had loudly proclaimed their superiority over northern manhood and the ease with which they would whip the Yankees. Now, in their victory, northern men could turn the tables, confirming not only their moral righteousness and superior civilization, but also their manhood. George Templeton Strong, for example, noted the stories that circulated through the North in June 1865 concerning the Confederates' military ineptitude. According to one account, "The braggarts of South Carolina were the slowest fighters, and are the most abjectly whipped rebels in all Rebeldom. They did nothing but whine . . . as Sherman's column marched over their plantations." Whitelaw Reid, a northern journalist who toured the South in 1865 and 1866, also pictured the Confederates as less than adequate soldiers, concerned primarily with social pretensions, "with feasting, and dancing, and love making, with music improvised from the ball room." Reid claimed that these light-headed socialites had "dashed into revolution as they would into a waltz"—thus taking an impetuous, even feminine, approach to war. The indictments of Strong and Reid against southern soldiers were echoed and expanded upon in pictorial images, especially in one lithographer's portrait of the surrender done immediately after Appomattox. Although later representations of the scene depicted a more dignified and restrained Confederate leader, this Lee was shown clutching a handkerchief while his Confederate aide covered his weeping face with his hand. In stark contrast to this emotional breakdown, Grant and his Union assistant calmly looked on.[16]

The postwar questioning of southern manhood involved much more than turning the rebels into whimpering cowards. Rather, this discussion reflected and extended northern society's critique, formulated in the antebellum period, of the southern social and economic system. At issue was the southern code of honor. Beginning in the eighteenth century, the southern plantation system had given rise to a strong tradition of chivalric and heroic behavior, as well as a code of masculinity, that affected the lives of all southern white men. In many ways, this southern code of honor became the standard by which white southern manhood, especially the aristocracy, was judged. Northerners had been steeped in a similar tradition of honorable commitment to family and community, although the social institutions had been different. But in the early nineteenth century, precisely when the economic distinctions between the regions became most pronounced, North and South parted company on the questions of honor and manhood. Yankees became more responsive to abstract institutions and laws and no longer felt compelled to settle differences through a show of physical strength before the immediate community. Masculinity in the North no longer rested primarily on maintaining honor before the community, but on the ideas of self-improvement and self-cultivation. "Respectability" became the new watchword for northern men, demanding a condemnation of vices that had formerly been considered honorable. Behind this notion of respectability lay a host of religious and moral

"Gen. Lee Surrendering to Lieut. Gen. Grant," by H. Thomas, published by J. Kelly and Sons (Philadelphia, 1865). Courtesy of the Prints Division, the New York Public Library, Astor, Lenox, and Tilden Foundations.

values, especially an emphasis on restraint and self-control. And, increasingly, respectability denoted economic status and the possibility of class mobility.[17]

This northern reassessment of manliness dovetailed with the developing free labor ideology of the early nineteenth century. Just as the new code of masculinity focused more on individual character, so the free labor outlook stressed the individual laborer's ability to improve his economic and social standing. Viewing themselves as economic individuals striving in an uncertain and unpredictable market, northern men became more concerned with tempering and restraining their individual passions and feelings, with exercising physical and emotional control in order to better assure their advancement and success. In short, economic self-improvement demanded and encouraged moral and religious self-cultivation, counseling the antebellum northern man to restrain his social and sexual vices. Failure to do so, many suggested, often resulted in economic ruin. The Republican press, for example, attributed the economic panic of 1857 not to the forces of the market but to "ruinous habits" and "luxurious living," personal failings which exemplified a lack of moral restraint.[18]

The distinct economic world views of the North and South, and their corresponding notions of masculinity, shaped the sectional debate of the 1850s. Southern men contrasted their highly touted fighting abilities with northern men's apparent lack of virility. Northern abolitionists, portrayed as men of talk and not of action, were especially subjected to this gendered ridicule. Antislavery lecturers, the Baltimore *Patriot* declared, had to be escorted by "a life-guard of elderly ladies, and protected by a rampart of whale-bones and cotton-padding." To counter this abuse, northern anti-slavery men welcomed John Brown's attack on Harpers Ferry for reinvigorating their cause with a spirit of manly vitality. Even anti-abolitionists like New York *Herald* editor James Gordon Bennett recognized what Brown had accomplished and hoped that southern men would now recognize northern masculine energy. "Truly," Bennett explained in an attempt to anoint the beleaguered abolitionist with the scepter of masculinity, "there is as much difference between the manly heart and the politician's gizzard, as physically between the massive form of the Abolitionist and the insignificant figure [of the average politician]. Would not a Southern gentleman respect the former far more than the latter?"[19]

As Bennett's anxious plea to the southern gentleman suggests, some antebellum northerners remained ambivalent as to which section had in fact produced a superior strain of manhood. At times their apprehensions about the expansive acquisitiveness of a growing market economy made them look with sympathy on the image of the southern gentleman, respecting his disdain for materialistic enterprise. This meant that northerners, especially in the early stages of the war, often stood in awe of southern soldiers. In April 1861 George Templeton Strong worried whether "the spiritless money-worshipping North" could be "kicked into manliness" in its confrontation with the South. Many northerners, of course, tried to counter southern claims of superiority, especially as the sectional crisis gathered steam in the 1850s. Receiving the brunt of the northern assault, the southern planter was assailed for his laziness and licentiousness, qualities which placed him at the opposite pole from the industrious and restrained northerner. Even the southern man's supposed physical vitality only affirmed his failure to adhere to the new masculine ethos of self-control. The southern slave system, explained one northerner, promoted "pride, indolence, luxury, and licentiousness. . . . Manners are fantastic and fierce; brute force supplants moral principle . . . a sensitive vanity is called honor, and cowardly swagger, chivalry." Indeed, both antebellum and postbellum northerners were keenly aware that the southern man laid claim to a certain aura of manliness, but by using the rhetoric of the free labor ideology, northern men attempted to reveal the fallacy of those claims.[20]

The war's conclusion, especially in the postassassination backlash, saw a resurgence of the attack by northern men on southern masculinity, a diatribe which continued and extended many of the North's critiques from the antebellum period. The northern victory, many claimed, proved that the assertions of antebellum southern men had been a sham, that all the talk about the southern gentleman's strength and chivalry had been mere bravado. Perhaps because some northern men had been taken in by this image, they sneered all the more at southern weakness and impotence at the war's conclusion. According to Union soldier John Phelps, "the Southern idea of manhood" was little more than "a self-assumed superiority and arrogance over the people of the South." The Chicago *Tribune* emphasized how the war revealed the true conditions of northern and southern masculinity. Before the war, the paper observed, the southern " 'chivalry' did not respect the Northern 'mudsills.' The Northern man did not come up to the Southern gentleman in his essential ideas of manhood. . . . [I]n manly courage, a noble sense of honor, and statesmanlike qualities a Northern man had no claims in the estimation of the South which the oligarchy were bound to respect." But now this gendered hierarchy had been turned on its head; northern "courage," claimed the editorial, "has commanded respectful consideration."[21]

Following Lincoln's death, northern men set out to confront a still hostile South with a continued show of masculine force. George Strong suggested that the North must prove its masculine superiority in crushing the rebellious spirit behind the assassination. He found the tone of the postassassination meeting outside the New York City Custom House to be "healthy and virile," and he approved of the resolutions condemning the southern leadership passed that day in Trinity Church as "masculine and good." Union soldier Edward Morley suggested that a less than stern approach to the South at this moment would be decidedly feminine. "I do not think," he wrote to his father a few days after the assassination, "much mercy will be preached by old women now."[22]

The "old women" that Morley had in mind were not southerners; they were other northern men, especially the forgiving and sentimental types like Henry Ward Beecher. In this sense, this postwar diatribe about manhood had as much to do with northerners' changing notions of manliness for themselves as with the attack on southern manhood. Indeed, as historians have suggested, middle- and upper-class northern men emerged from the war with a new regard for manly and vigorous action and a waning interest in intellectual and humanitarian objectives. Many, especially those who had been soldiers, became frustrated with what seemed to be the overly sentimental concerns of antebellum reformers. In contrast, the war gave some northern men a new appreciation for athletic prowess and discipline; to some extent, it even made them appreciative of certain "manly" qualities which they once believed to be monopolized by southerners. Hence they often seemed ambivalent in these years as to just what characterized genuine manliness: restraint or physical strength, self-control or aggression. Nonetheless, the war did impart one clear message about manhood: the real men who had fought and won the war were not just striving individuals, promoting themselves in an unstable market; they were men who took their places in a chain of command and organization. In this sense, they were men who would not just hypothesize about reform, whether in terms of abolition, utopianism, or self-culture; they were men who knew how to get things done. In the immediate postwar period, as Edward Morley's comment suggested, they were not the talkers and the preachers who dwelt upon humanitarian ideals; rather, they were the men who were prepared, if necessary, to deal harshly and directly with the South.[23]

Of course, as numerous historians have pointed out, northerners did not enter the postwar period with a clear and mutually agreed upon plan for reconstructing the southern states. Among most, however, there was agreement on the need to impose basic northern economic principles, especially the free labor plan. Most also agreed on the need to bring the South under a more coherent and more strictly enforced national political system. Consequently, as reports surfaced in 1865 of southern political abuses and of southern desires and attempts to restore something close to slavery, a growing body of northerners began to worry that their victory might have been in vain. They believed that northern might must continue to make its presence felt and that they would have to prove themselves again in whatever contests remained with unrepentant rebels.[24]

Likewise, southerners, especially southern men, had to be prepared to accept the new Yankee order—to learn the lessons of self-control and honest labor, as well as submission to a larger organization and a higher authority. They would have to accept the new chain of command, one which emanated from northern free labor principles, from federally determined political rules, perhaps even from Yankee rifles. Such a readjustment, many Yankees explained, involved a reimposition of proper gender behavior. "If there be any manhood among the ex-slaveholders," the New York *Tribune* editorialized, "we shall soon find it out. We mean the manhood which cheerfully attacks the difficulties of peace and wins victories not less renowned than those of war. . . . The sooner all Southern employers, whether 'gentlemen' or not, understand 'the new organization' the better for Southern production and prosperity."[25]

Apparently, most Yankees believed that southern white men could not develop a proper conception of manhood from within their own society, that a proper model would have to brought from the outside. In this respect, northerners were decidedly grim when it came to assessing the manhood of the rest of the South. A few, mostly from the abolitionist camp and the small northern black community, had at one time expressed some optimism about the manhood of southern black men, especially as the struggle for emancipation gathered steam. In the early years of the war, Republicans had often defined the black struggle as one for attaining human citizenship, even manhood. The struggle for black rights, explained the Republican governor of Wisconsin in 1859, "is a question of manhood, not of color." During the war, many saw the enlistment of African Americans in the Union army as another step on the road to black manhood. Even many nonabolitionists had been impressed by the courage of black soldiers and urged that this sector of the black community be recognized as citizens in the postwar period. In the period immediately following Appomattox, however, most northerners believed that the black man remained untested; he had only just emerged from the degraded state of slavery and had yet to prove himself a man. Most northern whites suspected that former slaves still bore signs of slavery—especially a weak character and a degraded sense of morality—which ran counter to a proper code of manliness. Northern journalist Sidney Andrews, who traveled in the southern states shortly after the war's conclusion, offered a typically mixed assessment of southern black men. On the one hand, he praised their dedication to hard work, believing that they showed a superior capacity for labor over many southern whites. Yet Andrews also believed that, because the freedman remained a product of slavery, he had "little conception of right and wrong" and was "improvident to the last degree of childishness." "The negro," in Andrews's final judgment, was "no model of virtue or manliness."[26]

Nor were many northerners willing to concede these manly qualities to the mass of nonslaveholding southern whites, who, as most in the North insisted, even after Lincoln's assassination, could not be blamed for the rebellion and even deserved considerable sympathy. This class, which had been tricked and deluded for years, which had allowed itself to be cajoled by the southern "chivalry" into fighting a civil war, could hardly be counted upon to provide a model of manhood for the postwar South.

Judged from the Victorian standpoint of proper gender behavior, the South was sorely lacking, and, as northerners were quick to point out, the problem went beyond the South's degraded sense of manhood. The South's confused notions of gender, compounded by the intensity and chaos of the war, had put southern women in a very sorry state as well. According to northern observers, especially men, southern women displayed an attachment to the Confederacy and a hostility toward the Union that far surpassed the disloyalty of southern men. As some in the North suggested, the trauma of the battlefield had at least partially transformed the thinking of some southern men. "The men who did the fighting," remarked Sidney Andrews, "are everywhere the men who most readily accept the issues of the war." The women of Dixie, on the other hand, who had been raised under a corrupted form of male leadership and had never experienced the defeat of the battlefield, apparently had shifted the war from the field to the homefront. As the most resolute advocates of sectionalism, southern women were seen as the final obstacles resisting and obstructing the northern victory.[27]

During and after the war, numerous northern soldiers and travelers frequently attested to the feminine anger and hostility that had gripped the southern states. Indeed, so standard had such stories become that by July of 1865 the German-American political leader Carl Schurz could remark that these tales "of the bitter resentment of the Southern ladies" had become "stale by frequent repetition." Perhaps the most frequently repeated account concerned the women of New Orleans. Publicly castigated in the early part of the war by Gen. Benjamin Butler for the "repeated insults" they heaped upon the occupying Union troops, the New Orleans women ultimately provoked Butler into issuing an order which likened their feminine intransigence to flagrant prostitution. Whitelaw Reid, in his postwar tour of the South, found the hostile mood of the New Orleans women only slightly alleviated. The southern women, Reid observed, "are very polite to Yankee officers in particular, but very bitter against Yankees in general." John Dennett reported to the readers of the *Nation* that certain Union officers "tell me that some of the women still carefully gather up the folds of their dresses when they approach a man in the Federal uniform," thus showing their anger through the swish of their skirts. Sidney Andrews also detected insult and anger in the flounce of southern women's dresses. These women, he found, "much more than the men, have contemptuous notions for the negro soldiers; and scorn for Northern men is frequently apparent in the swing of their skirts when passing on the sidewalk."[28]

The toss of southern women's skirts held more serious implications than a mere rebuff to Yankee authority. Postwar observers portrayed southern women as the very foundation of the Confederacy—its main supporters and defenders. In a society that held women's political participation in contempt, this notion of southern women's intense commitment to the Confederate cause only underscored the illegitimacy of that government. Moreover, postwar observers relied on the image of southern women's intransigence to suggest that the locus of war had shifted from the battlefield to the homefront. They implied that whatever honor had existed in battle was lost now that women became the chief combatants. Men, as Sidney Andrews had inferred, had accepted the outcome of the soldiers' struggles, but the women seemed determined to prolong the fight. In continuing to swish their skirts at Union soldiers, southern women further revealed the dubious nature of southern sectionalism. By refusing to accept the outcome of the war, southern women had turned the battle for the South into a petty demonstration of feminine nastiness.

In the eyes of some northerners, feminine sectionalism also confirmed the weakness of southern masculinity as it pointed to the failure of southern leaders to assert control over their womenfolk. In this spirit, the New York *Tribune*, in an April 18, 1865, editorial, commented on "the fiendish spirit evinced by many Southern women" who "had been told, and believed, that 'the Yankees' were the scum of mankind." Still, if this female bitterness could be traced, ultimately, to the misdirection of men, many northerners suggested that southern women's anger had taken on a life of its own, lending an abusive undertone to the postwar relations between the sections. Sidney Andrews, who claimed to "have seen not a little of feminine bitterness since coming into the South," viciously attacked the "bitter, spiteful women whose passionate hearts nursed the Rebellion."[29]

White southern women, at least those of the upper classes, undoubtedly were staunch defenders of their social system and of the Confederacy. It is no wonder that, having withstood destruction, devastation, and invasion by the enemy, southern women expressed a bitterness and antagonism that may not have been matched by northerners, men or women. Still, the images and accounts of female intransigence do not necessarily reflect the true emotional state of white southern womanhood. Southern men, taking comfort in the notion that their womenfolk had vehemently taken up their defense in this hour of defeat and emasculation, may have embellished and exaggerated these accounts of angry southern ladies. Likewise, northern men did not offer neutral appraisals of enraged southern women but used that notion as a symbol in their political discourse.[30]

Finally, by harping on the outrageous behavior of southern women, northern men once again revealed anxieties not just about the South, but about their own society as well. On a broader scale, the Civil War had wreaked havoc on the stability and rigidity of the Victorian code of gender. Not only had southern women brought their political allegiances out into the open, but women everywhere had assumed new responsibilities and new roles which ran counter to accepted notions of the feminine sphere. Even the cherished Union nurses had tampered with etiquette, bringing a female presence right onto the battlefields where previously no "respectable" woman would go. When northerners decried southern women's public role, they also spoke to a deeper concern about reestablishing a firmer sense of gender hierarchy and control throughout the reunited nation. Their concerns about both manliness and womanliness in the postwar South spoke to a deeply felt need to straighten out the disorder of their own war-torn society.

But for now, in the spring of 1865, the most obvious problem was in the South. Here, gender had gone haywire: men had been braggarts and hypocrites and women had assumed an unnatural degree of political authority. In the end, many came to believe that a sense of gendered order and hierarchy would only be reestablished in the South through the guidance and direction of northerners. In this sense, the "northernizing" of the South that was advocated in the postwar years was not just about bringing Yankee morals and work habits to the South. In the Victorian frame of mind, it was very much about appropriate notions of gender as well.[31]

Probably nothing reveals this gendered view of the postwar South better than the events surrounding the escape and capture of Jefferson Davis. Just one month after Lee's surrender to Grant at Appomattox, Davis's capture by Union troops helped to crystallize northern men's ideas about unmanly southern men and disruptive southern women. The Confederate president had long been a key symbol of northern resentment. The rage against him became especially pronounced in light of the "atrocity" stories circulating in the North at the end of the war, detailing horrendous crimes against Union prisoners-of-war. In most of these accounts, Davis figured as the archenemy. Lee, although not especially well liked, had at least paid a small part of the price for his transgressions when he surrendered to Grant. Sooner than other Confederates, he commanded a combination of respect and sympathy from some northerners who viewed him as a force for reconciliation and a model of submission. But Davis, who stalked the South as a fugitive from Union justice during April and part of May in 1865, received neither sympathy nor understanding. After Lincoln's assassination, all eyes turned toward Davis, who many believed to be responsible for this most atrocious deed. In early May, Andrew Johnson offered $100,000 for the Confederate leader's arrest.

On May 10, 1865, the 4th Michigan Cavalry of the Union army cornered Davis in a secluded spot in southern Georgia. Five days later, the *New York Times* printed a dispatch from the commanding officer that summarized the unusual events surrounding the capture:

> The captors report that [Jefferson Davis] hastily put on one of Mrs. Davis' dresses and started for the woods, closely pursued by our men, who at first thought him a woman, but seeing his boots while running suspected his sex at once. The race was a short one, and the rebel President was soon brought to bay. . . . He expressed great indignation at the energy with which he was pursued, saying that he had believed our Government more magnanimous than to hunt down women and children.

Historians have disputed the accuracy of these reports of Davis's unheroic departure, and certainly Davis himself took pains to counter his enemies' charges. Most scholars, however, agree that Davis donned some form of disguise that may have belonged to his wife—most likely a cloak or shawl (or both), commonly worn by both men and women. It is important to place Davis's capture in the larger context of Civil War cross-dressing. Mary Chesnut, for one, observed how women were "used as detectives and searchers" at various border crossings "to see that no men come over in petticoats." In 1861 pictures had circulated of Abraham Lincoln disguised in Scottish garb when he tried to evade the assassins who threatened him in the days before his inauguration; some accounts of the Union leader depicted him in a rather feminine-looking kilt. In other words, even if the Confederate leader had not attempted some type of disguise, it would not have been surprising to find ludicrous and unmanly portrayals of Davis in this, his most unheroic moment. What is significant here is not the accuracy of these accounts but the way in which northerners adopted and embellished the tale of the Confederate chieftain, fashioning an image that thoroughly confirmed their view of the postwar South.[32]

Davis certainly never wore a petticoat nor a hoopskirt, yet these were the frequently mentioned accessories in the Confederate's disguise. Such adornments allowed artists and songwriters to thoroughly delineate Davis's unmanly demeanor and get a good laugh out of it as well. Songwriters paid homage to "Jeff in Petticoats," in which the Confederate leader explained, "To dodge the bullets, I will wear my tin-clad crinoline." Poetic accounts of the petticoated "Jeff" abounded, again sounding the theme of exposing the southern man's false claim to manliness:

> Jeff Davis was a warrior bold,
> And vowed the Yanks should fall;
> He jumped into his pantaloons
> And swore he'd rule them all.
> But when he saw the Yankees come
> To hang him if they could,
> He jumped into a petticoat
> And started for the wood.[33]

During May and June of 1865, in magazines, in museums, and even on private farms throughout the North, images could be found of Jefferson Davis decked out in crinoline and skirts, offering a symbolic display of the northern view of southern gender confusion at the close of the war. P. T. Barnum, always eager to take advantage of a cultural phenomenon, depicted the unfortunate Confederate at his New York museum in a tableau

"*Jeff in Petticoats: A Song for the Times,*" *words by George Cooper and music by Henry Tucker (New York, 1865). Courtesy of the Louis A. Warren Lincoln Library and Museum, Fort Wayne, Indiana, a part of Lincoln National Corporation.*

THE HEAD OF THE CONFEDERACY ON A NEW BASE.

"The Head of the Confederacy on a New Base," published by Hilton and Company (New York, 1865). Courtesy of the Louis A. Warren Lincoln Library and Museum, Fort Wayne, Indiana, a part of Lincoln National Corporation.

scene showing a hoopskirted Davis surrounded by his soldier captors. Countless cartoons and prints offered similar impressions of "Jeff's Last Shift," "The Chas-ed Old Lady of the C.S.A.," and "Jeffie Davis—the Belle of Richmond." The prints frequently displayed soldiers in the very act of exposing the Confederate president, often depicting a single Union soldier using his sword to lift Davis's skirt, thereby revealing the hoopskirt and unseemly boots which had given him away. One print in particular, leaving little to the viewer's imagination, suggested that more than just boots had been responsible for Davis's undoing. Entitled "The Head of the Confederacy on a New Base," the cartoon pictured Davis with skirt drawn back, legs parted, a phallic sword between his legs, and a threatening Union soldier standing above him.[34]

The wide circulation of the cartoons suggests ways in which an initially middle-class image of inadequate southern manliness reached a broad audience of northerners. Some of the less sexually explicit cartoons appeared in journals such as *Harper's Weekly* and *Frank Leslie's News*. Most, however, circulated as separate-sheet cartoons and were sold as single prints. The cost of such prints (ranging from twenty-five cents to one dollar) probably precluded their widespread purchase by a working-class clientele, but they were accessible to the more highly paid artisans, professionals, and merchants, many of whom were shopkeepers and saloon owners who showed these pictures to a wide variety of patrons. Caroline Richards, a schoolgirl living in upstate New York, recalled how one man in her town drew a picture of Davis in women's clothes after reading the newspaper account and how another man made photographs from the picture and sold them. Richards's family bought one "as a souvenir of the war." As these images circulated, they drew on a pervasive hostility among northerners and a widespread desire among northern men to make a mockery of southern manhood.[35]

For northerners, Davis came to represent all the claims to manliness and chivalric courage of the southern ruling class. He proved false the claims made repeatedly by southern leaders who had boasted of their more civilized society, their greater concern for the weaker sex, their military prowess, and their manly courage. Because these assertions of masculinity had become defining characteristics of the southern aristocrat, a blow aimed at Jefferson Davis's manliness also targeted the class pretenses of the southern "chivalry." Northerners drew on the theme of depraved southern manliness, once again, as a way to establish their regional and political superiority in the postwar period. Northern observers thus noted the contrast between Davis the coward and Davis the southern aristocrat and alleged upholder of the manly tradition of southern honor. "Who is yonder aged, lean-faced female, flying through the woods, with skirts lifted of the wind, and with cloven feet disclosed in boots?" the New York *Independent* pondered. "That is no other than the masculine hero who promised never to desert the fortunes of the Southern Confederacy." Moreover, as many noted, Davis implicated the entire Confederate leadership through his actions. "We are going to have the president of the petticoat Confederacy imprisoned at this fort," wrote Union soldier Edward Morley to his wife from Fort Monroe, Virginia. Summing up this gender predicament, *Harper's Weekly* suggested a "new interpretation of the initials C.S.A.—Crinolinum Skirtum Absquatulatum."[36]

Southerners clearly recognized in the Davis imagery an assault on their manhood. John Dennett, a reporter for the *Nation* who visited the South in July 1865, encountered one southerner who was astounded to learn that "intelligent" northerners actually believed the story of Davis's disguise. As Dennett's informant explained, the Confederate president had merely taken a precaution against his neuralgia by throwing on a cloak prior to his arrest. Northern Democrats likewise took pains to defend Davis's manhood. One Democratic paper, the Cleveland *Plain Dealer*, questioned the veracity of the Davis disguise dispatches and noted that "it is now said that Davis had no disguise on at all, but was found in his tent dressed in a morning gown—and he absolutely had his boots on,—two articles of dress common to other men, less notorious than the rebel President."[37]

But for most northern Republicans, Jefferson Davis had become the petticoated president. Seeing Davis as the symbolic representative of the Confederacy, they interpreted the cartoons and reports as a metaphorical unmanning of the southern aristocracy. Just as gender and class had become bound together in the southern ruling class's self-identification, so did these categories become inextricably linked in the northern postwar portrayal of their former enemies. Only this time, definitions were turned on their heads. Davis may have represented the southern "chivalry," but now northerners were told that this chivalry could no longer lay claim to courage or a protective posture toward their women. Now it was Mrs. Davis who did the protecting as she advised the Union soldiers "not to provoke 'the President, or he might hurt some of 'em!'" The New York *Herald* believed that the very thought of Jeff Davis, coward in women's clothes, harming brave Union soldiers must have been "received with shouts of laughter," but, in extending the role reversal and proving the superiority of northern men, the *Herald* cast the Union soldiers as the truly manly and chivalric ones and so supposed that they might laugh— but only when "the lady's back was turned." Finally, to underscore the transformation of roles and the loss of the male aristocrat's power, the *Herald* informed its readers that Mrs. Davis's actions proved her to be "more of a man than her husband."[38]

These ludicrous scenes of "the last shift of the Confederacy" not only challenged Dixie's manhood but also ridiculed the position of southern women. On one level, these depictions satirized the chivalric ideal and the cult of southern womanhood. When northerners portrayed the Confederate leader as an awkward and ungainly female and then proceeded to crown him as "the belle of Richmond," they explicitly challenged the ideal

JEFFERSON DAVIS AS AN UNPROTECTED FEMALE!

"He is one of those rare types of humanity born to control destiny, or to accept, without murmur, annihilation as the natural consequence of failure."—*N. Y. Daily News, May 15, 1865.*

"Jefferson Davis as an Unprotected Female,"
Harper's Weekly, *May 27, 1865.*

of southern femininity, a notion which northerners had been familiar with since the antebellum period. But northerners also read into the Davis images the idea of southern women's commitment to the Confederacy, finding in them further affirmation that southern women had become the foundation of southern sectionalism. After all, if southern women had been the mainstay of the rebellion, then it seemed only natural for Jefferson Davis to reveal himself as one of the Confederacy's diehard supporters. The New York *Herald*, for example, combined the image of the petticoated Davis with the notion of southern fakery and a feminized Confederacy, deriding Davis as a true representative of southern hypocrisy and applauding his appearance in feminine disguise, which confirmed the contention that the Confederacy "was mainly supported by women and was as hollow as a hoopskirt."[39]

By casting Davis as a spiteful southern female, northern cartoonists found a way to stifle this feminine hostility, to squelch that aspect of the rebellion that could not be defeated on the battlefield. Hence Union officers often surrounded and looked leeringly at "Jeffie D.," who was frequently identified as a "lone" and "unprotected female." In other accounts, soldiers subdued the unruly "female" by stripping off the notorious skirt, or some form of feminine apparel, which had been rudely swished at Yankee soldiers. Even that epitome of bourgeois respectability, the *Atlantic Monthly*, maintained that, while the Union soldiers treated their prisoner kindly and considerately, Davis had been "stripped of his female attire." In effect, once the southern enemy had been pictured as a woman, northerners could punish that enemy in any manner they saw fit, including sexually aggressive behavior which came close to, but stopped short of, rape. Here, in short, was a clear indication of the North's need to continue to exercise authority over the South, even after the fighting had ceased. The continued insubordination of the feminine South required the firm hand of northern military and political leadership.[40]

Still, it did not reflect highly on the victor if all of his resources were needed to put down a population of angry women. Ultimately, northerners saw a more deeply rooted problem in the South: a disordered sense of gender behavior that extended to both men and women. In this regard, Jefferson Davis was portrayed as neither man nor woman, but some amalgamation of both. His capture, the New York *Herald* suggested, demonstrated an extreme state of gender confusion:

When [Davis] was finally brought to bay, he remembered that he was a man and flourished a bowie knife. . . . [But] the appearance of a Colt's revolver drove all his courage out of his heart, and reminded him that he was only a poor, lone woman. Consequently, he dropped his skirts and his knife . . . and blushingly proclaimed, in falsetto tones, his indignation at being so energetically pursued, saying that "he believed our Government more magnanimous than to hunt down women and children." From this statement we infer that the redoubtable Jeff. had confused ideas as to whether he was a woman or a child.

Davis had become a peculiar symbol of both southern men and southern women, at one moment depicting southern gentlemen's manly pretenses and at another representing those "bitter, spiteful women" loathed by northern journalists and Union soldiers. He thus became a figure whose subjugation could prove Yankee virility in several ways. As a man who might attack with his bowie knife, Davis was seized at gunpoint and defeated in a way that men subdue men. Knowing that Davis was really not a woman, northern soldiers could prove their superior prowess in bringing down this dangerous fugitive. Still, as a southern man, Davis had also been an impostor of manliness. Hence, appropriately enough, he was shown in a disguise, in a costume which hinted at his questionable masculinity. His cowardice, his false bravado, and his final "shift" showed the Confederate leader to be more like a woman than a man, a woman who had not fought on the battlefield but would viciously snipe at northern men from the sidelines. Davis-as-woman thus had to be subdued again; "she" either had to be stripped of her attire or, when portrayed as a "lone" and "unprotected" female, "she" would be leered at by Union soldiers. In any case, whether as sexual aggressors or as superior soldiers, northern men could prove themselves the manly superiors of Davis and all that he/she represented.[41]

Davis was not the only figure in the heated postwar literature who symbolized the sexual ambiguity of the South and invited the sexual domination of the North. In 1865 a popular northern author of boys' fiction, Oliver Optic, offered one of the earliest literary depictions of the Civil War as gender conflict. In the novel *Fighting Joe*, Optic's Union hero, Capt. Thomas Somers, meets Maud Hasbrouk, "a majestic and haughty young lady" of the South, who defiantly declares her allegiance to the Confederacy. Maud acts on her declaration, attempting to make Captain Somers a prisoner of Dixie, but finds she is not able to outsmart the wily northern man. Accusing Maud of conspiring in that southern female subversion of sexual and political order, Somers proclaims, "You are one of those brawling rebel women who have done so much to keep up the spirits of the chivalry in this iniquitous rebellion. You are one of the feminine Don Quixotes who have unsexed themselves in the cause of treason and slavery." True to her role as rebellious woman, Maud replies in the words of the disguised Jefferson Davis. "I had supposed," she says in an accusatory tone toward the Union forces, that "making war on women and children was merely a poetic figure, but it appears to be literally true." Somers, not surprisingly, responds in the language of the New York *Herald* when it had mocked the Davis capture. "Pray," he says to Maud, "am I to regard you as a woman or a child . . . or as both?" In the end, Somers subdues the feminine threat through his superior wit and force, achieving a victory which the author suggests is as significant as the subjugation of Confederate men. "It was something to see a brawling rebel woman," Optic told the reader, "the most pestilent and inveterate enemy the government had in the contest, in a pleading posture. It was something to expose the ridiculous pretensions of one of that army of female rebels, fiercer and more vindictive than the men, and to demonstrate that she had none of the courage of which she had boasted."[42]

These gendered images of the South, especially the depictions of a female-led and feminine-inspired Confederacy, offered northern men more than just a vehicle for subduing southern women's intransigence. Ultimately, they pointed to the northern man's conception of power relations in the postwar society. Whether portrayed as a Confederate president in women's clothes, as Oliver Optic's Maud Hasbrouk, or as that broader "army of female rebels," the southern Confederacy had been drawn into a complex web of gendered imagery which, to northern men, demonstrated the weakness and the illegitimacy of that government. These metaphors follow a pattern, observed by historians of politics and gender, in which gender has been used to represent "natural" and "legitimate" relationships of public power. In the aftermath of the Civil War, the various metaphors of gender revealed northern men's concerns about the disordered and chaotic nature of the postwar South, and about postwar society more generally, but through these discussions of gender, northern men also projected an image of power and control. Northerners could repress the belligerent southern women and project their understanding of the gendered, and thus apparently natural, hierarchy between the two sections. Significantly, they could bring the South back into a proper Victorian framework, and ultimately into the Union, by subjugating southern men and women under a proper model of northern manhood. In the spring and summer of 1865, this conception fit quite well with northern interests in bringing their own political and economic models into the South and, more directly, with bringing the South under northern military and political control. By the end of 1865, and in the years to come, northerners would begin testing and reshaping their observations in the course of some direct and practical experiences.[43]

2

A Reconstruction of the Heart

Reunion and Sentimentality during Southern Reconstruction

"A blooming daughter of an F.F.V. consents to wed a noble son of New Hampshire. When will wonders cease?" Here, indeed, was an amazing sign of just how much had transpired since Russell Conwell's last trip to the southern states. Having left the South after serving as a Union soldier, Conwell made a return visit in 1869. Through most of his journey, Conwell surveyed the sites of the great military confrontations and observed the conditions of defeated Dixie, forwarding his dispatches to the *Daily Evening Traveller* in Boston. Although he was primarily interested in seeing the old soldiers and the fields of battle, Conwell paused just long enough in his travels to attend this unique ceremony of inter-sectional union, a ceremony that was bound to hold a special fascination for his northern readers.[1]

The romance did, after all, make for a good story. The New Hampshire soldier had been injured during McClellan's Virginia campaign in 1862. When he was near death, a young girl of sixteen discovered him; although fearful of Union soldiers, she enlisted the aid of an elderly black woman and together they nursed him back to health. Anxious to keep her father, an avid Yankee-hater, unaware of the man's presence, the young woman aided him in secret, at one point disguising him in an old dress in order to mask his identity. The soldier, unfortunately maimed for life, ultimately returned to his compatriots and left the South. Soon after the war's conclusion, however, the Yankee returned to Virginia and sought out his young white savior (the older black woman had died). He found her, they fell in love, and, over the strenuous objections of the girl's father, they were wed in a modest but lively ceremony in rural Virginia.[2]

It was a story which must have been especially appealing for Conwell's Boston readers. True, they might not have liked the idea of the Union soldier being disguised in a woman's dress, an image that came a little too close to another man's unseemly use of feminine garb; nonetheless, they must have been happy to see the Union soldier make his romantic conquest. They also would have been happy to learn that the newlyweds, despite the father's objections, planned to settle up North, in Wisconsin. The story also presented a hopeful metaphor for the northern victory, especially about the ways in which former enemies might learn to accept the new status quo. In light of the political chaos and turbulence of Reconstruction, many northerners remained skeptical about the likelihood of a genuine reconciliation, one in which the Yankee triumph remained secure and southerners conceded their willingness to cement the bonds of union. But here, in the bonds of matrimony, there seemed to be hope that northerners and southerners would learn to come together. Here was a sign that what could not be accomplished through investments or through constitutional amendments might be accomplished through love. So powerful and compelling was the image of inter-sectional romance that it would be constantly repeated, refurbished, fictionalized, and dramatized for many years to come.

Still, in the early postwar period, stories depicting the close, emotional bonding of northerners and southerners were extremely rare. For the most part, when northerners looked South in these years, they were distressed with what they beheld. They saw, not surprisingly, a land of devastation and desolation, a region that had been ravaged by years of hard fighting and neglect. Moreover, when they looked at the people of the South, especially the white people and especially in the first stage of the Reconstruction process, they saw what seemed to be a defiant and angry group of Confederates, ever ready to turn against the people and institutions of the North. They certainly did not see a conquered and subdued mass of southerners. Writing in October 1865, one Union soldier was disgusted by the amount of treasonous and rebellious talk he continued to hear in Dixie. "Go where you will," he explained, "& you will hear bare-faced Treason uttered in the strongest terms. . . . There is not 9 out of 10 of the so-called 'Whiped' [*sic*] traitors that I would trust until I saw the rope applied to their Necks, [and] then I would only have Faith in the quality of the rope." Another northern man, who had emigrated South after the war, told the *Nation*'s southern correspondent, John Dennett, how his initial optimism about reunion had disappeared since his arrival in Dixie. "I came out with the kindest feelings for these people down here," he said. "We had whipped them, and I wanted it to rest there. I thought the South wanted it to end there. But I was tremendously mistaken. They hate us and despise us and all belonging to us." As many saw it, the northern victory would not be secure until southern whites acknowledged that they had been thoroughly and soundly beaten.[3]

Amidst the uncertainty of the uneasy postwar transition, especially after Lincoln's assassination, some Yankees even suspected that south-erners were once again preparing to wage a war against the Union. Indeed, with hostilities so recently concluded, northerners frequently interpreted southern anger and intransigence as signs that a rebellion might at any moment begin anew. Such fears, along with specific reports of southern violence against northerners, helped build support for the pro-gram of the Radical Republicans as elections approached in the fall of 1866. "It is a fatal mistake to hold that this war is over, because the fighting has ceased," exclaimed Richard H. Dana in a June 1865 speech arguing for an imposition of northern military rule in the South. Others detected signs of insurrection in 1866 and 1867 but noted that northerners were prepared to respond with equal force. In January 1867, following the electoral success of the Radicals, northern women's suffrage supporter Henry Blackwell penned a public statement "to the legislatures of the Southern states" in which he explained that northerners believed "that a majority of the white people of the South are at heart the enemies of the Union" and that if southerners "should resort to arms, the North would be practically unan-imous" in squelching any uprising.[4]

Thus the old animosities persisted as white southerners appeared to be the same treasonous rebels in Reconstruction that they had been in war. Many northerners continued to think in military terms, believing that northern might and military discipline were necessary to subdue the white South's intransigence and to insure that the Yankee victory would not be lost. "Isn't it just possible," remarked northern emigrant George Benham in 1866 in a letter to a Yankee friend, "that a little iron rule would be a good thing down here now? Just enough to compel strict obedience to the acts of Congress." Moreover, as long as northerners viewed the postwar relationship in a military context, they continued to see the problem in gendered terms, especially in regard to tempering and controlling the passions of southern men. As they had before, northerners mocked the notion of southern chivalry, often blaming the arrogance and excitability of southern men for the angry defiance encountered in this postwar period. Ultimately, they hoped to see southern men accept a Yankee model of behavior and manhood. James Lowell, for example, was exasperated with what he saw as the childish rebelliousness of southern men. "Is it not time," he wrote in October 1866, "that these men were transplanted at least into the nineteenth century, and, if they cannot be suddenly Americanized, made to understand something of the country which was too good for them, even though at the cost of a rude shock to their childish self-conceit?" In this same period, Oliver Wendell Holmes offered his own critique of southern manliness. "I hope that time will explode," wrote Holmes in a letter to Senator Albert Beveridge, "the humbug of the Southern Gentleman in your mind. . . . the Southern gentlemen generally were an arrogant crew who knew nothing of the ideas that make the life of the few thousands that may be called civilized."[5]

Such men, northerners believed, fomented much of the resistance to northern rule in the postwar period. Northerners interpreted Reconstruction strategies, or southern resistance to Reconstruction, in terms of gender and manhood, in much the same way that they had viewed the sectional relationship before and during the war. For many, the objective of Reconstruction apparently was to keep southern manhood in check while keeping the northern model of masculinity in the ascendancy. John Phelps, a former Union soldier, fumed at President Johnson's attempt in 1866 to allow the southern states to return to the Union "with all their manhood." Likewise, a transplanted southerner living in Boston in 1866 found that most northerners were loathe to acknowledge any type of southern masculinity. This former resident of Tennessee thus was enormously pleased upon hearing a lecture in which one northern orator "paid several compliments to Southern manhood." Much to this southerner's chagrin, however, these remarks were "the first . . . true manly avowal that there was such a thing as manhood in the South that" he had seen or heard.[6]

Exasperation and mistrust of southern whites led many northerners, at least initially, to put their hope for Reconstruction in southern blacks. By educating, enfranchising, and working with the African American community, northerners hoped to secure a foothold in Dixie which might pave the way for reconciliation. Convinced that the freedpeople would be loyal allies against the former Confederates and hopeful that they could be inculcated with Yankee morality, many northerners concluded that the only hope for the South lay with the former slaves. For some northerners, especially those who had moved to Dixie with reform motives in mind, the very presence of African Americans offered their only source of solace. "We always knew we were safe with the black man," remarked one northern teacher in the South, "but we feared the white, for the hatred of the 'Yankee' was still strong." Others emphasized the political security which southern black suffrage could offer northern interests. James Lawrence, writing to Horace Greeley in December 1866, summed up the attitudes of many northern Republicans as they took their first tentative steps toward Reconstruction. "Enfranchise the Blacks," wrote Lawrence, "and further rebellions at the South are impossible." Acting on these sentiments, the Radical Republican plan of Reconstruction emphasized black empowerment as one aspect of a program which would allow for Republican domination in the South. Initially, a significant portion of northern society supported this proposition.[7]

Northerners who looked to the South with more pecuniary interests in mind hoped that the freedpeople, unlike their lazy masters and mistresses, could provide the much-needed labor which would get the southern economy back on its feet. The former slaves, wrote Henry Lee Higginson to his wife in 1865, "are quite ready to work, are strong, energetic, as far as we can see, and will come to their bearings before long." Garth Wilkinson James, younger brother of William and Henry, moved to a Yankee planting community in northern Florida after the war, confident that the former slaves would work more effectively than they had under slavery. "The freed Negro under decent and just treatment," he explained in 1866, "can be worked to profit to employer and employee." Northern planters thus believed that, if nothing else, at least the freedpeople could learn the habits and methods of the Yankee system and thereby provide some hope for southern progress.[8]

Few northerners ever believed that a true Reconstruction and thorough reconciliation could be achieved just through this contact with southern blacks. Longstanding prejudices, as well as concerns about the turbulent nature of southern race relations, prompted many Yankees to believe that efforts would have to be made to reach southern whites as well. Although George Strong welcomed the initial granting of suffrage to southern blacks, he also suspected that this might not restore national harmony. Southern black political power, Strong noted, "may keep us unsettled for an indefinite period." Moreover, given how many more whites than blacks resided in the South, it was clear that such a large constituency could not be ignored. Some put their faith in discovering and working with middle-class southern whites, "a large party," explained one northerner "that will gladly cooperate with us." Yet, in these early postwar years, as in the antebellum period, northerners generally saw few signs of an emerging white middle class, certainly not one that personified the Yankee image of thrift, efficiency, and upstanding morality. Most saw only dirty and diseased "crackers" who possessed none of the moral characteristics that provided the foundation for a true middle-class society.[9]

With much of the southern population so clearly immune to Yankee influences, northerners faced a profound dilemma in the Reconstruction period. How could the northern victory be solidified and a genuine bond of union be created? On one level, the war had made the nation one—in that sense, reunion was an accomplished fact. On another level, however, many northerners realized that a true and thorough union had not been forged, certainly not in terms of deep-rooted emotions and feelings. "Enemies," observed the editors of the *Nation* in 1872, "are reconciled by the mutual determination to forget past differences, and by the springing up of a mutual liking." Through much of the Reconstruction period, most northerners would have found that anything but a "mutual liking" characterized the relationship between the sections. In particular, they suspected that a large percentage of southerners, despite what they might say or do, remained thoroughly hostile to the Union. While some northerners were willing to accept a prolonged imposition of military and political rule on the South, it was becoming increasingly clear to many that such an arrangement would hardly result in a "mutual liking" and would yield only hostility or a superficial bond across the Mason-Dixon line.[10]

For Americans coming to grips with a new concept of nationhood, this was an especially troubling situation. Gradually rejecting the legalistic conception of nationalism, many northerners had begun to see the nation as more of an organic and living entity, built upon its own distinctive moral will and sense of purpose. "The historical nation," explained economist Robert Thompson, "is an organism, a political body animated by a life of its own." Not all northerners studied the problem of nationalism from Thompson's intellectual vantage point; nonetheless, many had come to believe that the nation could not be bound together simply by the passage of laws or constitutional amendments, that northerners and southerners had to seek out that common will and moral energy which made them one. In effect, northerners sought to reforge what has been termed the "imagined community" of the nation, a harmonious and idealized collective whose unity rested more on an assumed natural affinity than on political ties. Thus, many believed, nationalism must spring from the true feelings of the people. It certainly could not rest for long on the force of arms. "I long for a heart-union between the North and the South," wrote abolitionist Gerrit Smith, "but . . . it cannot be enforced."[11]

Such feelings reflected a more general, and growing, disillusionment which Americans displayed toward their political system. An increasing number were becoming convinced that American politics were not equipped to handle the challenges of Reconstruction, that the system led only to chaos, confusion, and corruption. Northerners suspected that the political system which they imposed upon the South, as well as the one that existed in many of their own communities, attracted only charlatans and opportunists. By 1874 George Strong was just one of many complaining about the "bogus state governments" and the "corrupt carpetbaggers" who ruled in Louisiana and South Carolina; he found this situation only slightly better than the degraded "Celtocracy" which ruled New York City. Clearly, a political solution that encouraged pretense and corruption could not lead to a genuine harmony of northern and southern feeling or to a true sense of nationalism.[12]

As the Reconstruction years progressed, many northerners wondered just how those nationalistic feelings could be forged. Some had faith in the redemptive power of money and investments, suspecting that northern capital might bring Yankee ways and customs to the southern people and that this would solidify the two societies. Indeed, in the context of tremendous wartime and postwar growth, and the spread of northern capital throughout the continent, the economic route to reunion did inspire a great deal of optimism. Edward King, the northern author of the 1873 *Scribner's* series on "The Great South," made frequent reference to Dixie's industrial possibilities and believed that as these opportunities were exploited the region would become "more progressive and liberal every year." Yet money and economic growth bred intense feelings of ambivalence among Americans, prompting hopes of expansion and prosperity as well as fears of greed and corruption. Northerners began to question the efficacy, as well as the propriety, of a victory that rested primarily on a financial foundation; few northerners believed that money alone could completely transform the sectional relationship. In fact, many feared that a reunion that spoke only to pecuniary interests might do even less than a purely political solution toward producing a "mutual liking" between the sections.[13]

Specifically, northerners worried that a monetary reunion would produce sham and pretense more than genuine feelings. As many saw it, southerners' love for the Union seemed to be only as deep as a carpetbagger's pockets. One Republican newspaper expressed profound annoyance with what was called the "pocket loyalty" and "cupboard love" of the former Confederates who had regained influence in much of the South. Reporter Whitelaw Reid believed that many southerners "were willing to forego manifestations of Rebel spite for the sake of furthering their chances of a good bargain." Analyzing this state of affairs, John Dennett believed that the Yankee investor could never be completely sure if he had made a true friend or just another southern wolf in sheeplike clothing. Many southerners, Dennett found, openly proclaimed their hostility to the North, yet "frequently men make a merit of disclaiming it" even though "no one denies its existence."[14]

Indeed, as time passed, northerners suspected that they had not tapped into a genuine sentiment of reunion at all. Rather, they feared they had only uncovered a sham and hypocritical show on the part of many southerners, a tendency, which Dennett noted, of "disclaiming" hostility despite its existence. In the introduction to his 1866 volume of Civil War poetry, Herman Melville warned northerners against forcing the South into this hypocritical posture. "The only penitence," he observed, "now left [the South] is that which springs solely from the sense of discomfiture; and since this evidently would be a contrition hypocritical, it would be unworthy in us to demand it. Certain it is that penitence, in the sense of voluntary humiliation, will never be displayed." Like many, Melville longed for a genuine change in southern feelings; unlike many, however, he questioned how deeply and completely southern attitudes would ever be transformed. Most Yankees desired a thorough alteration of the South's disposition, and they wanted it fairly quickly. Certainly, as real estate promoters discovered, emigration was not advanced by southern hypocrisy. "Many at the North," wrote one promoter in his attempt to explain the declining appeal of emigration, "believe that the words and deeds of the Southern people are far from showing that they have really intended to" follow through on their professed commitment to peace and conciliation. Others suspected that the spirit of hypocrisy would only be strengthened by northerners pouring money into the South. In 1869 Russell Conwell found that southerners seemed to treat northern men with respect, not out of any true fraternal feelings, but mostly because of their money.[15]

Nor was southern hypocrisy the only problem. John Dennett not only warned against southern deceptions but also implied that the northern newcomer must learn to be less than forthright in his own dealings with the South, "to restrain the free expression of any social or political opinions distinctively Northern." Former Union soldier John Phelps was also alarmed that pecuniary interests might encourage northerners to adopt a false facade with the South. "It looks," he observed in January 1867, "as if the New Yorkers, discovering that their trade is at the mercy of the South, are resorting to acts of kindness as a means of winning over their obdurate brethren." To use Melville's words, many Yankees seemed to be making themselves "unworthy" of their victory as they manipulated their own and their former enemies' feelings for the sake of a quick and economically satisfying reunion. In short, northerners feared that economic interests, accompanied by this false display of affection, might cheapen the high-minded nobility which had been associated with the Union victory.[16]

Clearly, then, this concern for southern and northern pretense was not a trivial matter. In the 1860s middle-class northerners continued to pay homage to a sentimental culture which warned against the wily and deceitful ways of the "confidence man." Etiquette manuals of the antebellum period informed them that no transgression was worse, no defect more unChristian, than hypocrisy. Moreover, money and market relations were frequently targeted as the source of hypocrisy; people, it was feared, would adopt whatever attitude was necessary simply to make a buck. By turning away from public and pecuniary affairs, by looking toward the emotions and the concerns of the heart, middle-class northern men and women believed that one got closer to true feelings and sentiments.[17]

In the aftermath of war, as northerners faced a problem that went beyond personal hypocrisy and extended to the sectional and national levels, an intensely sentimental discourse resurfaced. Northerners, in effect, confronted the dilemma of how to be victors in war yet still retain their honesty and magnanimity. How, they wondered, could the northern victory be upheld without unleashing an orgy of opportunism and corruption? And how could they cut through the pretense at fraternalism and uncover the true feelings that would lead the way toward a more genuine and personal reunion? In this regard, they were not opposed to showing kindness to their former enemies, but increasingly they believed that such kindness had to spring, somehow, from the heart and not from the pocketbook or from the barrel of a gun. John Underwood, for example, was one northerner who wrote of his desire to counter southern treason with northern nobility and goodwill. "May we learn to return good for their evil," Underwood wrote from Richmond in November 1867, "blessings for their cursings and try to imitate the glorious example of our divine Lord and Saviour." A growing number of Yankees thus hoped that their own noble and forgiving sentiments might set the nation back on its proper course. [18]

With this emotional objective in mind, northerners gradually reevaluated certain sectors of southern society as they searched for those more personal bonds of union, hoping to present themselves as more magnanimous and high-minded victors. They became more respectful of and sympathetic toward many southerners who had only recently aroused their anger and suspicion, including the former elites of the plantation society. This is not to suggest, despite many pronouncements to the contrary, that Yankees suddenly learned to like their former enemies. In some cases, perhaps they did; in other cases, they certainly did not. What is significant, however, is that northerners learned to be sentimental about those whom they had once despised and that they often did so in order to assure themselves of their own capacity for sympathy and goodwill. For many, what might have been more important was not that the former Confederates suddenly became "likeable," but that they, as the victorious Yankees, had learned to be forgiving and emotional. "O, strong and true and tender is the North!" proclaimed a Chicago orator in 1869, "and this is the time for tenderness." Likewise, Harriet Beecher Stowe observed how this sympathy for southern suffering revealed the better, and more sentimental side, within the commiserators. "The man who defied the slaveowner when he was rich, haughty, and powerful," she wrote in reference to Henry Ward Beecher, "had a right to speak a kind word for him now when he is poor, and weak, and defeated. The instinct to defend the weaker side is strongest in generous natures."[19]

Reflecting their increasing concern about postwar economic and political corruption, northerners displayed a growing affinity for those southerners who were, in their view, disconnected from unscrupulous political and economic entanglements. In other words, they expressed an intense sympathy for southerners who had in no way profited from war and Reconstruction and who were now removed from the web of postwar hypocrisy. Plantation women became special objects of northern pity. Although many northerners continued to condemn them as unreconstructed rebels, the women of Dixie held out a unique appeal to the sentimental strain in northern culture. Having lost their menfolk at war, as well as many of their worldly possessions, they were believed to be suffering profoundly, especially as they struggled to maintain a semblance of ladylike behavior. Moreover, sentimental culture placed special value on feminine emotions, stressing that women, removed from the public sphere, had a closer connection to sincere and sentimental feelings.

Many northerners thus began to see the women of the postwar South as naive pawns in the evil world of market relations, as innocent creatures cruelly forced into the economic arena. After traveling in South Carolina, the Massachusetts resident Abigail Waters wrote to her son James regarding her encounter with white southern womanhood. She had met southern ladies, she wrote, "industriously striving to support themselves and to obtain the comforts and . . . the elegancies of their former position. Our sympathies were strongly awakened by their recital of the wrongs which they had endured from our army." In Abigail Waters's view, northerners themselves had often been responsible for the suffering of southern women. Even more, their suffering made it impossible for them to live by accepted codes of womanhood—in some cases, they were being forced to fend for themselves and receive wages for their labors. Edward King, traveling in the South in 1873, found himself sympathizing with "ladies of culture and refinement, whose incomes were gigantic before the war, who are 'washing' for their daily bread." Many sympathized with women who, because of the hardships of war and Reconstruction, tried but were unable to live up to the model of womanhood which northerners themselves professed to uphold. And they sympathized with this image of women as caretakers of the private sphere of sentiment and emotions, now forced into the unsavory public world of the market.[20]

By stressing the sentimental nature of southern women in the postwar period, northerners gradually learned to overlook their sectional animus. At least, many seemed to imply, these women showed their true feelings; they would not hide behind a pretended civility. They had endured genuine suffering and could now be excused for showing some genuine hostility. Mary Abigail Dodge revealed many of these notions in her own account of the postwar South. An ardent abolitionist, Dodge had written extensively for a number of magazines during the war years. In her postwar writings she maintained a critical view of the values of the antebellum South; yet, like so many others, she now stressed the sentimental side of sectional healing. According to Dodge, northern anger would disappear, and righteousness become manifest, once people became aware of the depths of southern suffering and of the material deprivations which many southerners endured. "The poverty and the misery of the South," she wrote, ". . . make a deeper impression on the traveller than anything else." In particular, she believed that northern sympathy must reach out to southern women, despite their devotion to the lost cause. "If women wish to walk in the middle of the streets, up to their ankles in mud and mire," wrote Dodge, "following the funeral train of a favorite general," then northerners should show some understanding. "These things lay hold of their deepest, truest, tenderest sentiments."[21]

Although others might not have been quite as understanding, there was, nonetheless, a growing tendency to identify this type of open defiance with the more emotional nature of southern womanhood and no longer see it as a dangerous threat to northern rule. Indeed, despite the value placed on feelings and emotions, it was not unusual for northerners to depict southern women's attitudes as nothing but emotion, and therefore lacking in reason and logic. This was especially true of any political opinions which southern females might express. Explained in these terms, southern women were transformed from dangerous rebels into emotional and beguiling creatures. Northern reporter Albert Webster described one such rebel girl who kept up the old diatribe against the Yankee conqueror. But her defiance, explained Webster, could not be taken too seriously because "when pressed to define her charges she would plunge into the very middle of the monstrous tangle, and wind herself up like a poor fly in a web." Caught in the irrationality of her emotions, the southern woman in the end was forced to profess her truest sentiments: "At heart we all love what is now our country."[22]

To some extent, the Victorian ethic of suffering encouraged northerners to look with increasing sympathy at the circumstances of plantation women and even, in some instances, of plantation men. In the sentimental frame of mind, suffering represented a genuine emotion which cut through economic and political pretenses and revealed true human feelings. Victorian Americans were drawn to certain types of distress, such as the nervous disease of neurasthenia, which were indicative of one's weakness to withstand the ordeal of a bustling, materialistic society. It was felt that those who suffered, as well as those who were sympathetic to suffering, were emotional and caring people, not just vicious competitors in the public sphere. Southern plantation women, now cast as sufferers in a market economy, became, in northern eyes, sympathetic victims. In a more general sense, the whole class of former slaveholders also underwent a rather remarkable transformation—they, too, became the potential victims of greed and corruption. Thus, while many Yankees kept up a virulent attack against the smug and arrogant aristocracy, some of this anger began to wane as northern contact with this class increased during Reconstruction and as northerners watched the southern elite make a painful adjustment to their new, materially constrained conditions.[23]

Unlike certain questionable business leaders in the North who had clearly manipulated and profited from the Civil War experience, the former planters now knew only poverty and loss. The northerner who recognized this revealed some genuine sentiment and moral understanding. Amazingly, and often in the interest of conveying their own magnanimity, northerners conferred a moral victory upon their former enemies. In April 1867 northern schoolteacher Elizabeth Botume observed the return of the former slave owners to her South Carolina district. "Many of the old residents had returned to the town," she reported, "despoiled of everything they had once possessed. . . . with all our hearts we pitied them and deplored their misfortunes." Northerners found it especially poignant to witness the anguish of those who had once enjoyed luxuries and advantages not unlike their own. Indeed, the more southern planters lost, and the more removed they now seemed from the world of economic entanglements, the more they inspired sentimental pity. "Y[ou]r present privations and hardships," wrote one well-to-do northerner to a member of a once-prominent South Carolina family, "could not fail to wring the hearts of those who remembered the proud position, the charming attractions, and social advantages of y[ou]r family." Edwin Corning of New York wrote to his former college classmate, Louisianan Henry Slack, "I often commiserate in my own mind, with the Southern people, as I hear of one case of distress after another."[24]

To some extent, sentimental suffering merely masked a deeply rooted sense of class snobbery. Many middle- and upper-class northerners claimed to be captivated by the idea of southern suffering, but most were fascinated by the image of wealthy southerners who had experienced such great losses. Southern planters aroused northern pity because of their drastically altered circumstances and because it seemed so unfortunate for such a well-mannered and highly bred people to have suffered so much. In this sense, northerners occasionally suspected that the loss of fortunes only enhanced the elite southerner's sense of good breeding. Deprived of money and possessions, they apparently became true aristocrats, far removed from the world of middle-class money-grubbing. Unsullied by such crass concerns, the southern planters could now openly exhibit the true hallmarks of class. John DeForest, for example, observed the southerner's "suavity of manner" and lamented that the money-hungry northerner had "not been better educated in such gentilities." Others also affirmed the appeal of southern etiquette while they bemoaned the lack of refined manners amongst northerners. Anxious about the apparent cultural stratification which plagued their own society, and fretting about the growing disparity between the refined and the unrefined, some members of the northern elite embraced the southern aristocracy as long-lost compatriots in cultivation. George Templeton Strong, a man notorious for his snobbish hankering for "culture," moderated his dislike for former rebels as he got to know some of the more refined refugees of Dixie who had moved to New York. And Mary Abigail Dodge wrote admiringly of "the elegant manners to be found in the South," something with which she believed the "rough" Yankee emigrant was unfamiliar.[25]

This affinity for the South's upper class often left little room for feeling sentimental about southern blacks; at least, it was unclear as to which group deserved more understanding. Even some who had been fired by the old abolitionist spirit reckoned with ambivalent sympathies as they witnessed postwar encounters between impoverished planters and former slaves. Schoolteacher Margaret Thorpe expressed a newfound concern for the old master class and the predicament they faced as new employers. Noting that "white people seldom pay the negroes whom they employ," Thorpe also believed "that they really have no money with which to pay their debts. Everyone is poor and the suffering is heart-breaking." Others, less sympathetic to the plight of the freedpeople, saw the black population positioned at the opposite pole from their former masters—they stood to profit from the war's outcome and from the policies of Reconstruction and thus became immersed in the very unsentimental practices of the postwar period. Perhaps, as many claimed, the former slaves were not to be blamed for their moral failings; nonetheless, northerners no longer felt compelled to cast them in the role of sentimental sufferers. As many saw it, the freedpeople were now able to take advantage of their new roles and manipulate their new economic relationships. Whitelaw Reid, who set himself up temporarily as a Louisiana planter after his journalistic excursion through the South, found the former slaves to be just as deserving of sympathy as insolent domestic servants from Yankeedom. "The wretches," wrote Reid in reference to the freed blacks, "tyrannize over their master precisely as they do in other well regulated households, further North, which proves the excellence of the advantages they are now enjoying." The fact that Reid's assessment had only a slight basis in reality is beside the point; what is significant is that Reid and others like him now perceived the former slaves as savvy competitors in the market while their former masters had become poor, unfortunate victims. Even more damning was the sense that the freedpeople might now take advantage of poor plantation women. Elizabeth Devereux, a northern transplant in the South, thus bemoaned the racial implications of the southern lady's impoverishment. Devereux was especially struck by "the quaint, old-fashioned dresses the ladies wore . . . as they are so penniless many of them, as not to be able to afford a better style." Like other Yankees, Devereux's pity intensified upon seeing these ladies go to work, "even . . . for the darkies themselves."[26]

Nor was there much sympathy for the freed slaves' new political position. Indeed, northerners' commitment to black suffrage in 1866 and 1867 gave way to a tendency, just a few years later, to scapegoat the black politician and voter for all the problems of the South. In northern eyes, the former slave had become immersed in the questionable policies of the Reconstruction period and had profited from corrupt and hypocritical entanglements. Again, regardless of the black community's actual political position, there was little about this perceived situation that would arouse Yankee sympathy and compassion. Many northerners made frequent comparisons between the politics of southern Reconstruction and the corrupt practices of Tammany Hall. Many saw the black politician immersed in the politics of greed. Even William Lloyd Garrison, Jr., traveling in the South toward the end of the Reconstruction period, was dismayed at how well the freedmen had learned to play the game of political corruption. "Most of the office-holders here," he wrote to his wife from South Carolina, "white and black, are 'on the make.'"[27]

In general, the newfound pity for the white South also made many northerners look with growing disfavor on the whole Reconstruction experiment, not only on the elevation of African Americans but also on the Yankee carpetbagger. Increasingly, the carpetbagger seemed little better than a hypocritical "confidence man," a wicked opportunist who played upon the poverty of elite white men and women. To many he represented the ugly and materialistic side of the northern victory, always ready to exploit the Yankee triumph and lacking any sense of human compassion. "One wonders," wrote John DeForest, "that the South did not rebel anew when one considers the miserable vermin who were sent down there as government officials." A growing body of northerners found many of the Reconstruction officials unworthy of their respect, especially when compared to the unfortunate, yet apparently still dignified, plantation class. Mary Dodge was not surprised to find that many of the South's "higher classes" expressed contempt for Yankee emigrants, believing "that very many of the Northerners who go South are ignorant or careless of good breeding."[28]

Finally, amidst the sentimental reconsiderations of the Reconstruction period, northerners even learned to sympathize with the former Confederate soldiers. Yankees suspected that the common soldier, perhaps more than any other southerner, had known the suffering and hardship of war. As some saw it, the southern soldier's suffering was especially profound in that he had lost the final contest and could not revel in the victory. Clearly, if anyone had been cut off from postwar profiteering, it was Johnny Reb. Even more, the defeated soldier earned respect not only for his suffering, but also for what seemed to be an honest, although tragic, willingness to accept his loss. "Nothing was more touching," remarked Whitelaw Reid, "in all that I saw in Savannah, than the almost painful effort of the rebels . . . to conduct themselves so as to evince respect for our soldiers." Even Robert E. Lee, by the time of his death in 1870, earned respect for his submission to defeat, although he was still denounced for his secessionist actions. "By his unobtrusive modesty and purity of life," wrote the

New York Times, Lee had won respect for his postwar endeavors, even from "those who most bitterly deplore and reprobate his course in the rebellion." Northerners showed compassion not for the Confederate cause, but for the sacrifice and ultimate failure which that cause had generated. Again, Yankees seemed especially proud of their own ability to commiserate with the losing side. "I confess to a strong sympathy," James Lowell wrote to E. L. Godkin in 1868, "with men who sacrificed everything to a bad cause which they could see only the good side of; and, now the war is over, I see no way to heal the old wounds but by frankly admitting this and acting upon it."[29]

By the time the Reconstruction period came to a close, the sentimental notions of the 1860s and early 1870s had left a decided imprint on the tone and rhetoric of the reunion discourse. As northerners abandoned their intention to force a purely political or economic solution on the South, they enhanced the sentimental vision of reconciliation, stressing the joining of hearts and souls as opposed to a bonding through words and legislation. Northerners took tentative steps, usually symbolic ones, to demonstrate the re-creation of national bonds, always being careful to highlight the sentimental side of the reunion process. During the 1875 centennial celebration at Bunker Hill, as former Confederate soldiers marched through the streets of Boston amidst the cheers of Yankee spectators, speakers stressed these conciliatory sentiments. "You are come so that once more we may pledge ourselves to a new union," John Quincy Adams II told the enthusiastic crowd, "not to a union merely of the law, or simply of the lips: not to a union . . . of the sword, but gentlemen, the only true union, a union of hearts." The politics of Reconstruction, Adams implied, had attempted a superficial conciliation through laws and through force. A true and everlasting reunion rested on none of these, but rather on the emotions and sentiments of the heart. Setting the sentimental language of reunion against the political rhetoric of Reconstruction, conciliators managed to depoliticize the ideas and notions of reunion, suggesting that it was a concept so sacred and abstract that it could not be dirtied by the mundane specificities of politics. Certainly northerners attached a political significance to their understanding of reunion, but they also submerged those politics beneath images and metaphors that wallowed in compassion and claimed to take the high ground of emotion as opposed to the low ground of party positioning. In this way, they hoped to re-create the heartfelt, and supposedly more natural, foundations of a truly national community.[30]

For the most part, then, when reunion was discussed in the Reconstruction years, it was couched in the language of sentiment and emotion. Yet this was by no means a universally accepted proposition in the 1870s. Indeed, many found the sentimental rhetoric offensive and believed it degraded and detracted from the northern victory. "I for one," declared the orator at the centennial celebration in Detroit, "do not wish to clasp hands with the plotters and authors of the terrible strife." The main orator at a Philadelphia Memorial Day ceremony in 1879 sounded a similar theme and railed specifically against the gushing tone of sentiment. "We protest," he intoned, "against the sentimentality which seeks to promote harmony by belittling the cause for which we fought and these [Union men] died." On the same day in Dubuque, Iowa, that town's principal Memorial Day speaker, a Mr. Cooley, took an extremely dim view of the reunion sentiment and urged that "the spirit of forgiveness . . . not be degraded to the spirit of apology." He had no interest or desire, he claimed, in being part of the abhorrent new fashion, the "sentimental 'clasping of hands,'" which seemed to imply that both sides had been right in the Civil War.[31]

Why were some northerners happy to "clasp hands" with their southern brethren while others were not? It would be easy enough to discount the words of Lambert, Cooley, and others simply by classifying them as "bloody shirt" orators, by identifying them as nothing more than political opportunists out to score some points against the Democrats as they revived the bitter memories of the recent war. But to do so is to overlook the genuine appeal which this type of rhetoric undoubtedly held for a number of northern constituencies and the ways in which this language spoke to their own personal memories of the war and their concerns about reunion and the meaning of the Union victory.

Not surprisingly, some of the staunchest opponents of the early reunion sentiment were former abolitionists, especially those who continued to work for, or feel strongly about, racial reform. Imbued with an ideological commitment to racial justice, many of the old antislavery reformers remained extremely wary of the new conciliatory feelings and policies of the 1870s. In particular, they feared that the North's antislavery victory would be subsumed by the new atmosphere of fraternalism. Of all the old abolitionists, William Lloyd Garrison was one of the most resistant to the reunion mentality; he warned his fellow abolitionists against the "siren-cry of 'conciliation,'" which he believed was "humoring the old dragon spirit of slavery, and perpetuating cast distinctions by law." Garrison made his views known in preparation for an 1874 national antislavery reunion, a meeting that was called for the express purpose of denouncing the conciliatory spirit. Yet, even in this group, there were those who found the sentimental approach persuasive and were anxious to show that they would be noble and peace-loving victors. "Let it not be our fault," wrote the poet John Greenleaf Whittier, "if we are not henceforth a united people in feeling as well as in name."[32]

Of course there were some, especially in the ranks of the Republican party, who did "wave the bloody shirt" for opportunistic reasons. Republican campaigners in the 1860s and 1870s used the image of southern aggression to warn voters away from the Democratic party. Reminding them of Democratic resistance to the war, and of that party's support of secession in the southern states, these politicians insisted that a vote for the Democrats represented a vote for treason. Such Republican orators often made a special appeal to one distinct sector of the northern population, a group that had little patience for the maudlin sentimentality of reunionism, the Union veterans. While there were undoubtedly some who fed on the soldiers' hostility to the South to promote the Republican ticket and to secure political office, the veterans themselves were much more than knee-jerk bloody shirt wavers. Rather, the former soldiers' thinking often reflected a profound sense of frustration and alienation from the postwar society, an attitude that was closely bound up with the socio-economic changes that affected so many northerners of the 1860s and 1870s.[33]

The Reconstruction period witnessed intensive industrialization and capitalist expansion. An integrated market system spread into all corners of society, an extensive transportation network took shape, and large-scale industry catapulted forward. Moreover, as the economy experienced repeated cycles of expansion and bust, the chasm between classes widened tremendously. More than ever before, American society witnessed vast accumulations of wealth, gut-wrenching poverty, and heated class conflict. Appropriately, Reconstruction reached its formal conclusion amidst the most volatile labor showdown the nation had ever witnessed. As numerous observers explained it, the class war had begun to replace the civil war.

Inevitably, these dramatic changes created personal crises for large numbers of Americans. Faced with the loss of older, preindustrial skills, and sometimes with their very ability to earn a living, many northerners experienced postwar industrialization as a crisis of identity. Workers who had once prided themselves on finely honed skills often found themselves becoming little more than cogs in a chain of large-scale production. And where they had once looked forward to becoming independent artisans, now few found this to be a realistic objective. Soldiers, too, were caught in this postwar industrial crisis. Many, of course, were workers caught in the same crisis of eroding independence, but many also faced a distinct set of problems as veterans. Where once they had been the pride and the hope of the nation, now many veterans found themselves dishonored and disgraced, unable to secure jobs from which they could derive a similar sense of pride, and left to suffer with wounds or disabilities for which they received little or no assistance. Indeed, for many, the image of the returning Union veteran was that of the weak and disabled cripple, now forced to roam aimlessly through society. "These 'sad wrecks of war,'" explained Captain Fee in a Michigan ceremony, "meet us in every avenue of society. Empty sleeve and crutches are painfully common sights."[34]

The economic changes of the 1860s and 1870s precipitated a personal and ideological crisis for many of these former soldiers. Anxious to recapture the notions of dignity and self-sufficiency which had been part of the free labor rhetoric of the 1850s and a central feature of the Union soldier's identity, veterans often interpreted their present circumstances as a crisis of manhood. With their well-being and livelihood often challenged, former soldiers tried to resist this threat to their masculinity—that is, this threat to their self-defined image and role in the world. In this regard, they faced a crisis which ate away at their sense of independence, at their ability to provide for themselves and for their families, and at their sense of themselves as the same self-respecting citizens of the nation which they had always been; they evaluated the war, and the reunion process, from the standpoint of this social and personal crisis.[35]

The organizations which the veterans created, most notably the Grand Army of the Republic, and the rituals which they established all served to bolster the veteran's standing, as well as his sense of manhood. Memorial Day, or Decoration Day as it was often called in these years, became a day that was crucial for preserving the Union veteran's sense of identity and for establishing his image of manly heroism in the broader community. On June 22, 1868, John Logan, GAR commander and Radical Republican representative, proposed before Congress the celebration of Memorial

Day. Calling on local GAR chapters throughout the North to lead in the ritualized mourning, Logan sanctioned May 30 as a day for the "commemoration of the gallant heroes who have sacraficed [sic] their lives in defence of the Republic." Logan's official pronouncement reflected a trend that had already been established unofficially; local communities had organized over 100 ceremonies in 1868, a number which grew to 336 in 1869. Within a few years the number of observances increased even more as the GAR fanned out across the North and several northern states designated May 30 an official holiday.[36]

With the GAR usually assuming the main responsibility for organizing the event, the Decoration Day ceremony represented a prime moment for underscoring the soldier's sense of self-worth. Speakers often reminded their listeners of the manly accomplishments which the soldiers had achieved in war. "We measured men by a new standard," explained the Reverend Mr. Hall in Worcester, Massachusetts, in 1869; "we applied a new test of manhood" to those who upheld the Union cause. In calling on soldiers to make a deeply personal sacrifice for a noble and abstract cause, the war, many veterans believed, had pushed them to a new level of manliness. In the postwar period, however, it had become increasingly difficult to maintain a semblance of manly dignity, either in the form of independent wage-earning or in sacrificing for the greater good. "You have to task your wits," remarked one Memorial Day sermonizer in 1872, "to keep bread enough before our comrades and their families, to save the veterans of our nation from vagrancy, and the orphaned girls and widowed wives of soldiers from the dreadful by-ways of a woman's life."[37]

As this speaker suggested, the veteran's ability to watch over the war's female victims provided at least one affirmation of manhood. In fact, Memorial Day orators frequently referred to the helpless widows and orphans who were now forced to rely on the veterans for manly protection. Expressing this view in symbolic form, Memorial Day ceremonies usually placed orphaned children and widows in important roles—though often in a silent and supportive capacity—in a way that would highlight their dependence on the manly heroism of the former soldiers. All women, not just widows, were urged to participate fully in Memorial Day events, to turn out for the ceremonies and especially to make the floral tributes. In effect, they were expected to support the menfolk much as they had done during the war itself and to affirm that sense of feminine sacrifice which was devoted to masculine courage. "The ladies of Hartford, whose patriotic services during the war were second to none in any part of the country," were thus applauded by that city's newspaper for the tremendous floral contribution they made to the 1871 ceremony. In ritualized ceremonies where leading men of the community counseled male survivors to care for the neglected widows and sisters and where grieving northern women showed their devotion to the former soldiers, the Union veteran's manhood received public attention on at least this one day of the year. "We trust that the manly virtues of those who perished," editorialized the Illinois *State Journal* on Memorial Day in 1871, "may never be forgotten."[38]

Decoration Day's focus on the former soldier's manhood and dignity meant that sentimental reunion talk was often out of place at these gatherings. There was a sense, touched on by many Memorial Day speakers, that the Union soldier's honor, and manhood, would be tarnished if any regard or sympathy was shown to the Confederate soldier. For them, the Union victory was more than the triumph of abstract principles; it also entailed a personal level of success that could not be ignored. Hence a tone of gushing sentimentality did not seem fitting for those focused on themes of masculine sacrifice and nobility. One Philadelphia speaker, doing little to uphold the city's image as a place of brotherly love, claimed that the Memorial Day "spirit is violated, and our beautiful ceremonial made either meaningless or a mockery when the same honor is shown those who died to destroy as those who died to save." Memorial Day's official sponsor, John Logan, likewise believed that "'conciliation' and 'forgiveness' . . . have gone on the rampage and apologies have been as thick as autumnal leaves." Such pardoning, Logan believed, only dignified the southern cause and dishonored the Union soldiers' struggle. And, speaking in Worcester in 1868, the Reverend R. B. Stratton also sounded the anticonciliation theme and suggested how excessive sentiment might run contrary to the soldiers' more manly objectives. "Too much forgiveness, too much leniency," he claimed, "has well nigh ruined us."[39]

But even among the diehard sectionalists of the GAR, signs of conciliation could sometimes be detected in their Memorial Day speeches. Many orators suggested that, because the Union soldier had been victorious, it did not detract from his dignity to recognize the bravery of the southern fighter. Indeed, by acknowledging that a truly courageous enemy had been defeated, the Union veteran could only enhance his own sense of heroism. "We who have met a brave foe, who fought with such misguided valor," remarked John Vanderslice in an 1872 Philadelphia ceremony, "can extend to him the olive wand of peace, and ask him to unite with us." Under these circumstances, when the bravery of both sides was clearly accentuated, it even became possible to hold joint memorial ceremonies. Cincinnati's 1875 Decoration Day was a memorable one for its citizens because "for the first time since the war the brave men who were arrayed against each other in deadly war met at the graves of their comrades." Other speakers suggested that the Confederate fighting men could be forgiven precisely because they, more than anybody, now appreciated and understood the Union soldier's manliness. "The soldiers of the gray," declared Colonel Hopkins in 1875, "having learned to respect the determination of the northern people and the mettle of the northern armies, are the truest in their loyalty and the readiest to extend the hand of fellowship." By the 1870s, then, it was possible for the former soldiers and Memorial Day organizers to speak, at least occasionally, of reconciliation, as long as it was a reunion which was not overly sentimental and which stressed the masculine superiority of northern men.[40]

Although Union veterans and Memorial Day organizers maintained a more strident tone in their attitude toward reconciliation, it apparently reached a fairly small circle of Yankee society. By the end of the Reconstruction period, many northerners had little, if any, contact with the memorializing ritual. By 1875 newspapers in Worcester, Massachusetts, and Providence, Rhode Island, were reporting on the lack of funds being set aside for May 30 observances and the suspension of Decoration Day activities in many communities. "Many well-meaning people," explained the Providence *Daily Journal* in 1876, think that the war should be forgotten and "are opposed to the now national custom of annually decorating the" soldiers' graves. In 1877 the Worcester newspaper lamented the cancellation of Memorial Day activities in Westboro, Massachusetts. "Progress in forgetfulness," the paper observed, "is wonderfully rapid." Increasingly, the Memorial Day event became an activity that revolved almost solely around the GAR members and their female supporters. Outside of this circle, forgetfulness did, in fact, seem to characterize the popular mentality. Many northerners, especially those in the laboring class, were more interested in relaxation and entertainment on this one spring holiday of the year and thus spent more time at baseball games or "strawberry and ice cream" festivals than at veterans' parades and graveside ceremonies. Others were turning away from the memorial ceremonies and self-consciously celebrating a policy of historical amnesia.[41]

While the veterans, often to no avail, urged the community to remember their manly wartime sacrifices, many northerners prided themselves on their ability to forget the past. They believed that it was a sign of greatness and magnanimity that the victorious Yankees could overlook the history of sectional animosity and see only a future of national progress and harmony. In 1878 the *New York Times* chastised the old abolitionists, especially William Lloyd Garrison, for not learning how to forget. "Does he really imagine," the paper editorialized, "that outside of small and suspicious circles any real interest attaches to the old forms of the Southern question?" This type of preoccupation with the past was for useless prattlers, not for broad-minded thinkers; it was for "antiquarians," not for "statesmen." Countless speakers at centennial celebrations throughout the country likewise picked up on this theme, pointing out that a great and progressive people would know how to forget. "Let us imitate the wisdom of the ancients," declared the centennial speaker in Wilmington, Delaware, "and pledge ourselves here, upon this joyous, glorious day . . . to bury the dead past . . . [and] hand in hand . . . march forward with unity of purpose, to enlarge the prosperity, garner the glory, increase the intelligence, deepen the patriotism, and render more enduring than an Egypt pyramid, our Republic." Indeed, it seemed especially incumbent upon the winning side to show their ability to forget, as this would reveal just how broad-minded and progressive they were.[42]

Clearly, forgetfulness offered certain comforting features to the Yankee mentality. As historian David Blight has suggested, the culture of individualism and the sense of newness that had long preoccupied many Americans encouraged northerners to reject the Civil War past and look only toward the future. Forgetfulness also fit well with American notions of progress and expansion, notions which were often celebrated, albeit with a certain ambivalence, in the Reconstruction period. The ability to forget revealed that northerners, and the Union for which they stood, embraced a future of growth and development and were not obsessed with the fractures and divisions of the past. And the theme of forgetfulness could also fit the sentimentality of the postwar period. Just as the reunion sentiment urged northerners to look only at the immediate hardships and sufferings of the southern people, it also encouraged them to ignore and overlook whatever past transgressions and errors might have been committed. As many saw it, the compassionate victor should look only at the misery of the defeated; it would be petty and mean spirited to continue to harp on southern wrongs.[43]

Thus, as the Reconstruction period drew to a close, few northerners thought it noble or worthwhile to dwell on the past history of sectional hostilities. Forgiving and forgetting were the order of the day. In the context of this mentality, northerners frequently made recourse to one specific reunion metaphor, an image which suggested a rebirth of national harmony. Indeed, in the rhetoric of reunion, the family metaphor possessed a special significance for a people imbued with sentimental notions of emotions and sincerity. It had, of course, been a staple of prewar and wartime discourse. In the 1850s, as George Forgie has pointed out, statesmen frequently contemplated their failure to uphold the paternal legacy of the Founding Fathers. In the postwar years the family metaphor gained new potency as northerners searched for signs of genuine reunion sentiment. Like the new organic view of nationhood, the family metaphor emphasized a natural and moral locus for the spirit of the nation. And, removed as it supposedly was from the world of crass public interest, the family could apparently nurture and regenerate the type of emotional bonds that would truly and completely heal the national rift. Northerners and southerners, once joined like a family, would rebuild a domestic union, which would provide the truest and most sincere basis for national harmony. In the 1876 centennial celebrations, the family metaphor was a frequently recurring theme in the many reunion proclamations. Northern orators repeatedly paid homage to the notion of the North and South, both descended from the common "fathers," now reunited in the family circle. "People from all parts of our recently divided country," proclaimed Bishop William Stevens of Pennsylvania at the Philadelphia gathering, "will meet around the old family hearthstone of Independence Hall and pledge anew heart and hand in a social and political brotherhood never to be broken."[44]

Increasingly, however, the family metaphor rested less on images of brotherly cooperation or paternal legacies and more on images of marital bliss. This shift occurred for several reasons. For one, a marriage of North and South would be freed from the burdens of a familial past; reunion, in this context, was seen as a new familial entity for the present and the future. In addition, northerners used the marriage metaphor as a way to convey their image of a Union victory, one which was not rooted in greed but in feelings and emotions. Northerners played on the sentimental appeal of white southern womanhood and began to project a vision of reunion that joined northern husbands with southern wives. Northern manhood thus remained predominant, although now in the much more agreeable role of husband and romantic suitor. And, as they developed the notion of southern women's highly emotional nature, northern observers suggested that southern women could be won over by the truest sentiment of all—love. In other words, southern women who were at one moment rebellious could in the next moment become loving and committed spouses and hence a force for unification.

Russell Conwell played on these themes in his description of the intersectional marriage between the Virginia belle and the New Hampshire soldier. The southern bride, Conwell noted, was at first resistant but was soon converted by romance. And the northern husband, standing up to the unreasonable objections of the bride's rebel father, registered a victory for northern manhood as well as for national unity. Of course, despite some literary flourishes, Conwell's story reflected a real-life incident that was being repeated in many parts of the South. With so many southern men killed in battle, it was not unusual to find southern women interested in, or being encouraged to accept, Yankee husbands. Conwell met another southern gentleman who, unlike the Virginia bride's Yankee-hating father, hoped to see both his daughters take northern grooms. Nor was it odd to find northern men, especially those who were in the South for one reason or another, interested in finding a Dixie bride. Mary Easterly, an Alabama resident, wrote her northern brother in 1871 and approved of his "intention to come South to seek a bride if you ever married again." And numerous northern soldiers often wrote of the attraction they felt for southern women, a feeling which prompted some to propose marriage.[45]

Out of these real-life stories northerners gradually began to fashion an image of reunion that built upon sentimental values and developed an explicit vision of gender and power. That image, as in Conwell's story, assigned the weaker and more emotional role to the South. In contrast, the northern man revealed the finest qualities of manhood—a commitment to high moral principles and an unswerving strength of character. It was an image, in other words, that emphasized the Yankee triumph while it apparently elevated the sentimental bond above all others. Significantly, it was precisely as the Reconstruction experiment waned that this image of marital reunion became more popular. In other words, just as northern men began to back off from their direct roles as planters, political advisers, or military officers in the South, they began to fashion an image which, metaphorically, perpetuated their power and influence over Dixie.

One year after President Hayes removed the last federal troops from the South in 1877, the language of romantic and sentimental reunion reached a crescendo. This time it was prompted by a devastating yellow fever epidemic which swept through much of the South in the summer and fall of 1878. The northern press was filled with accounts of southern suffering, while northern churches and charitable organizations were urged to make their contribution toward southern relief. As an occasion of profound misery and devastation, the yellow fever epidemic prompted repeated expressions of the sentimental view of reconciliation. *Harper's Monthly* responded to the South's misfortune and set the tone for the heartfelt reunion that was supposed to come. "The whole [northern] community was stirred as in the bitter days of sixteen and seventeen years ago, but with what a different emotion!" observed *Harper's*. "This, at least, must be one of the great consolations of so melancholy a situation . . . it tends to confirm the union of hearts, without which that of hands is fruitless."

Many southerners by this point were equally susceptible to the sentimental appeal of the emerging reunion culture, especially when they were speaking to northern audiences. Southern writer Paul Hamilton Hayne gave a poetic rendition of his image of reunion in one piece of "yellow fever verse," aptly titled "Reconciliation," which appeared in journals throughout the North:

> Once wedded thus, O North! O South!
> Should Discord ope her Marah mouth,
> Smite the foul lips so basely fain
> To Outpour Hate's sharp salt tides again:
> Long raged the Storm, long lowered the Night
> O Faction fly our morning Light!

Hayne combined sentiment with the family metaphor, sounding a theme which would be repeated by many, during the yellow fever epidemic and afterward for years to come. With the factious and bitter politics of Reconstruction behind them, northerners and southerners emphasized reunion in soft, romantic tones. The union of hearts became a wedding of the North and the South, a marriage which, when described by northerners, almost always paired the feminine South with the masculine North.[46]

3

Sick Yankees in Paradise

Northern Tourism in the Reconstructed South

In August 1889 "Bab," "the Popular Society Correspondent," wrote to her readers in the Springfield *Homestead* direct from her exclusive location at the White Sulphur Springs in West Virginia. Describing the "pretty Southern girls" at this famous southern health resort, Bab wrote, "Somebody, inclined to speak very plainly, said: 'The Lord made the White Sulphur Springs and then the Southern girl, and rested, satisfied with his work.'" The speaker, Bab continued, "was a Northern man who came down here, heart whole and fancy free, and is now given over to the rule of a small woman . . . who thinks, but is not quite 'shuah,' that she's fond of him." After capturing her readers' attention with this tantalizing hint of a North-South love affair, Bab went on to tell her northern audience about the lighthearted, exciting summer at the springs, where life revolved around one enticing romance after another.[1]

In her own way, Bab captured the spirit and the sentiment of southern tourism as it appeared to northern travelers, and to readers of travel literature, in the 1870s and 1880s. No longer preoccupied with wartime anguish and destruction, northerners of the post-Reconstruction years increasingly thought of the South in tourist terms, as a land of leisure, relaxation, and romance. Bab also implied that tourism and reconciliation went hand in hand, as hands were often literally joined together in much of the literature which promoted an explicitly romantic notion of North-South reunion. Celebrating the wonders of the southern landscape and the leisure and refinement of southern health resorts, northerners in the late nineteenth century learned to appreciate the picturesque, relaxing, and seemingly feminine features of Dixie.

Southern travel, of course, was not an entirely new experience for northerners. Frederick Law Olmsted, traveling through the rice district of Georgia in the 1850s, observed that increasing numbers of Yankees had begun to seek a southern refuge from harsh northern winters. He astutely predicted that as this trend increased it would be necessary to provide "more comfortable accommodations along the line of travel . . . if not by native, then by Northern enterprise." These improvements were slow to materialize, and in the prewar years the southern tourist experience remained fairly limited in scope. For the most part, the resort life of the antebellum South centered on the Virginia springs, where wealthy plantation families made their summertime pilgrimages for relaxation and healthier air. Northerners who traveled South in these years, including men like Olmsted, seldom focused their sights on the tourist potential of the region. Rather, they concerned themselves with southern problems, especially with the political crisis that had begun to pull the nation apart. In the period immediately after the Civil War, journalist-travelers such as John Trowbridge, Sidney Andrews, and Whitelaw Reid continued this tradition by focusing on the new social problems that emerged in the war's aftermath, most notably the South's adjustment to the new demands of the free labor system.[2]

In the 1870s the South became something other than a social problem; it became an accepted sojourn on the tourist's itinerary. In this sense, southern tourism reflected a more general change in American travel. Once an intellectual and adventurous pursuit of the very elite, travel became, in the second half of the nineteenth century, a mass industry predicated on transporting herds of people through strange and unusual scenes in comfortably predictable tours. Tourists, unlike the earlier travelers, were assumed to take a passive approach to their trips, seeking out restful and comfortable accommodations and waiting to be impressed by scenery or entertained by their surroundings. Although extensive travel remained inaccessible for most of the working class, growing numbers of middle-class people could afford this type of travel by the end of the nineteenth century. As travel itself became more affordable, more Americans also had the time to take trips: after the Civil War, an increasing number of middle-class northerners regularly received a one-week paid vacation.[3]

Several factors encouraged Yankees to look southward for their vacation enjoyment. For many, the objective of a southern trip rested mainly on the question of health. In an age when countless middle-class Americans had begun to fret about the possible signs of "neurasthenia," or the nervous exhaustion to which the fast-paced modern man and woman were said to be susceptible, the southern health appeal was a persuasive one. Doctors often advised their respiratory patients to seek the warmer climate of the "sunny South," especially in Florida. Other wornout victims found their way to the mineral springs of the mountain districts, where they learned that the waters could do wonders for any number of modern ailments. The White Sulphur Springs, explained one correspondent, are "peculiarly suited . . . to the nervous and other diseases resulting from the headlong pace of modern life." Likewise, as another writer explained, "a very considerable area of the South is regarded as a sanitarium by much of the country at large, for diseases of the throat and lungs." Certainly it took significant promotional skills to convince the traveler that a region which had long been known for malaria and yellow fever could offer a miracle cure. Travel writer Charles Cory, for example, believed that northern travelers often exaggerated the benefits of the southern climate. "Some of them," he observed, "crowd the temperature up a little" to impress their friends at home. Still, as Cory suggested, the image of southern healthfulness was a powerful one and may have been enough to convince many travelers that they had found the perfect climatic corrective, even if their southern trip failed to live up to the advertisements.[4]

Aside from the salutary appeal, the southern tour also spoke to the northern tourist's desire for a more exclusive vacation. Resorts like Saratoga had long touted their own healing properties, but by the 1870s a number of travelers craved something different. Saratoga, as well as other northern spas, had simply become too common and too accessible. "The old families" at Saratoga, noted a French visitor as early as 1860, "attempted . . . to reserve the privilege of the Congress House, supposedly the most 'closed' hotel, but nouveaux riches and politicians succeeded in creeping in to the despair of the inhabitants." Hence the "old families" sought the distinction of a new tourist spot, and the middle-class traveler desired the association with a more exclusive crowd. Northern traveler Anthony Keasbey found that the vacationers in Jacksonville, Florida, were "mostly people of more retirement and wealth than are seen at those more accessible places [in the North]." Likewise, travel writers enticed visitors to some of the exclusive southern spas by drawing an explicit comparison with the increasingly ordinary resorts of Yankeedom. The Virginia springs, they explained, had "less of that Northern shoddy-ism" and none of that "Saratogian route of carriage and drag; no crowded street, with ultra style predominant in every costume." No fanciful display was required, they implied, because only true quality had gained admittance to the southern vacation spot.[5]

In this regard, the South held a unique class appeal which other tourist spots seemed to lack. Unlike the American West, also a popular tourist destination in the late nineteenth century, the South could offer an association with true aristocracy, even if it often meant the remnants and ruins of an aristocratic past. The South, as opposed to either the West or the North, seemed to have no nouveaux riches, only a bona fide elite, deeply rooted in southern tradition. Consequently, for middle- and upper-class northerners, the South became a land in which the class tensions of their own industrializing and stratified society could evaporate. The South was not a place of frantic scrambling and vying to attain status and prestige; it was certainly not a place where one's class rank was up for grabs. Rather, it was a place that had a time-honored respect for deeply ingrained social positions.

Even more, the South provided an escape from the distressing uniformity and alienation of the mass consumer society. The South, to use historian Jackson Lear's concept, offered an antimodern refuge, a place of distinctive character and real experiences, where life had not been homogenized by a corporate and commodified culture. In an age which Alan Trachtenberg has described in terms of the incorporation of American culture, northerners found their own society haunted by standardization. Railroads, industry, and department stores were, more and more, homogenizing northern life. The South, in contrast, offered the chance to experience something unique and very different. Occasionally, for the northern tourist, this meant enduring the real experience of drafty old houses and broken-down beds, but it might also mean an up-close encounter with the ruins of an old plantation, a rundown former slave cabin, or an old Confederate soldier. In the tourist's eye, these sites were seldom problematic and they were certainly not political; they only heightened the image of southern distinctiveness which the northern traveler craved. In short, the South became less the subject of sociological or political scrutiny and more the source of entertaining and intriguing travel destinations, a land filled with unique sites and attractions that stood in stark contrast to the commodified uniformity of northern society. In the tourists' eyes, the South ceased to be a sectional problem and became more of a regional antidote to northern distress.[6]

Still, it would be hard to imagine anything further removed from a tourist paradise than the American South in 1865. Sidney Andrews, Whitelaw Reid, and John Trowbridge complained repeatedly of the bad food, poor accommodations, and lack of hospitality which they encountered in their travels. By the 1870s southern accommodations still suffered, but several factors had contributed to the revival of tourism in the reconstructed South. The railroad lines that Sherman's soldiers picked apart were pieced back together in the postwar years, and several new lines were added. This transportation revolution not only made southern travel easier, but, even more important, it put the railroads, financed mainly by northern capital, in a position to control the southern tourist industry. The health resorts and mineral springs in the Virginia mountains quickly came under the close watch of the Chesapeake and Ohio (C&O) Railroad, which extended its lines to the doorstep of West Virginia's White Sulphur Springs as early as 1869. The advent of the railroad, suggested one northern writer in 1880, had made the Virginia springs a popular destination for northerners, so that "the White Sulphur is now less distinctively a Southern resort." Undoubtedly encouraged by this transportation invasion, several spas undertook extensive renovations and enlarged their facilities in the early 1870s. In the 1880s the C&O Railroad purchased three of the Virginia spas—Warm Springs, Hot Springs, and Healing Springs—forming a joint stock company to oversee the management of these resorts. Following these changes and improvements, a writer for *Harper's Weekly* agreed that "a larger proportion of Northern and Western people" now came to these retreats.[7]

Yet, throughout the late nineteenth century, the Virginia and West Virginia spas did an uneven business. The White Sulphur Springs faced financial difficulties even after the railroad line was extended. A letter writer to the *Nation* in 1877 hoped to see "an enterprising and competent

"Sketches at the White Sulphur Springs in West Virginia,"
The New York Daily Graphic, *August 22, 1874.*

proprietor" lift the White "out of its present bankrupt condition." The resort remained economically troubled until it was purchased by the C&O Railroad in the early twentieth century. Other springs, however, especially in the western Carolinas, apparently increased their business as the Virginia springs declined. In 1890 northern writer and traveler Henry Field found that Asheville, North Carolina, was "taken possession of by Northerners" in the winter months. As early as 1874, northern correspondent Anthony Keasbey discovered Aiken, South Carolina, to be a "famous resort for northern invalids." Nor did word of these spas remain confined only to well-to-do northerners. In 1889 a widely read Populist newspaper from Kansas contained an extensive discussion of resort life at the Hot Springs in the North Carolina mountains.[8]

But it was Florida which eventually became the focal point of southern tourism. Northerners poured into this southern state as early as the 1860s, searching out real estate and citrus growing possibilities as well as the healthful climate. By the following decade, Florida's tourist claim was well established. Writing in 1873 from her new Florida home, Harriet Beecher Stowe observed that the state was fast becoming a popular winter retreat for northerners. In the same year, Edward King found that "fully one-half of the resident population of Jacksonville is Northern, and has settled there since the war." Jacksonville remained an important center for northern tourism, especially after the completion of a luxury hotel in 1880. In the 1870s Jacksonville also provided the jumping-off point for what became the standard Florida vacation: a trip down the St. Johns River, with visits to some of the important landing points, including an essential stopover in St. Augustine. Certainly if there ever was a prototypical southern tour, this was the one. To embark on this trip, northerners traveled by rail or steamboat to Savannah, occasionally stopping in Charleston en route. From Savannah they could continue either by train or by boat to Jacksonville. However they traveled, the route began to swarm with Yankees. Charles Landis, a Philadelphia businessman who took the tour in November 1883, found that the boat on the St. Johns was so crowded with "emigrants, tourists and consumptives" that he could not secure himself a private room and was forced to make do with a cot. Anthony Keasbey, traveling in 1874, discovered that because rooms were scarce on his boat trip, some of the passengers slept under tables. Keasbey was also turned away at hotels along the way for lack of room. Still, the tour remained so popular that books for children even promoted the joys of this standard route to Florida. "People from New England," explained Hezekiah Butterworth, author of the Zig-Zag series of children's books, "find a favorite route to Savannah by the Boston and Savannah Steamship Company's elegant boats." From there, Butterworth explained, it was a quick trip to Jacksonville and the St. Johns River, "thus making for $100 a Southern tour as historic and romantic as it is warm and flowery."[9]

The popularity of the St. Johns tour created a boom in commercial tourism in Florida and in certain select spots along the way. Hotels sprang up throughout the state and in southern Georgia. Northern industrialist Henry Flagler created the Florida tourist industry practically singlehandedly; beginning with the construction of a luxury hotel in St. Augustine in 1885, Flagler proceeded to accumulate Florida railroad lines and build a string of hotels along the Florida coast. In 1870 the federal census listed only forty-six hotel keepers in Florida; by 1890 this number had increased to 208. Even these figures do not tell the complete story, as many tourists boarded with local people in their homes during the busiest points in the travel season.[10]

Although northern investors like Flagler often held a controlling interest in southern tourism, local southern leaders occasionally jumped in to reap the benefits of the Florida boom before outsiders got the chance. During the early 1870s travelers en route to Jacksonville had begun to stop in Thomasville, Georgia, known and appreciated by many for its dry climate. Conscious of the need to target the growing wave of northern tourists, town leaders urged construction of suitable accommodations. By 1875 the city's first luxury hotel had been built by one of the wealthiest men of the community. Perhaps to insure a northern clientele, he maintained it under northern management through the remainder of the nineteenth century. In 1880 former Georgia governor Joseph E. Brown visited Thomasville and advocated that even more be done for tourism. These northern travelers, Brown explained, "will be numbered by your capacity to entertain them." Residents heeded Brown's appeal so well that by 1886 one Minnesota newspaper estimated that the town had hosted 11,000 tourists that year. One visitor supposedly remarked that the people of Thomasville lived, for the most part, "on sick Yankees." By the 1890s many of those Yankees had built winter homes in the area, thereby encouraging President McKinley to make Thomasville one of his official vacation spots in 1895 and again in 1899.[11]

Thomasville, like other southern resort areas, undertook vigorous campaigns to inform northerners of its attractions. Indeed, by the 1870s the northern reader was bombarded by an abundance of travel and "local color" literature from all over the country, all of which seemed to be directed to the potential tourist. Northern magazines stocked their pages with this descriptive fare, some of it in the form of tourist accounts and some as illustrative landscape literature loosely woven into a fictional plot. Hotel owners in the southern mountains frequently invited local colorists to visit, hoping that these writers would be inspired to advertise the scenic wonders of their particular locale in a new magazine story. Even the literature that examined social and political problems revealed only thinly disguised tourist motivations. Robert Underwood Johnson, editor of *Scribner's Magazine* in the 1870s, recalled the lofty motivations of that journal in the conception of Edward King's massive 1873 series on "The Great South." "It was the first high note of nationalism struck by the magazine," Johnson wrote, "and was conceived in magnanimity and sympathy." Perhaps, but King's series also made frequent mention of the resorts, their facilities, and the railroad routes that one could take to get there. Writing of the Virginia springs, King made sure to note that "the Northerner is especially welcomed at all these watering places." Nor did the Richmond and Danville Railroad miss the point of King's series when, nine years later, the railroad's travel writers published a tourist brochure which suggested that King had done as good a job as they could in describing the scenic wonders of western North Carolina.[12]

Of course, there were many for whom the promotional literature offered only a vicarious journey through the South. Not everyone could heed the advice of the travel promoter and catch the next train to Charleston or Savannah. The cost of the trip—$24 to travel by rail from Philadelphia to Charleston in 1869—impeded many who might have had the urge to travel. Nor were southern hotels inexpensive. In 1871 Sarah Putnam, daughter of a wealthy New England family, commented on the relatively high cost of southern accommodations—usually about $4 per person per night. In New Orleans in 1884, Charles Landis found that many travelers had cut their visits short, "as charges for all kinds of service are too high." Apparently, even for the expanding group of middle-class vacationers, the costs of a southern tour may have been somewhat prohibitive, a fact which might have enhanced the sense of exclusiveness for others. Moreover, although travel to the South might have become more accessible for some New Yorkers and New Englanders, midwesterners do not seem to have been as affected by the urge to visit Dixie. "We of Kansas," observed one journalist in 1881, "do not go South."[13]

Even for those who made the trip, there were times when the actual experience never really lived up to the promotional enticements. "The trip up the St. Johns," observed New Hampshire traveler Charles Washburn, was "not as pleasant as where we were last summer on the Winnipisiogee . . . but considerably like it in many places only more monotonous." Chicago traveler Erastus Hill also expressed disappointment during his 1877 sojourn. "I haven't found Florida," he noted during February, "to be a land of flowers at this season of the year anymore than Illinois." More often, travelers enjoyed the scenery but were unhappy with their accommodations, especially if they traveled in the wake of postwar chaos. Charles Cory found that "in Florida 'to bed' and 'to sleep' are not synonymous terms; 'mattresses' and 'stock farms' may be." As another northern travel writer put it, "The recognized standard of comfort is lower at the South than it is at the North." William Lloyd Garrison, Jr., traveling through the South in 1875, would have agreed. The southern hotels, he wrote to his wife, "make no provisions for heating, and a cold dampness pervades them." Nonetheless, and somewhat to his amazement, "crowds continue to pour down here from the North. The cars and steamboats are loaded and the hotels are reaping a harvest."[14]

As Garrison suggested, the southern tour remained popular despite the inconveniences. Indeed, there were some who even found the primitive conditions appealing. For them, the southern tour offered the chance to live simply and without the abundance of fashions and material objects found up North. The rooms at the Old Sweet Springs, explained northern travel writer Mary Dodge, were seldom "lavishly supplied in respect of carpets or other unnecessary furniture. Yet the fact that we can be so very comfortable with only the necessaries for material enjoyment is something worth learning in a Virginia trip by the pampered daughters of metropolitan success." Writing of the Arkansas Hot Springs, another travel writer likewise appreciated the simpler style of southern fashions. "There is very little dressing done by the ladies," he observed, "and the gentlemen lounge about dressed solely with regard to comfort." Northerners were apparently drawn to what they saw as a more genuine and personal feeling which characterized southern resort life, a condition now rarely found up North. Many northerners had come to find their own personal interactions to be less than genuine and direct; consumerism and materialism seemed, more and more, to mediate human relationships. In contrast, the southern resorts offered a more dynamic and individual quality. "In the midst of the fast and somewhat pretentious and 'shoddy' existence of the present time," wrote Virginian John Esten Cooke of the White Sulphur Springs, "you find here the same air of high-breeding and rational relaxation . . . which characterized the White Sulphur during the ancient regime, before the modern spirit of democracy had levelled everything to so distressing a uniformity." Cooke called it democracy, but, to a great extent, he was speaking of the alienation experienced by many northerners in a society increasingly characterized by mass consumption and industrial conformity.[15]

In the end, people often were prepared to overlook some of the personal discomforts if their travel experience afforded them some type of distinctive personal interaction, one that rose above the mundane middle-class conventionalism of the North. Hence many relished the social interactions they had with southern residents just as much as the chance to take the healing waters or breathe the soothing air. One *Nation* writer encouraged his northern readers to vacation in Dixie, noting that they would be pleasantly surprised to find that southern manners possessed an "ineffable charm . . . indicating a recognition of the fact that even if you are no better than any other man, you are different, and that your peculiarities are respectable." In contrast, Yankee manners apparently revealed the same blandness and anonymity that had fallen upon northern society, a tendency "to avoid anything which is likely to lead you to forget that you are simply a human male."[16]

Northern travelers also demanded that the South convey its distinctive and more intimate qualities in the scenery and the landscape which they saw. Ultimately, what was appreciated in a southern journey was its unplanned and unregulated quality, its lack of northern conformity and standardization. As many observed, the South might lose its special tourist appeal if it adopted too many northern features. Edward King thus fretted about the damage which the railroad might do to southern scenery. He objected, for example, to the construction of a railroad between Jacksonville and St. Augustine, claiming it "would rob good old St. Augustine of its romance." And in Texas, a land "of beautiful rivers and strange foliage," King again warned that "the railroad will yet subdue you! Then there will be no more mystery in your plains."[17]

Every tourist seemed to yearn for an encounter with something that was distinctively southern, with something that would awaken in them a sense of life and drama that had been lost amidst the morass of Yankee conformity. Inevitably, this quest encouraged a tendency to stereotype the old South, to highlight the familiar features of the antebellum legend such as the sweeping plantations, the columned mansions, and the beautiful belles. In the 1870s and 1880s the quest for the distinctive South also encouraged travelers to overlook the social and political problems of the region, to see the vestiges of the slave system or even the monuments to the lost cause as touching and charming sites. These things spoke to a dramatic, sometimes tragic past, one which could not always be admired, but which offered a sense of history that now seemed absent from the northern landscape.

Not surprisingly, Yankee travelers yearned to see the old plantations and planter estates. New Englander Caroline Barrett White traveled with her husband in 1880 on the Mississippi River and was thrilled when Mrs. Barrow, "a charming . . . very ladylike and intelligent" fellow passenger invited her ashore to visit the family plantation. "I would like so much," replied White, "to see something of the old plantation style." Other northern travelers were especially moved by the image of plantation ruins. Charleston, explained travel writer Albert Webster, "is full of picturesque surprises and unique architectural combinations, and the disasters that have overtaken it have left their traces in ruins that are, in some cases, wonderfully beautiful." Following the European tourist's compulsion to seek out charming and decrepit ruins, the traveler in Dixie often did the same. In fact, the sight of decay and ruination in the South frequently encouraged northern travelers to compare those sites with the fashionable tourist vistas of Europe. Sarah Putnam, for example, believed that Charleston, "with its ancient looking, moss covered walls . . . might pass for some old Italian town." But perhaps more important than the comparison with Europe was simply the presence of ruins, which again offered that distinctive contrast to Yankee blandness. Ruins indicated the absence of anything modern and industrial and typically northern. The South, in other words, had room for ruins while the North did not. Such was the image which came to Constance Woolson's mind in her description of Charleston. "The neighborhood," she wrote, ". . . is rich in colonial memories and Revolutionary legends, verified and emphasized by the old houses and gardens which still remain, not having been swept away by the crowding population, the manufactories, the haste and bustle, of the busy North."[18]

Ruins, even of a slave market or a plantation estate, appealed to the tourist's aesthetic demands and thus became devoid of political content. In the same vein, even Confederate history could make for pleasant sightseeing. Because the relics of the lost cause again spoke to something that was old, historic, and distinctively southern, northern travelers often made a point of seeing, and even enjoying, these images. In Augusta, Georgia, New York attorney William Davies stopped to see the Confederate monument. "The whole work," he wrote in his 1882 travel diary, "is in perfect taste and admirably executed." Charles Washburn was bored by the St. Johns excursion but was impressed with the Confederate sculptures in Savannah. The city, he found, was "quite Southern" and "got up in good style," an effect that was apparently enhanced by the statues of "distinguished heros" of "the 'Lost Cause.'" It was not long before the old and traditional features of the South became the objects of northern commercialization. By 1888 one promotional account was using the lost cause to advertise the charms of Richmond. Here, it was said, "the spirit of the Lost Cause might almost be supposed to haunt Capitol Hill."[19]

Perhaps most important, the joys of southern tourism and the beauty of the southern landscape had the power to obliterate one of the thorniest, and most sectionally divisive, problems in this postwar society. In their endless and enthusiastic descriptions of southern scenery, northerners frequently lauded the contribution which the freedpeople made. At a time when many northerners continued to concern themselves with the plight of southern blacks and when some still raised a cry against southern abuses of African American rights, travel writers—from both the North and the South—helped to soften and sentimentalize the "negro problem" amidst an abundance of flowery prose. In the eyes of the northern traveler, blacks became less of a problem and more of a "picturesque" element on the southern scene.

Many travelers chose to view African Americans as simply another feature of the landscape. One northern visitor described her scenic journey down the Mississippi, noting "the beautiful plantations that lined both sides of the river, the numerous boats passing . . . the singing of the negroes as they discharged and took on cargo." Southern blacks became the objects of the tourist adventure, the "attraction" that no visitor to the sunny Southland should miss. The vision of black people, spotted from the train as it headed southward, heralded a traveler's arrival in the true South. "The negro huts along the way, with a grinning, turbaned colored woman standing in each doorway," one travel guide explained, "apprises the Northerner that he is certainly 'right smart down South.'" Likewise, in order to prove their adherence to the tourist regimen, northern visitors sought out pictures of these genuine southern articles. In one fictional travel piece, a northern girl "found opportunity to use her camera, and obtained a number of new Florida types,—negroes busily lading the boat or lazily looking on, too well-to-do for active exertion." And, as an early-twentieth-century article explained in regard to northern visitors of an earlier period, "It used to be the fashion in Thomasville to go out in the country to the cabin of an old 'mammy' who was a famous cook." In this way, the more adventurous tourist could have an up-close encounter with a part of the southern scene.[20]

A number of tourists believed that one of the most distinctive interactions with African Americans could be had by attending a black church service. Especially during the 1870s, and perhaps influenced by some of the concerns of the Reconstruction period, many travelers made this a regular stop on their tourist itinerary. In 1870 Amory Lawrence, then a student at Harvard College, made a tour of Richmond, Virginia, and visited "a negro church in [the] afternoon; a very impressive service, an occasion of a funeral." Sarah Putnam, traveling as a young woman through Florida in 1871, attended a black service in Magnolia. She vividly described the energetic ritual she witnessed, the singing and foot stamping which "was enough to make you laugh, yet it was all done in such an earnest, kindly way, you ought respect it too." For many northern tourists, this experience may have provided the type of personal encounter which they craved while it also confirmed their ideas about black spirituality. Little else that they would see could offer such a point of contrast with Yankee blandness and conformity. "We went to Zion Church with Br'er Brown," wrote northern industrialist Edward Atkinson while traveling in Chattanooga in 1880. "The service was regular African and the singing genuine. . . . one cannot help being moved by it all."[21]

Most tourists, however, especially after about 1880, preferred to meet the "negro element" in less direct encounters. After years of reading travel literature which had objectified southern blacks as features of the scenery, most northerners became convinced that they needed only to "see" black people, not interact with them, in order to have the tourist experience which they craved. What became more important was how the black presence enhanced the southern scene and made it more unusual. Consequently, writers and travelers seldom restrained themselves from declaring a gathering of black people, or even a lone black worker, to be "picturesque." No adjective was used more often in the descriptive literature than this one, indicating that American travel writers had become thoroughly imbued with European aesthetic standards. Widely used by European artists and writers as early as the seventeenth century, the concept of the picturesque had offered observers the chance to appreciate the ordinary scenes of daily life, including dilapidated ruins or simple peasant folk, in the context of this new aesthetic standard. By the late nineteenth century, both Europeans and Americans used the picturesque formula to render possibly threatening features of society—such as poverty and the underclass—safe and amusing. Not surprisingly, travel writers in the American South found potentially troublesome blacks to be prime targets for picturesque descriptions.[22]

Indeed, travel writers could hardly mention the "negro" without attaching a picturesque adjective. Celebrating the "romance" of one "remote and isolated plantation," Edward King focused on "the tall and stalwart women, with their luxuriant wool carefully wrapped in gayly colored handkerchiefs; the picturesque and tattered children . . . the groups of venerable darkeys." Referring to all southern blacks, Charles Dudley Warner found that "these people somehow never fail to be picturesque, whatever attitude they take, and they are not at all self-conscious." Mark Twain, who relished the chance to ridicule the most banal and hackneyed descriptions of the South, pounced on this racial use of "picturesque." Pinpointing two of the most frequently noted sights in the tourist litany, Twain described a New Orleans canal where one could see "an occasional alligator" and "an occasional picturesque colored person on the bank, flinging his statue-rigid reflection upon the still water and watching for a bite." Twain may have borrowed his setting from a travelogue written the same year as his own in which this very sight prompted a more serious and bucolic treatment. Watching New Orleans blacks fish from the open sewers, this author wrote, "The scenery becomes picturesque, and the sewers turn poetical."[23]

Despite the increasing recourse to this uninspired expression, it frequently insinuated itself into very specific settings. Since the urge to seek out European-style "ruins" could be satisfied in the search for the extremely modest (if not impoverished) architectural relics in the southern landscape, homages to the picturesque often appeared in connection with the shabby, dilapidated "huts" in which the freedpeople lived. In this way, the poverty and hardship of the southern black experience became a scenic delight in the eyes of the northern traveler. Edward King commented on the "picturesque grouping of coarsely thatched roofs [which] marked negro 'quarters'" as he passed the setting of a former Louisiana plantation. Describing a gathering of black corn-shuckers, another travel writer set the scene with the appropriate aesthetic elements: "Some ten or twelve roughly-constructed yet picturesque [black] cabins were nestled at the foot of the hill, under the wide-spreading branches of a group of noble trees." Emphasizing that a truly picturesque scene had been discovered, he thought it "worthy the pencil of a master-artist." And a traveler in Richmond marveled at the artist's ability to capture the picturesque. Regarding an illustration of black dwellings, he wrote, "One cannot help recognizing in this sketch how much more effective in the hands of the artist is dilapidation than tidiness, and a ruin than a perfect structure. The ramshackle porches of the negro tenements here have a higher effect than would a neat row of white-painted houses with green blinds in a well-kept New England village." Again, northerners had found the distinctive qualities of southern life, even black impoverishment, worthier of description than Yankee homogeneity.[24]

Black people at work apparently assumed especially picturesque qualities. As one writer explained, "There is something picturesque in a field of darkeys at mid-day; their women work, and work furiously too; the men wear flaunting hats of yellow straw, and the other sex bright bandana handkerchiefs bound high upon their heads." At a time when most northerners had begun to surrender many elements of the free labor ideology, especially in regard to black people's ability to advance by the formula of hard work and middle-class success, these images suggested that grueling, physical labor was the African American's natural lot in life, indeed, that such work was picturesque. Although he refrained from using that adjective in his description, Edward King experienced a similar scenic excitement from the cotton fields, where he saw workers and cotton blend together in panoramic pleasure. "Nothing can be more beautiful than the appearance of a cotton-field . . . when the snowy globes of wool are ready for picking, and the swart laborers, with sacks suspended from their shoulders, wander between the rows of plants, culling the fleeces."[25]

But southern blacks did not need to be hard at work in order to be picturesque. Following the European prescription, Americans' appreciation of this aesthetic standard allowed them to relish the sight of an idle, nonindustrious work force. Combined with a minstrel stereotype that had long made fun of black people as lazy, the worship of the picturesque in the 1870s and 1880s reinforced northern whites' image of indolent African Americans. Numerous travelers thus joyfully observed idle black workers, described by John Muir during his 1867 trip as "easy-going and merry, making a great deal of noise and doing little work." Photographer Rudolf Eickmeyer offered pictorial endorsements of this view in his scenes of southern black life taken in the 1880s and 1890s. In countless photos he portrayed his subjects, frequently in the fields, but seldom at work. Rather, he captured them in happy and carefree moments, when they were thought to be shirking their responsibilities. Once more, the aesthetic standard placed African Americans' claims to the free labor ideology in jeopardy. As many northerners undoubtedly concluded, these apparently lackadaisical workers could never hope to ascend the ladder of economic progress.[26]

There was, of course, no happy and carefree work force up North, nor a picturesque urban slum. But the South, caught in a premodern and preindustrial era, had the ability to turn what would be an urban eyesore in a northern setting into something charming and appealing. In this way, the South seemed to offer a refuge from northern social tensions. While the North represented industrialism and class conflict, the South seemed of a different time and place—if such a time and place ever existed—when life was simpler and more leisurely and when class differences seemed to be more natural and acceptable. In other ways, too, the South offered a welcome retreat from northern modernity. Especially in the 1870s and 1880s, when the northern middle class increasingly voiced concerns about their frenetic work pace and sought the benefits of relaxation and play, the South seemed the ideal refuge from the grind of hard work. It was, in effect, the perfect place for leisure. Yet, as historian Daniel Rodgers has explained, northerners never felt completely comfortable about abandoning their ethic of hard work in what seemed to be a perpetually depression-prone economy. By regionalizing leisure and relaxation in the southern states, northern vacationers seemed to solve some of their problems, applying themselves avidly to their work life in the North and unwinding peacefully in their vacation life in the South. As they created this dichotomy between northern work and southern leisure, middle-class northerners also assigned to the South a set of attributes which further divided the regions on a whole range of issues, mirroring the nineteenth-century split between public and private, work and home, and, ultimately, between masculine and feminine spheres. In effect, northerners imposed a traditional, Victorian dichotomy on the two sections, finding in the South a haven for those feminine and domestic ideals which seemed to be disappearing from Yankee society.[27]

By viewing the South as a leisurely retreat from the northern workplace, northern travelers created an image of the southern vacation which conformed to classic, Victorian notions of domesticity. Only one year after the end of the Civil War, *Appleton's* tour guide suggested some of what made the southern sphere so distinct. Describing the "old Dominion" style of life on Virginia's Eastern Shore, replete with "manorial homesteads" and "lordly acres," this guide urged "the business man, careworn and wearied, [to] slip down from New York, Philadelphia, or Baltimore . . . [to] land lazily at ancient Accomac, or thereabouts, and forget for a little while the wrinkling perplexities of cabinets and commerce, in the quiet pleasures of simple domestic life within doors." Here, emulating the life of aristocratic southern planters, northern businessmen and professionals could discover the perfect formula for rest and relaxation in the South's unique domestic setting. The southern health resorts, in particular, offered this feeling of relaxed domesticity in an atmosphere of historical romance and refinement. Like the idealized middle-class home of the nineteenth century, they offered the busy northerner an escape from the workplace, something which the northern home no longer seemed to provide. If anything, the northern middle-class home had become more like a showplace of consumerist excess, hardly a place of refuge from economic worries. In contrast, the southern vacation spot, often lacking in furniture and creature comforts, could be even better than home. Travel writer Mary Dodge, for example, wrote approvingly of the lack of lavish furnishings in the Virginia hotels. She found this to be indicative of the slow, deliberate pace of life at the resorts and of the unique quality of the southern vacation experience. "At first," she wrote, this lethargy "frets one who may be tuned up to Northern speed, as though the last trump were sounded . . . but you grow rapidly used to this unhurried life." According to another travel writer, the "flavor of domesticity, so rare in hotel life, the White Sulphur Springs has never lost." As numerous observers suggested, the antebellum aristocrats of the South had mastered the art of domestic relaxation, a skill unknown among the unwashed masses or the nouveaux riches of the North. Fortunately, the overworked (but presumably well-bred) northerner could still find this refined relaxation at the nearby southern spas.[28]

It was, of course, more than just age or distance which made the southern resort a unique Victorian refuge. These resorts maintained an image of domestic comfort, largely due to a distinctively southern orientation toward leisure. As a writer for the *Nation* explained, "The traditions of the old [southern] system are . . . unquestionably a better basis for good hotel-keeping than anything we have at the North. . . . To be well cared for you must expect it and be used to it, and this condition the Southerners fulfill in a much higher degree than we do." Significantly, the aristocratic South had known true domestic comfort under slavery, the remnants of which could still be seen in the service rendered at the southern resorts. One visitor to the Warm Springs was thrilled at the attention she received from "the stately old Dinah who bore our burden of shawls and bags with the step of a queen as she ushered us into the old-time parlor." In describing the Arkansas Hot Springs, another writer made certain to mention that vacationers could enter the mineral baths "with the help of the negro

"Diven Rowing Us up Peter's Creek, Wed., April 26th, Fla.," by Sarah G.
Putnam. Reprinted from Sarah G. Putnam Journal, vol. 11, April 1871–
March 1873, courtesy of the Massachusetts Historical Society.

bath-man." And the *Nation*'s writer concluded that, in the South, "the
waiter world, partly from habit, and partly, no doubt, from race tempera-
ment, render [their service] with a cheerfulness we are not familiar with
here [in the North]." Clearly, what the South lacked in domestic furnishings, they made up for in domestic service.[29]

This emphasis on the domestic side of southern tourism suggested only
one component of the region's feminine appeal, a quality travel writers
made more explicit in their descriptions of both the scenery and the
resorts. In this respect, the tourist in the South seemed to share the
sentiments of the western tourist who demanded that his vacation spot
"correspond closely to standards that were . . . generally feminine rather
than masculine." But, perhaps even more in the South than in the West,
the lush, wild, and relaxed qualities of the landscape, as well as the
romance of its history and domestic setting, called up an excess of feminine
adjectives in the descriptions of travel writers and local colorists. The
historic rivalry between North and South may have also encouraged
postwar travelers to continue to make stark and explicit comparisons

between the two regions, the southern setting offering a feminine contrast to the North's more masculine way of life. Charles Dudley Warner, for example, found New Orleans to be unabashedly seductive and possessed of an apparently feminine sensuality that more northern-style cities seemed to lack. "I suppose we are all wrongly made up," he explained, "and have a fallen nature; else why is it that while the most thrifty and neat and orderly city only wins our approval . . . such a thriftless, battered and stained, and lazy old place as the French quarter of New Orleans takes our hearts?" Most travel writers found this feminine romance not in urban settings, but in the gardens or the country, where nature lay in sensual abundance. Describing the gardens of Savannah, Georgia, Edward King wrote, "There is nothing that reminds one of the North in the deliciously embowered [*sic*] chief city of Georgia, surrounded with its romantic moss-hung oaks, its rich lowlands, and its luxuriant gardens, where the magnolia, the bay and the palmetto vie with one another in the exquisite inexplicable charm of their voluptuous beauty." Likewise, a turn-of-the-century travel guide stressed the feminine qualities of the Virginia springs. "There is a feminine grace in all such beautiful scenes," this pamphlet explained. "The exquisite forms of the waving current, the crystal depths of the silent pools, . . . the snowy purity of the descending torrent, the freshness of the living foliage, the happy life of birds and flowers, all made glad by the presence of the stream, suggest the feminine idea, which ever gives life and grace and beauty to that which without it would be but a barren wilderness."[30]

The natural opulence of the South prompted numerous writers to see the woman's touch in the southern landscape. More often, however, writers employed feminine descriptions to suggest the languid and idle qualities of the region. Indeed, the whole notion of southern leisure suggested a more feminine style of life. To Edward King, a group of beautiful, "dusky" women in Florida embodied the feminine and idle spirit of Dixie. This gathering, explained King, was "the South, slumbrous, voluptuous, round and graceful." And King frequently called up the image of "Eve" and "Eden" to feminize the South's less industrious side. Contrasting the garden South to the factory North, King wrote, "If you wish once again to find the lost gate of Eden, if you wish to gain the promised land, if you wish to see in this rude, practical America of ours an 'earthly paradise,' where life is good, because Nature has invested it with everything that is delicious and fairest . . . seek the Teche country [of Louisiana]." If Louisiana suggested Eden, the proof of this metaphor could be found in visions not of Adam, but of Eve. "Sometimes," King wrote during his stay in New Orleans, "through a portal opened by a slender, dark-haired, bright-eyed Creole girl in black, you catch a glimpse of a garden, delicious with daintiest blossoms . . . a mass of bloom which laps the senses in slumbrous delight. Suddenly the door closes, and your paradise is lost, while Eve remains inside the gate!"[31]

As they had done with the black population, travel writers in the 1870s and 1880s sang the praises of the South's feminine inhabitants as if they had become part of the regional landscape. Several authors exploited the feminine names of southern states to make the analogy between femininity and southern geography explicit. There was "Virginia of Virginia" or, as seen on the stage, *The Heart of Maryland*. Other writers chose favorite states which, so they claimed, excelled in their production of feminine loveliness; the women of the region were described along with the flora and fauna of the land. "I think the women of the Alabama valley," wrote traveler Stephen Powers, "especially at Selma and on the great plantations west of it, are the best type of American beauty." Edward King agreed that Alabama was "a land of beautiful women," but Charles Warner seemed to prefer Kentucky. He found women there to be "attractive in another way from the intelligent New England women" and believed "it would be no disadvantage to anybody if the graciousness, the simplicity of manner, the refined hospitality" of Kentucky's women spread to the women of other states. Another travel writer made the scenic implications of southern femininity even more explicit. Comparing the women in one Savannah garden with the delicate vegetation, he described "the beauteous maidens, the bloom on whose fair cheeks would shame the blushing rose, and in whose bright eyes are deeper, tenderer things than ever artist limned or poet sang." Lovely as flowers and soft as dew, southern women, in the language of travel writers, epitomized the southern landscape.[32]

Some writers and tourists went so far as to suggest that, under the influence of the South's unique domestic and romantic heritage, a superior strain of femininity had been created. Certainly by the 1880s northern women seemed far removed from some of the stricter Victorian standards of womanliness. Found with increasing frequency in the ranks of college students, laborers, and political activists, women in the North were yet a further indication of the distressing modernity that had befallen Yankee culture. As many feared, there now seemed to be little demarcation between the male and female spheres, at least among middle-class northerners. In contrast, southern women retained distinctive feminine charms. A northern editor, for example, found the superior femininity of southern women revealed in their physical beauty. "The young ladies of the South," he noted, "are, with very few exceptions, beautiful, and we see no sickly, ugly or consumptive-looking females, such as are to be found in all similar gatherings in the North." *Cosmopolitan* writer Marion Baker worried about "the masculinity and independence of too many Northern women" and found them "less charming, less womanly" than their southern counterparts. Yankee modernity had apparently homogenized the northern population, robbing women of their distinctively feminine attributes. In the South, however, a sharper line had always divided the masculine and feminine spheres, thus making the traveler more aware of the region's unique femininity. The women of antebellum Savannah, explained I. W. Avery, "were pure, luxurious, modest, and thoroughly feminine. They were absolutely helpless, so far as the practical world was concerned, and wholly dependent upon father, husband, brother, or son." Stressing the superiority of this strict Victorian division of gender, he noted that "there has never been a finer strain of ladies."[33]

Ultimately, the finest strain of southern womanhood could be seen—in full flower and glory—at southern resorts and hotels. In their bombastic broadcasts for the health resorts, tourism promoters seldom neglected to mention one of the spas' principal attractions—the incomparably lovely southern belles. Just as no tour of the South could be complete without viewing a picturesque grouping of blacks, no visitor to the resorts could feel satisfied until those beautiful belles had been seen in all their magnificence. Comparing the southern resort belle to her colder northern sister, Mary Dodge wrote of the White Sulphur Springs, "It is a paradise indeed for unmarried belles, who rule there with a sway undivided by their Benedictine sisters, such as queen it at Saratoga or Newport." Impressed by the feminine allure of both the scenery and the springs, Edward King compared the two while visiting the Greenbrier. "In early autumn," he wrote, "the leaves of the maple, the hickory, the oak, the chestnut, the sweet gum, and the pine, vie in color with the gay toilets in which the Southern belles clothe themselves." Overwhelmed by this bevy of beauty, King described the dinner scene at this resort, where "hundreds of beautiful girls from every part of the South, clad in ballroom costume, are seated at the round tables in the long hall." The resident physician at the White

Sulphur Springs also advocated the feminine charms of the spa, hoping perhaps that what the waters failed to cure might be healed with the feminine touch. "Here congregate the fairest of the fair from every state," explained the doctor, "and one can gaze, and gaze on beauty until the heart reels in its very fullness."[34]

In the antebellum period men had generally outnumbered women at the southern spas, but in the late nineteenth century women predominated among the tourist crowd and were well-represented at the southern resorts. One travel writer in the 1890s found that at the Florida hotels "there were more often three than two women to a man." Civil War deaths had significantly reduced the male population, a fact which placed single women in the majority at numerous southern gatherings. "It is nigh about the death of a fellow to go to a party," one southern man told Russell Conwell. "There never fails to be three girls to one fellow, and such a squirming, kissing, hugging as we do get!" Moreover, women came in especially large numbers to the health resorts, drawn by the well-advertised medicinal features that made special promises for female clients. The springs in Arkansas, for example, were apparently "in great repute among the fair sex, who fancy that it improves their complexions." As the increasingly hectic pace of life led many to fear for even southern women's susceptibility to the prevalent nervous diseases, the mineral springs were quick to advertise their curative powers for the nervous constitution of the modern woman. The publicist for the Red Sulphur Springs thus noted the water's healing effect on "female diseases," which lately seemed to be "increasing in frequency and severity." Coinciding with a general call in the society to improve women's physical well-being (and not to tax their mental capacities), the southern springs promised a healthier and livelier womanhood, a point to which many women seemed to respond.[35]

Still, as most travelers and guidebooks revealed, the women turned out at the springs more for mingling than for medicine. Edward King found two separate groups of women and invalids monopolizing the scene at the Greenbrier springs. "At the early morning," he wrote, "the parlor is filled with ladies who make their engagements for the day, and with the customary rows of invalids who chat cheerily." As Bab of the Springfield *Homestead* explained, "There are three things which the girl of the White Sulphur Springs must do," and none of them had much to do with improving her health. "She must dance well, she must be even-tempered, and she must understand the coquetry of the thimble." Once a woman had mastered these arts, she had a good chance to become the belle of the season, an implicit competition which, if the publicists are to be believed, held every female vacationer in its grip. Indeed, the reigning belle of the Virginia resorts received publicity throughout the land. The New York *World* thus promoted Mary Triplett, the resort belle from 1868 to 1874, as the South's "unrivalled beauty." Through the 1870s and 1880s, a succession of reigning belles captured Triplett's title. Irene Langhorne went from resort belle in the 1880s to become the famous "Gibson Girl" in the 1890s, after marrying the artist Charles Dana Gibson. Prominent northern families entered the fray as well, attempting to mold their daughters into the part of the southern belle. Rhapsodizing over the romance of the White Sulphur Springs, one tour guide found that belles from both North and South could be found at this resort because "a girl is scarcely equipped for a social campaign until she has had her season at 'the White.'" As this brochure suggested, the life of the belle—especially the reigning belle at the Virginia resorts—offered a model of charming and sociable femininity to which all American women could aspire.[36]

Apparently the rivalry among the belles, especially between the representatives of the North and the South, could be fierce. The undue attention which newspapers and tourist promoters paid to the reigning belle undoubtedly contributed to an intense competition among the women from opposing sections. Moreover, the growing tendency to rank southern women more highly in regard to feminine charms may have made the northern female traveler even more combative. Col. James Walton of New Orleans, a visitor to the White Sulphur Springs in the summer of 1883, found the bout between the women one of the main events of the season. "The line of demarcation between the Boston, New York and Philadelphia ladies and those aristocrats of the South was thoroughly marked and defined," he wrote to his family. "I thought the War was over until my experience at the White." Colonel Walton then reported his conversation with one New York woman who proclaimed of the opposing feminine set, "We are a different race, the difference is as marked as between a Parisian and an Egyptian! She said, 'we are not one people,' and there was malice in her rude speech." Julia Newberry, a young Chicago socialite of the 1870s, was also extremely conscious of the implicit competition that had sprung up between the sections. "I was not edified," she observed after attending a Savannah ball, "with either the Southern beauty or chivalry of which one reads and hears so much." While several writers promoted the sectional harmony that supposedly reigned at the resorts, apparently it did not include feminine concerns. Some, however, may have consoled themselves with this image, even viewing this feminine competition as a sign of the progress of reunion, as an indication that sectionalism was now little more than a sparring among women.[37]

If the women did not openly embrace each other, there was still an opportunity for the northern man to become better acquainted with the southern belle. Enticed by the mystique of southern womanhood, northern men were encouraged to head for the springs in search of their own Dixie bride. Travel writers gushed over the marital matches, usually pairing a northern man with a southern belle, that had been and could be made at the spas. Indeed, the springs had long been known for their romantic potential, but, as several writers suggested, the absence of young southern men in the postwar years created an unforeseen demand for eligible bachelors. "The Springs . . . became very early, and are now, a great marrying-place," a writer in the *Nation* explained. "The 'desireable young men . . .' go there in search of wives, and are pretty sure to find there all the marriageable young women of the South. . . . Widows abound at the Springs just now—by which I mean widows who would not object to trying the chance of matrimony again." By the 1880s northern men were being urged to make romantic conquests at Dixie's spas. In the Springfield *Homestead*, Bab described the agony of the northern man, hopelessly in love with some delightful southern woman, but unsure if his love was reciprocated. Still, explained Bab, he "will go back to his home fettered with rose chains and swearing that when a man wants a wife this is the only place to go and get the right kind."[38]

Thus, Bab suggested, the northern man could return home upholding the image of romantic conqueror. Indeed, this notion of marriageable southern women offered northern men the chance to play out a role with numerous symbolic implications. For the younger men of the 1880s and 1890s, here was a chance to live out the image of crusading hero, to become the victors in a regional contest, not unlike their forebears who had fought the Civil War. In short, they could cling to the title of regional dominance through this conquest of Dixie's females. Moreover, here was also a chance to exercise power and control, which many northern men felt they had lost in their own society. Lacking any sense of control over their careers and economic futures, and feeling increasingly like useless clerks in a massive and mysterious system, many middle-class northern men

"*A Reminiscence of the White Sulphur Springs,*"
by C. S. Reinhart, Harper's Weekly, *August 4, 1888.*

chafed at their new powerlessness. If nothing else, at least now they could
conquer the southern belle. In "A Reminiscence of the White Sulphur
Springs," *Harper's Weekly* presented a picture of one northern man gaz-
ing at his lovely southern bride, gently swaying in her hammock while
delicately strumming a banjo. Here again, a romantic regional alliance had
been formed. But, despite the coquettish charms of the belle, the northern
man clearly emerged as victor, a point which the *Harper's* writer emphasized by noting the Yankee husband's "assured look of possession." Some
years later, the conquering image was made even more explicit in the
description of a trip made by the Illinois National Guard to Charleston,
South Carolina. "Every chap," observed the Chicago *Daily Tribune* reporter, "has made a conquest among the young ladies of Charleston,
judging from the sights one sees on the streets and in the hotels."[39]

Thus, while the women of the North and South may have bickered
amongst themselves, romantic reconciliation reigned at the resorts of the
South, or so the travel writers would have their readers believe. In 1883
Georgia journalist and orator John Temple Graves penned a tourist brochure for the Savannah, Florida, and Western Railway Company. Clearly
aimed at northern travelers, Graves's work contained the usual travel

descriptions but wove them into a fictional account of a northern family's southern vacation. Like so many other promotional pieces, this one began with discussions of the superior health conditions in the South and mentioned the possibilities for economic investment that the financially inclined tourist might find. But, in the end, it was romance that characterized the Revere family's southern vacation, as every member of the clan—including the old, widowed father—became embroiled in a southern love affair. Not surprisingly, the practical, money-conscious Roland was captivated by the most romantic figure of all, "the high-bred Southern belle" with "deeply, darkly, dangerously brown eyes."[40]

Through the tourist literature and experience, the northern upper and middle classes thus came to view the South and reconciliation through a romantic and depoliticized prism. Influenced by European aesthetic standards, American travelers and travel writers discovered the picturesque side of the South, one in which blacks, their poverty, and, indeed, many of the region's political problems disappeared in an abundance of romantic description. Northerners also became increasingly aware of the South's femininity, which alluringly flitted across the landscape and emerged in full romantic glory at the springs and spas. In the 1870s and 1880s tourism became one of the principal roads to romantic reconciliation, helping to shape a formula for sectional harmony that dominated the American cultural scene in the years between Reconstruction and the Spanish-American War.

4

THE CULTURE OF CONCILIATION

A MORAL ALTERNATIVE IN THE GILDED AGE

Born in 1857, Augustus Thomas came into a world that seethed with political conflict. His family was staunchly Republican in St. Louis, a city with strong pro-South sympathies. During the war Thomas's father led a Union regiment which fought the guerrilla rebels in Missouri, and he later served as a Republican representative in the state legislature. The young Augustus, however, did not have vivid political recollections of the sectional conflict. Instead, he recalled the war through the eyes of a child and clung to vague and romantic images in which lives were sacrificed for unknown and mysterious causes. He was awed by the soldiers and by the lively campaigns of the period, and he was much impressed by the stories of the "border romances," the tales of northern and southern fighting men who became smitten with the charms of girls from the opposing side.[1]

By the 1880s Augustus Thomas had become an aspiring actor. Like many actors of the period, he toured the South, and, like many tourists of the period, he was struck by the distinctive, premodern legacy which the region seemed to possess. He was moved by the appearance of the old plantation estates and charmed by the ruins of the old society. "The sight of a razed gateway to one old estate impressed me," Thomas recalled of a stopover in Talladega, Alabama. This particular vision stayed with the young thespian, especially as he changed his theatrical interests from acting to writing. The devastated Alabama plantation provided the central image for his first major success as a dramatist.[2]

Augustus Thomas's *Alabama* opened at the Madison Square Theatre in New York in April 1891. The play drew on the author's own experience in the South and on his vague and romantic recollections of the Civil War as well as on the increasingly popular genre of the reunion drama. Such productions as *The Blue and the Gray* (1884), *Held by the Enemy* (1886), and *Shenandoah* (1888) had introduced northern audiences to lush southern settings, opulent plantation mansions, fierce military conflict, and, as always, romantic love threatened by sectional division. *Alabama*, however, inspired its own special praise, especially for its apparent evocation of a genuine southern setting. "We breathe the languorous jessamine-laden air," one reviewer explained; "we see the scars of old wounds; we feel the influence of the blight that hangs like the Spanish moss over this stunned and devastated district." Making the experience even more vivid, patrons at one performance of this plantation melodrama came away with an authentic piece of southern scenery. Courtesy of "the ladies of Talladega," the women of the New York audience each received a cotton boll.[3]

This latest dramatic delineation of Dixie offered audiences yet another glimpse at the romance of reunion, replaying the well-worn tale of the love affair between a southern belle and a northern man, initially torn apart by sectional prejudice but eventually reunited, with an abundance of sentiment and sympathy. It was a theme which corresponded to the author's own vague and sentimental reflections on the war. In addition, Thomas encouraged the idea that this tenderhearted approach to reconciliation represented a more noble and genuine path to national harmony. "The play," explained one of its actors, "has touched upon the truest way in which to obliterate forever the sectional feeling between the North and the South. It shows the heart of our people; the love of father for son, of husband for wife, of lover for sweetheart. . . . Let love come in and the question of sectional feeling is put aside for a stronger principle." Once again, the sentiment of reunion would conquer the politics of sectionalism.[4]

Alabama appeared at the apex of the late nineteenth century's culture of reconciliation, a movement that had roots in Reconstruction but did not fully blossom until the 1880s and 1890s. In those two decades the reunion theme was strong in many quarters throughout northern society—in popular culture, in political movements, even among war veterans and former abolitionists. One version of this reconciliation culture, as seen in *Alabama*, reflected a mainstream bourgeois view of the conciliatory process. Appearing in scores of novels, plays, and popular songs, and appealing mainly to middle- and upper-class northerners, this reunion message drew heavily on the old southern myths and the tourist image of the plantation experience, as well as on an explicitly gendered view of inter-sectional union. Outside of this mainstream culture, numerous other groups also paid homage to the ideology of reunion. Among struggling farmers, unemployed workers, and female activists the reunion theme proved especially appealing. It offered these groups a vehicle for repositioning themselves closer to the center of American political life and for presenting their own views on current social issues. Such groups fashioned a unique image of reunion which allowed them to express their own demands for dignity, recognition, and moral rejuvenation.

Thus, inside as well as outside the mainstream, people sought to pay homage to a culture of healing and unity, largely in response to the troubling fractures and divisions of the Gilded Age. The reunion theme spoke to a wide variety of northerners concerned with what they saw as troubling signs in their society: increasing numbers of strikes, growing waves of immigration, and further revelations of economic and political corruption. A great many northerners in the late nineteenth century felt that their society had lost its moral center and sense of purpose. Instead of an older, artisanal commitment to skill, they saw only economic grasping or cynicism among workers and business leaders; instead of the moral foundation of marriage and the domestic sphere, they saw only a new breed of self-promoting women who had plunged into a world of public display and consumption; instead of the unity and harmony of older communities, they saw only class and ethnic conflict and community disintegration. In short, many northerners feared that economic and power-oriented concerns had replaced human values. The culture of conciliation, along with the accompanying celebration of the South, offered a soothing alternative to this moral dislocation. The goodwill expressed toward various groups of southerners—the honor bestowed on Confederate veterans, the respect conferred on southern farmers, or the regard expressed for southern women—helped to elevate the moral platform for a variety of

Gilded Age Yankees. In effect, such feelings of fraternity indicated that one placed certain moral values—personal dignity, familial integrity, or pure and simple romance—above the political and economic turmoil which seemed to keep people divided. In the end, many different individuals and groups of Americans turned to the practice and ideology of reunion as a way to rearticulate their sense of America's distinctive moral purpose in the late nineteenth century.

By the 1880s various political and reform groups in the North found it necessary to reach out to a southern constituency. Participation in American politics required a position on the reconciliation question, and a vast array of northerners were moved to purge themselves publicly of any past sectional proclivities, realizing that their political relevancy hinged on their acquiescence to the reconciliation process. More and more, northerners expressed the view that forgetfulness, at least as it pertained to the old sectional animosities, conferred greatness and that a failure to forget made one petty and narrow-minded. "The past is dead," explained the editors of the Trenton *State Gazette* in 1882, echoing the words of many other Yankee pundits. "Let us live in the present and act the part of men." Few, when the situation was expressed this way, would choose to be irrelevant and unmanly antiquarians.[5]

Even a number of former abolitionists made open and public avowals of sympathy for their southern brethren. Edward Atkinson, a Boston industrialist who had at one time been an avid supporter of John Brown's antislavery crusade, devoted his post–Civil War career to expanding the New South's economy. Seeking to prove his own sincerity and his faith in the southern people, Atkinson accepted an honorary membership in the Society of Ex-Confederate Soldiers. Former abolitionist Thomas Higginson, anxious to demonstrate his own relevance to postwar politics, also consorted publicly with former slaveholders and made a point of openly proclaiming his new regard for the South. Even an aging Ralph Waldo Emerson, perhaps hoping to secure a more noble place in the nation's history, could be found making a well-publicized visit to the University of Virginia, where he spoke kindly of the southern people.[6]

Union veterans also joined in the conciliatory rituals of the 1880s and embraced the new policy of forgetfulness. Throughout the decade, Union and Confederate troops held numerous joint reunions, meeting in both northern and southern locations, on battlefields, and in common Memorial

Day ceremonies. The assassination of President Garfield, a former Union general, brought Union and Confederate troops together in 1881 in a moment of mutual mourning. To some extent, the GAR also began to accept the idea that the wise and noble northerner was willing to forget the days of long ago, or at least to overlook the transgressions of specific southern actors. "Let us to-day," remarked Col. Robert Ingersoll in an 1882 Decoration Day address, "be great enough to forget individuals."[7]

Although they joined in some of the reunion rituals, GAR members found themselves in an uncomfortable situation. Like others, they wanted to demonstrate their continued relevancy and vitality in American life, to show the American people that the Union soldier was great enough to put the past behind him. Yet, since their identity was so bound up with past activity, the Union veterans could take this theme only so far. Because they were interested in highlighting their own manly contribution to history, GAR members often found the orchestrated sentimentalism of the reunion culture to be degrading and manipulative. Above all, they voiced their opposition to the northern leaders and politicians who, they believed, had little respect for veterans' needs and who maneuvered the reunion antics for their own benefit. Thus, as the conciliatory culture of the 1880s became increasingly florid and maudlin, GAR men expressed growing skepticism about the reunion ritual and blamed politicians for forcing the soldier to forsake his military dignity. "In view of the repeated manifestations of the veterans' inveterate hostility toward these maudlin affairs," explained the GAR national newspaper in 1891, "it is amazing that certain shallow sentimentalists and blatant politicians will continue to try to force the survivors of the Union army into them." The GAR drew the line at the conciliatory process when it downplayed or overlooked their own unique and courageous role in history.[8]

Throughout the 1880s and into the 1890s, the Union veterans and the GAR thought mainly about preserving their sense of honor and self-respect. Concerns about manhood and dignity became especially pronounced in the 1880s amidst their struggle to receive pensions from the federal government; by stressing their manliness as soldiers the GAR members perhaps hoped to counter the image that they had become helpless government dependents. To the extent that reunion with former rebels allowed them to maintain their sense of dignity, they joined in the celebration. But when President Cleveland proposed in 1887 to return captured battle flags to the former Confederate states, the GAR balked at the conciliatory gesture. Again, the issue was not the veterans' hostility toward the Confederates, but their anger at the machinations of the Cleveland administration. The decision, they believed, represented an official rebuke to the Union as well as the Confederate soldier's manly accomplishments; it ignored the individual soldier's heroic actions and allowed the administration to orchestrate the reunion drama for its own benefit. "We seem to be sinking into the slum of namby-pambyism and practicing self-emasculation," said one GAR member. The national organization echoed these sentiments. They respected the rebels, they maintained, but opposed this government-sponsored ritual when accompanied "by displays of sloppy and gushing sentimentality. . . . the men who fought us are full-grown, common-sense men, who look at things in a manly way. . . . Their self-respect and consistency are best maintained when we maintain our own consistency and self-respect." Ultimately, the point of all this talk had more to do with enhancing the manhood of the Union veterans than of the Confederates. Nonetheless, the GAR made certain to pay respect to the former rebels, realizing that the virility of the southern soldiers reflected on the virility of the Union veterans. Indeed, the Union veteran appreciated the manhood of the ex-Confederate, better than the government ever could, because he shared with him the dignity and honor that sprang from military service. In the end, Cleveland's decision was never implemented. In the process of discussion, however, the GAR had begun to stake out its own position on the reunion question, taking a stand which often kept it outside the mainstream of reconciliation politics, celebrated the dignity and manhood of the Union veteran, and, on occasion, showed respect for the former rebel soldier.[9]

The GAR participated in reunion politics from the perspective of its own moral vision, which celebrated the manly self-sacrifice of the soldier but condemned the self-promoting political and economic practices of the Gilded Age. This vision, like that of many northerners, was rooted in an idealized image of the American past, an image of individuals who worked for themselves and their communities and who shunned crass, materialistic objectives in giving their lives for purely altruistic reasons. It was a morality which, in particular, cursed the big, incorporating tendencies in American life and celebrated the days when the individuality of the American worker or farmer was not subsumed by corporate and political greed. Voicing many of the same concerns as the veterans, a number of reform organizations of the late nineteenth century joined in the conciliatory chorus in the 1880s and 1890s, articulating their own distinct moral vision of society. Steering a treacherous course through the murky waters of class and sectional politics, these reform groups were united in their opposition to big business and big party politics. Many, however, were also subjected to charges of anarchism and disloyalty for explicitly recognizing the existence of class antagonisms. The reunion theme offered a variety of reformers—with agrarian, working-class, and middle-class constituencies—a way to undercut accusations of disloyalty and to position themselves on a higher moral ground of patriotism.

The Farmers' Alliances, and later the Populists, often waved the banner of sectional harmony, using this message to speak to the common interests of troubled farmers in the South and the Midwest and to launch their attack on the sectional interests of the two major parties. Indeed, the reunion theme was deeply embedded in Populist politics and gave voice to some very specific concerns about patriotism, morality, and manhood. Hardly the anarchists which they were often portrayed as, Populists claimed to be true upholders of "a broad and liberal patriotism, [recognizing] but one flag and one country." In this period of intense class and party conflict, Populists felt that they, more than anyone, could effect a genuine patriotic spirit by explicitly calling for all Americans to unite in recognition of their common interests. As patriots, they projected themselves as the moral superiors to the Democratic and Republican leaders who played upon sectional politics to keep the masses of people divided and ignorant.[10]

The Populists also insisted on a policy of forgetfulness, which they believed was the only morally correct stance to be taken, as it insured an impartial view of the farmers on both sides of the conflict. Every newspaper or magazine that ran some sentimental series of wartime memoirs prompted Alliance wrath. Even these nonpolitical offerings, members claimed, were further evidence of party scheming designed to keep the bloody shirt waving and the American people divided. For their part, Populists played up the drama of reunion by sending northern crusaders to lecture in the South while southern leaders, including some former Confederates, spoke to the Alliance's northern constituency.[11]

The Populist approach to reunion politics also combined the issues of morality and manliness. Like many of the Civil War veterans (and indeed, many Populists were veterans), agrarian men frequently decried the loss of stature, independence, and control which preyed upon them in the late nineteenth century. They often described their present circumstances as a form of slavery, one in which the millionaires became "our new slave masters" and the people, both northern and southern, became pawns in their financial games. In particular, Populists attacked those business and party leaders who used the politics of sectionalism to keep the people in an even more weakened and downtrodden state. Sectionalism, they claimed, deprived the farmers of their manhood; it kept them, according to Alliance president—and former Confederate soldier—Leonidas Polk, "divided" and like "a Samson shorn of his locks." B. H. Clover, a Kansas man and the Alliance vice-president, employed the same analogy, noting that "Samson, while listening to the siren song of the party Delilah, was shorn of his locks, of his strength, of his manhood, and virtually of his freedom." This challenge to the farmers' manhood was even more galling because it was concocted by political manipulators, men who had used the passions of war to set the people against each other but who had themselves shirked the manly duties of soldiering. The sectional agitator, Polk often told his audiences—both northern and southern—was "the man who never smelt gun powder or heard a minnie ball." Echoing some of the GAR's themes and addressing both the northern and southern veterans' annoyance with the stay-at-homes, Polk appealed to his agrarian audiences as fighting men. He spoke of an equality of manliness, of the equal contributions of both northern and southern farming men, careful never to elevate one above the other. Indeed, he implied that all farming men possessed a more deeply rooted sense of manliness than the cowardly political agitators, one rooted in moral obligation rather than political gain. In the Populist vision, the farmer, especially the farmer-veteran, epitomized the American moral ideal through his commitment to hard work, community cooperation, and unselfish sacrifice. Now, Polk suggested, the farmers needed to recapture their sense of manhood and morality by uniting in the Farmers' Alliance and joining with their allies on the other side of the Mason-Dixon line.[12]

The reunion message was a potent one for the Populist cause, especially in its appeal to the manhood of both northern and southern farmers. Like the GAR, the Populists championed the moral integrity of the common man as opposed to the moral bankruptcy of the party politician. Ultimately, however, the organization could not surmount the underlying tensions of American politics in the Gilded Age. In some parts of the country, notably in the old Northwest, sectional politics prevented farmers from affiliating with an inter-sectional alliance. Many northern farmers worried that a power bloc of Confederates—now using the vehicle of the

Farmers' Alliance instead of the Democratic party—was out to achieve political prominence and thereby undermine the accomplishments of the former Union soldiers. Perhaps a more serious obstacle was the racial politics of the movement, especially the refusal of many southern white Populists to promote the more enlightened racial agenda which some northern Populists favored. In the end, reunion sentiments could not mask the fact that southern Populists were committed to a brand of racial politics that was often antithetical to some of the northern farmer's reform-minded traditions.[13]

Nonetheless, the reunion theme continued to hold a certain attraction for Gilded Age reform groups. Northern labor unions, anxious to build up a southern constituency, often spoke of forging a union with their southern brothers and made an explicit appeal to the common ties of laboring men.[14] Likewise, in 1894, one year after the onset of a devastating economic depression, another reform movement advanced the cause of uniting the common people in a consolidated moral crusade. In organizing his march of the unemployed, Jacob Coxey drew on many of the themes which the Populists and the labor unions had used before him. Coxey himself was neither a farmer nor a laborer but a forty-year-old self-made businessman who had campaigned relentlessly for currency reform. He organized the march on Washington, D.C., specifically to pressure Congress into passing his most recent piece of currency legislation. Unlike the Populists or the unions, Coxey had no popular base, but he did have a talent for symbolism and for seizing those symbols which he hoped would convey unity and national loyalty. Indeed, perhaps more than the Populists, Coxey tried to distance himself from the charge of anarchism and socialism which surrounded his endeavor. He was anxious to stress his, and his followers', patriotism, hoisting high his allegiance to the flag and to time-honored American values.

Again, reunion offered a powerful vehicle, allowing Coxey to show that he intended to bring all the people, northern and southern, together in a spirit that was truly American, even militaristic. At the head of Coxey's march was a black man, carrying an American flag; Jesse Coxey, Jacob's son, followed close behind, wearing an army suit that blended Union blue and Confederate gray. This was Coxey's ultimate symbol of patriotism, of Americans united in that most selfless of patriotic quests, giving their lives for their country. As an enlisted man's uniform, Jesse Coxey's attire also symbolized an appeal to the common, hard-working white people of

Jesse Coxey riding at the front of Coxey's Army, wearing a suit of Union blue and Confederate gray. Courtesy of the Library of Congress.

the two regions. Unlike the Populists' or the labor unions' crusades, however, Coxey's efforts seem to have been almost wholly symbolic, never leading to the creation of an inter-sectional alliance of the unemployed. Yet, like the unions and the Populists, he had found a way to articulate the common American's approach to national reunion.[15]

The moral message behind reunionism, advanced by the Populists and, to a lesser extent, by Jacob Coxey, offered an important source of strength to movements of the dispossessed. It opened up the pool of allies who could be united in a common struggle and made a large mass of "ordinary" people the caretakers of genuine "American" values. The reunion message gave these reform groups a voice in a national dialogue from which they had felt increasingly excluded. It also offered them a way to express their sense of moral indignation with the status quo. One of the most successful promoters of this moralistic approach to reconciliation, however, was an organization that had the least formal political clout. The Woman's Christian Temperance Union (WCTU) used the reunion message to articulate its own distinctive brand of moral politics and to provide disenfranchised women with their own vehicle for participating in the national political scene.

Beginning in 1881, and largely due to the herculean efforts of Frances Willard, the WCTU undertook an extensive southern campaign to bring its antidrinking message to the people, especially the white women, of the southern states. Born in 1839 in upstate New York, Willard had been influenced by antebellum feminism but had been too young to be part of the drama of prewar abolitionism. In the 1870s she combined her interests in religion and feminism to participate in the growing female temperance movement; in 1878 she became president of the WCTU. In this capacity, Willard undertook the southern organizing campaign and spoke in dozens of southern towns and cities, met with numerous community and religious leaders, and organized a number of local WCTU chapters throughout the South. The campaign culminated in October 1882, when the organization held its first southern convention in Louisville, Kentucky. Here numerous orators paid tribute to the conciliatory sentiments that had brought the women of the North and South together in this heroic and noble effort.[16]

The nuances of Willard's campaign speak volumes about the appeal and potency of the reunion message, especially for women and especially for reform politics in the late nineteenth century. Willard faced a formidable obstacle in undertaking her southern tour—namely, the fact that many southern communities frowned upon women in public roles and as public speakers, especially one who was known to take feminist and prosuffrage positions. By emphasizing the moral, sentimental, and domestic features of the WCTU message, Willard seems to have triumphed over both anti-Yankee and antifemale prejudices. "The true womanliness of this gentle lady," reported the Charleston *News and Courier*, "did much to charm away the prejudices" against female orators. Southerners found themselves hard-pressed to reject the message of the WCTU leader, no matter how much she represented the typical female Yankee reformer, because of the morality and the sentimentality of her statement, especially her touching appeal regarding the suffering of women and children from male alcohol abuse. Willard herself recognized that she could best accomplish her aim of winning southern sympathies by stressing the moral and downplaying the political. "My work," she wrote, "is to take the sentiment as I find it, and crystalize as much of it as possible into organic form. The woman's ballot is not a living issue in the South outside of Arkansas—and even there I do not think it best to agitate it." Willard softened the organization's views on women's suffrage in order to make it clear that she was not forcing Yankee politics onto the South; rather, she was making her appeal at a more fundamental, and more sentimental, level—to women's desires to preserve, protect, and nurture their families. Willard, of course, was not just playing up to the craving for something sentimental; she truly believed that women had a distinctly moral contribution to make to civilization and that women's moral influence must actively counteract the dominant masculine traits in society. Thus, even as she minimized the organization's explicit political message, she still provided women with a powerful vehicle and ideology for entering the political arena.[17]

The WCTU ultimately enjoyed a success in reaching out to southerners which other groups did not. Presenting the reunion effort in moral terms, the WCTU managed to draw on what were believed to be women's uniquely sentimental qualities. In this way, women's capacity for love and tenderness became an effective and reliable force not only for moral rejuvenation, but also for sectional healing—indeed, as many saw it, a more effective force than anything that could be mustered by men. "With tens of thousands of mothers of different parts united in a common moral effort," explained the *Christian Statesman*, "the men will more readily surrender to each other." The WCTU gave women a position of power and moral authority which made them especially well-suited to bridge the sectional chasm. Because women experienced the suffering of alcohol abuse and its effect on home and family, the organization argued, there was a moral imperative for the women of the country to achieve a national bonding. Moreover, as women, they helped preserve the nation's moral fiber and could counter the sectional power brokering of corrupt and immoral politicians. "Unlike the quarreling Senate of the United States," Willard explained, "we have no time for mutual recrimination. It takes every breath of our waking hours to plan for the . . . defense of homes equally endangered on both sides of Mason and Dixon's line." Thus, as an organization of women, the WCTU found the moral component of the reunion message especially empowering. It allowed them to present their conciliatory efforts as more honest and genuine than those of scheming politicians. It also elevated women's role as national healers and gave southern white women, in particular, a vehicle for social activism. Given the enthusiastic reception and organizing success which Willard enjoyed in most of the South, the WCTU message was apparently successful: it appealed to both southern white men and women, without unduly arousing sectional prejudices. "When I know your mission to our Sunny South is 'love and peace,'" wrote one Arkansas woman to Willard, "we wellcome [*sic*] you warmly and we feel that our hearts beat in unison with yours."[18]

In the end, the WCTU's campaign made clear the power of morality in American reform politics and used that morality as an effective bridge in the reunion process. Like other Gilded Age reform groups, the WCTU responded to the moral qualms and dislocations which many Americans experienced during the Gilded Age, in this case the anxiety many felt about family dislocation and alcohol abuse. Like the Populists, the WCTU built its reunion message on that moralistic foundation and helped to create an alternative vision of reunion that differed considerably from the message of the mainstream culture of the late nineteenth century.

A sense of moral anxiety could be detected not only among the active reformers of the period—like the Populists and the WCTU—but also among those who were more closely tied to mainstream northern culture and who were exposed to some of the more bombastic and romantic offerings of the conciliatory culture. Here the reunion message came dripping with sentimentality, especially in the novels and plays of the late nineteenth century, and here, again, northerners looked at the reunion process with their anxieties about social and moral chaos uppermost in their minds.

Many of the sentimental cultural offerings enjoyed by middle-class Americans at this time were predicated upon the theme of national reconciliation. Few of these works qualify as sophisticated cultural contributions; they were often little more than worn-out repetitions of a highly contrived formula. Nonetheless, these presentations of reunion were very popular in Gilded Age America. Novels devoted to reunion and plantation themes sold extremely well and their now-forgotten authors—such as Edward P. Roe, Charles King, and Winston Churchill (the American)—enjoyed enormous success. Likewise, the New York stage seldom witnessed a season that did not feature some type of Civil War drama, usually one with a plantation setting. Year after year, well into the 1890s, audiences flocked to these theatrical, and extremely sentimental, displays.[19]

On one level, these cultural offerings perpetuated much of the sentimentality and romance of the old southern myth, continuing to emphasize morals and values that no longer seemed as important in the personal and business interactions of late-nineteenth-century America. In this sense, they fit a broader historical pattern of a culture that values tradition over change, preferring a familiar and reassuring alternative to a modern, grasping, industrial society. But the reunion culture embodied more than just a desire to look backward. Its sentimental and romantic features were also consistent with a tendency in the Gilded Age to create a more soothing culture—what Alan Trachtenberg has identified as a feminine style of culture. Faced with a society wracked with political and economic conflicts, as well as an increasingly alienated work force, middle-class Americans attempted to construct a culture that could heal their social and moral wounds—a culture that could uplift human emotions to create a sense of selflessness that would appeal to all. According to Trachtenberg, middle- and upper-class northerners believed that an elevated sense of culture, especially when it emphasized domestic harmony and virtue, could bridge the chasm of class conflict and social unrest and raise the disgruntled factory hand or the angry immigrant worker to a new plane of civilization. While few factory hands ever had much contact with the middle-class magazines or the Broadway stage of the late nineteenth century, herein might lie the unique appeal of the plantation reunion drama. Based upon a cultural formula that enshrined domestic harmony and traditional femininity, it presented the metaphor of healing in its most direct and explicit form. Thus, as middle-class northerners made their peace with the South, they also found a way to come to terms with many of the moral anxieties, especially in regard to issues of class and gender, which they had about their own society.[20]

The plays and novels of conciliation imparted a clear message about class and the nature of a class society that was very different from the one offered by the Populists, by the unions, or by Jacob Coxey. The dramas of reunion focused, almost exclusively, on the old southern aristocracy, underscoring the notion that reconciliation remained the province of the social elite. When poor whites and blacks appeared in the dramatic and written material on the South which middle-class northerners devoured in these years, they usually were not the principal characters and they seldom were the subjects of reconciliation.[21]

Northerners revealed an intense fascination for the southern aristocracy, especially for their precarious social position. In the late-nineteenth-century North, a society with firsthand experience in social and economic instability, middle- and upper-class Yankees found the plantation aristocracy especially deserving of sentiment and sympathy because of the tremendous losses that class had endured. Continuing a trend that had appeared in the Reconstruction period, the cultural offerings of the 1880s and 1890s bemoaned the postwar devastation of the southern planters, who, many believed, achieved a certain nobility through their financial ruin. Notably, the political views of this class took on a diminished significance as northerners became primarily interested in their economic suffering. This sentimental concern found one form of expression in the newly established United States National Museum (later a part of the Smithsonian) in Washington, D.C. Seeking to add to the institution's Civil War collections, and forgoing some of the guns and cannons which the museum already had in great number, one curator in 1886 hoped to acquire materials that could "illustrate the privations and poverty endured throughout the South during the war." Noting the special sentimental value of such items as "home made shoes and homespun cloth," museum curators showed concern for the hardships of a southern aristocracy forced to rely on such common and tawdry items, which had always been part of the standard domestic stock for many of the South's poor. Thus, in a relatively short span of time, the southern elite had become a people deserving of the nation's heartfelt sympathy rather than their political abuse.[22]

Similarly, in the plays and novels of reconciliation the southern aristocrats inevitably endured a heartbreaking fall from wealth, often receiving aid and comfort from a northern protagonist. Although economics ranked below romance, the literature of reunion fulfilled the New South promise of bringing North and South together through financial cooperation, an effort usually paid for by northerners. In *The Bloody Chasm* (1881), written by former Union officer John DeForest, the impoverished southern belle has been brought so low by the war that she must live in "the house of one of their slaves." Her northern uncle, however, holds out the key to her financial salvation by agreeing to leave her part of his fortune when she has married a northern man of his choosing. The play *Alabama* followed a similar formula. Set on the devastated postwar plantations of Colonel Preston and his neighbor Mrs. Page, the drama offered financial security in the form of Mr. Armstrong, the northern railroad agent, who falls in love with Carey Preston, the enchanting daughter of the colonel. This play revealed, according to one reviewer, "the somnolent South awaking under the influence of a new generation and an incoming railroad." Economic considerations, of course, were always linked with romantic ones, thereby underscoring the fact that the reunion was sealed by genuine emotion rather than insincere financial motives. But, conveniently, these presentations pointed the way to the new and improved South through the union of the southern belle with the business-oriented northern man.[23]

Middle-class northerners learned to love the old plantation aristocracy, especially in their economic deprivation and eventual redemption through northern assistance. But, in their devotion to the southern elite, Yankee audiences also came to love elements of the old South's racial code, and this, too, formed a crucial part of the healing metaphor of the reunion process. Specifically, the overriding racial motif of the reunion culture stressed the loyalty and devotion of the old black servant to the southern family. Usually played by white actors and actresses, these "black" domestics showed an unflagging commitment to their masters in both antebellum and postwar settings. Uncle Rufus, described as a "tried and true servant of the old-time southern type," assumed this part in William Gillette's play, *Held by the Enemy*. Uncle Rufus presented "the picture of dog-like fidelity," one reviewer wrote, "that is a strong characteristic of the southern negro." Significantly, family loyalty and commitment made these old-time servants the most fervent supporters of the Confederacy. Joe, the black servant in Charles Townsend's *Pride of Virginia* (1901), was not only a loyal underling, he was also "a rank secessionist." Indeed, in their fierce dedication to their white masters, such servants demonstrated a more intense devotion to sectionalism than many Confederate women or soldiers. Just as northerners relished the images of rebellious southern women, they revealed a similar fascination for this notion of Yankee-hating black servants. In effect, both depictions minimized the threat of sectionalism, implying that now, in this era of conciliation, only women and blacks clung to anti-northern sentiments and might potentially block the path to national reunion.[24]

Moreover, as depicted in some of the more fanciful travel descriptions and in the novels and plays of reunion, southern blacks not only demonstrated their class loyalty, but they also helped to maintain the class position of the old southern aristocracy. By making southern blacks the defenders of class privilege, northern writers again took the burden of responsibility away from the southern elite, thus making it easier to effect a heartwarming reunion with the upper class. Charles Dudley Warner, for example, found that the black nursemaids at the southern health resorts played an essential role in establishing the class hierarchy. According to Warner, it was "these dignified and faithful mammies upon whom seemed to rest to a considerable extent the maintenance of the aristocratic social traditions." If, as Warner suggested, these black women had shaped the South's aristocratic system, then northern whites could embrace the southern elite with a minimal amount of guilt.[25]

Above all, the defining feature of the black presence in these dramas of reunion was the role of blacks in the class structure, as servants committed to their own social caste as well as to the class status and position of the masters. For the northern middle and upper classes of the late nineteenth century, all too familiar with labor unrest and turmoil, these depictions of faithful African American workers, passionately committed to their employers and to their own inferior social rank, held a special significance. They spoke to northerners' concern for a certain type of class obligation, for a system that rested less on physical or economic coercion and more on personal feeling. These slaves (and former slaves), after all, did not obey their masters out of fear of punishment or whippings, but out of genuine human concern. Nor did excessive wealth hold the key to a harmonious master-servant relationship, as even the most impoverished of planters continued to command the overwhelming loyalty of former slaves. Indeed, it seemed that the old planter class, now economically devastated, possessed an innate sense of class obligations, as did their underlings. In *Held by the Enemy*, the actions of Uncle Rufus received frequent and sustained applause from a Boston audience, "particularly his pathetic appeal for his master's life to the major general in command of the Union forces." Significantly, this play made its appearance in 1886, a year that saw some of the most intense labor unrest of the nineteenth century. In a society that was experiencing tremendous conflict and division along class lines, it might have been comforting to envision the seemingly "natural" sense of class that existed in the South, to see that class was not simply the creation of economic extremes but had a strong human component as well. Ultimately, and somewhat ironically, northerners accepted a soothing picture of the antebellum South where people were seen to adhere to their class positions out of a sense of free choice and free will.[26]

While the culture of conciliation encouraged northern whites to cast their sympathies with upper-class white southerners, prior to the turn of the century it did not offer an unqualified endorsement of these former enemies of the Union cause. Striking a note of compromise, the basic formula of the dramas of reconciliation rested on a gendered framework which mediated the rush to reunion by making rebellious but ultimately compliant southern women the main subjects of sectional bonding. In treating reunion mainly as an amorous endeavor, this cultural recipe further contributed to the increasingly depoliticized assessment of the Civil War and its aftermath by hiding all political and sectional viewpoints behind the rubric of romance and sentiment. The culture of conciliation thus continued to represent reunion as sentimental, and hence more genuine than the attempted political settlement of Reconstruction. The gendered and romantic formula for reconciliation made, as one character in *Alabama* explained, the hearts of the participants "a little bigger than sectional resentment." Again, human emotions could heal a sectionally and socially divided society.[27]

Prior to the late 1890s, most dramas of reunion revolved around the story of a northern man's conquest of a rebel belle. Imre Kiralfy's *America*, presented at the Chicago World's Fair in 1893, reduced this standard story line to its essential elements. Depicting the Civil War and reunion, act 4 of this theatrical pageant opened on "Lilian, a planter's daughter," and a group of sleeping soldiers. Observing the reposing recruits, Lilian "is distressed upon seeing the condition of the wounded man she loves. Yet she hesitates because he is a Union soldier and an enemy in arms, but her heart conquers, and with trembling footsteps she draws near to say farewell to her beloved." In a moment's worth of acting, *America* synthesized the tale repeated over and over in the culture of conciliation: the love between a northern, often Union, man and an initially resistant, but ultimately submissive, rebel woman.[28]

The formula of romantic reunion appeared as early as the 1860s in northern Civil War literature. John DeForest placed it at the center of his novel *Miss Ravenal's Conversion From Secession to Loyalty* (1867). As in so many other novels and plays in this genre, the loudest champion for the Confederacy was the southern heroine, Lillie Ravenal. Lillie, wrote DeForest, was "a rebel. Like all young people and almost all women she was strictly local, narrowly geographical in her feelings and opinions." True to her womanly nature, Lillie Ravenal defended the cause of southern secession against the better judgment of almost every man she encountered, including her father, her southern husband, and her northern lover. Only after an unhappy marriage, a considerable amount of coaxing, and a Civil War did Lillie finally turn her back on the Confederacy, joining in a romantic union with the northern man. In this early tale of reconciliation, Lillie's womanly commitment to the Confederacy lent a uniquely feminine quality to southern sectionalism and all that was distinctly southern.[29]

The novels and plays of the next three decades (and beyond) extended this notion of southern women's rebelliousness with a vengeance. De-Forest himself refashioned Lillie Ravenal into Virginia Beaufort in his novel *The Bloody Chasm* (1881). Like Lillie, Virginia was a dedicated secessionist who, upon hearing of Lee's surrender, exclaimed, "The soldiers have abandoned the fight, and only the women continue it." According to DeForest, this staunch sectionalism made women like Virginia the true representatives of the South. Underscoring the gendered regional duality, DeForest had one character describe Virginia's estranged northern husband, Colonel Underhill, as "the North incarnate," to which he replied, "And my wife is the South." As if the point had not already been driven home, Underhill's southern friend offered this reflection on the symbolic pairing: "'Yes—a woman,' sighed the General, 'a generous and impassioned woman. The South has been just that, and only that, all my lifetime. I see it now.'" DeForest's message was clear: the passionate and emotional commitment to sectionalism, compounded by the fervid defense of its females, cast a feminine spirit over the entire southern region.[30]

In countless plays and novels, scores of novelists and playwrights followed DeForest's lead, making rebel women the human emblems for the South and southern sectionalism. One review of *The Heart of Maryland* explained, "As is usual in plays of this sort, the heroine is a loyal southern girl, and the hero a soldier of the North." Writing in 1891, one northern observer found the rebellious female stereotype so pervasive that it impeded his ability to discuss the true conditions of southern womanhood. "I am asked a dozen times a week, by excellent people, in all parts of the North," lamented the Reverend A. D. Mayo in an article about the women's movement in the South, "if I do not find the southern women filled with bitterness over the results of the war, and if the southern girl of the period is not that . . . artful conspirator against the peace of the nation."[31]

Mayo found many northerners in the 1890s still clinging to postwar images of bitter southern women, but the new creators of the fictional southerners did not present their heroines in precisely those terms. Writers in the 1860s, resentful of what they perceived to be white southern women's sectionalism and aristocratic demeanor, had portrayed Dixie's females with a spite and vengeance that was tempered by the conciliatory sentiments of the 1880s. Previously, northern writers had focused on angry southern women as the new locus of sectional conflict, suggesting that the terrain of war had shifted from battlefield to homefront. Now, as the literature of the 1880s and 1890s implied, this part of the postwar battle was finally subsiding. Hence, the rebel women of the 1880s might still lay claim to aristocratic pretensions, but now northerners were more inclined to see that aristocracy as defunct and deserving of sentimental pity. Moreover, these women clung tenaciously to their sectional principles, like some of their real-life sisters, but eventually gave them up under the influence of a northern man's affections. Consequently, their rebellious spirit became more of a cute and flirtatious pretense than a bitter and spiteful rebuff. In the drama *The Pride of Virginia*, Kitty, "a bright, wilful [sic], impetuous daughter of the South," planned "to sweep the Yankees into the ocean if they invade Virginia." Kitty Carrington, the heroine of Charles King's *Kitty's Conquest*, was a "rebellious little fairy." And a reviewer of *Barbara Frietchie*, whose heroine was transformed by theatrical license from an elderly Unionist to a youthful supporter of the Confederacy, praised actress Julia Marlowe for her portrayal of "the impulsive, passionate, coquettish, tender, and high-spirited Southern girl." In a sense, these women were shadows of the "bitter, spiteful women" described by Sidney Andrews in 1865. Like those women, the heroines of the culture of conciliation maintained that peculiar, and apparently womanly, devotion to the South; they continued to lend the Confederate cause that distinctly feminine spirit which observers had noted twenty years earlier. But, under the influence of the romantic images of the 1870s and 1880s, as well as a general tendency to belittle female emotions, this bitter feminine spirit had become "passionate," "coquettish," and "tender," offering the perfect opening for the romantic hero.[32]

The romantic formula that joined the southern belle with the northern hero meshed well with this early period of conciliation, when northerners still expressed caution and skepticism about the war aims of the South and when many still had vivid memories of the sectional conflict. Indeed, some of the creators of this culture had actively participated in the war: authors John DeForest and Charles King were both Union veterans. Others, even if they had not been so directly involved, were aware that sectional prejudices still had an influence on northern emotions. Consequently, they did not envision a reunion with virile southern men devoted to the ideas and practices of the old South, but merely a match with women, southern yet submissive, and ultimately willing to accept the superior wisdom and national vision of the northern man. Several architects of this conciliatory culture implicitly understood the implications of this standard story line. Playwright William Gillette, for example, apparently knew a good formula when he saw it. Like his contemporary, Augustus Thomas, Gillette had lived through the Civil War as a youngster and took away from the experience his own vague and childlike recollections of the event. Striking out as a dramatist shortly before Thomas, Gillette was one of the first to use the North-South love affair in his productions. He successfully employed this romantic device in *Held by the Enemy* (1886) and returned to it nine years later in his Civil War drama, *Secret Service*. Gillette seemed fully aware both of the gender implications of this plot arrangement and of the mood of northern audiences. He was, one reviewer explained, "one of the first writers to recognize the fact that the time had come when an audience would admit that the wearers of the gray and their women were both human and heroic. He temorized [*sic*], though, as did all his followers, and cleverly gave his heroine to the South, reserving the hero for the North." Gillette had recognized just how far northern audiences could be pushed down the path to reunion and so made the sectional bonding easier by casting the South in the feminine role.[33]

Virginia author Thomas Nelson Page, one of the most widely read composers of reconciliation fiction, revealed a similar self-awareness in using this standard romantic recipe. Born on a plantation near Richmond, Virginia, Page had also been a child during the sectional conflict. Soon after the war ended, he moved quickly to establish himself as a writer, especially through northern magazines and publishing houses. Like many southern authors of the period, he became acutely aware of his dependence on a northern literary market. "The great monthly magazines," Page recalled, " . . . were not only open as never before to Southern contributors, but welcomed them eagerly as a new and valuable acquisition." Page, for his part, was extremely grateful and would often consult with his northern editors in developing his fiction. In 1885 he wrote to *Century* editor Richard Gilder to describe one of his short stories. "A Virginia girl is the heroine and a young Union Captain the hero," he explained. "The scene is laid during the war, and the story is told by an old negro after the war. It deals with the female rebel element, but I think will not wound any one, and I will vouch for its fidelity." Southerners like

Promotional flyer for William Gillette's play Held by the Enemy, *which focused on a tale of inter-sectional romance. Courtesy of the Billy Rose Theatre Collection, the New York Public Library for the Performing Arts, Astor, Lenox, and Tilden Foundations.*

Program cover for J. K. Tillotson's play The Planter's Wife, *a drama of romantic reunion. Courtesy of the Billy Rose Theatre Collection, the New York Public Library for the Performing Arts, Astor, Lenox, and Tilden Foundations.*

Page, whose livelihood rested on the northern literary market, had to be continually aware of whatever sectional bitterness lingered in northern audiences. As his letter implied, Page realized that he might offend regional sensibilities in depicting reconciliation with rebels. Yet Page also suggested that his story using "the female rebel element . . . will not wound any one," and herein lay the beauty of this standard plot device. Relying on accepted cultural stereotypes of women's emotional but submissive nature, Page, Gillette, and other authors allowed northern audiences to reconcile themselves with a South that could never really threaten the North, to ally themselves with a "rebel element" that offered mainly a flirtatious defiance of Union principles. In this way, real sectional antagonisms could now be displaced and defused by promoting harmony with these coquettes of the Confederacy.[34]

In using this formula, these writers relied on a gendered metaphor to make a political statement about the power relations between the sections

in the postwar period. The North, they suggested, had tamed and subdued and would now control the South in much the same way that husbands were assumed to take control in marriage. The marriage metaphor,
in effect, stood in for the economic and political leverage which the North
did exercise, and which many hoped it would continue to exercise, over the
southern states. Thus, the sentimental reunion image did not obliterate
political issues but transformed them into a romantic metaphor. According
to journalist John Trowbridge, the romance of reunion was more than a
fictional or dramatic device; it was part of the political solution of the post–
Civil War crisis. Writing his memoirs in the early twentieth century,
Trowbridge recalled his travels in the postwar South, offering a gendered
interpretation of what he had seen. "I found those who had been in the
Confederate ranks," Trowbridge wrote, "generally the most ready to
resume their loyalty to the flag." These were the men who, apparently,
had experienced the might of northern manliness on the battlefield and
could thus be reformed of their sinful ways. But, Trowbridge pointed out,
"the female secessionists were bitterest of all" and "to appeal to their
reason was idle." Still, reunion with southern women could be accomplished because, as Trowbridge noted, "they were vulnerable on the side
of the sentiments; and many a fair one was converted from the heresy of
state rights by some handsome Federal officer, who judiciously mingled
love with loyalty in his addresses, and pleaded for the union of hands
as well as the union of States." Hence, in Trowbridge's formula, Union
men could twice conquer the South—once in war and once in love. And,
through their second conquest, the problems of Reconstruction could be
neatly obliterated under the rubric of romance and the sentimental joining
of northern and southern hands. The "union of hands" also broadcast a
sense of power and order on the path toward a stronger and reunited
nation. Marriage, signifying an arrangement of proper, well-ordered,
and hierarchical gender relations, became the metaphor for the reunited
states, for a nation of clearly defined laws and hierarchies in regard to both
North and South and men and women.[35]

While the marital bond conveyed a message about power in the reunited
nation, it also spoke to late-nineteenth-century morality. Indeed, by the
1880s and 1890s many feared that marriage was no longer fashionable in
northern society and that family concerns were on the decline. "According
to a Chicago judge," one newspaper reported in 1890, "divorces are
rapidly on the increase, and five women apply for divorce where one man

applies. It is said that marriage is becoming an unpopular institution in the North and West among the upper and middle classes." Studies which circulated during the 1880s found that college women in particular were either postponing or avoiding the marital institution. The reunion drama, in reviving the seemingly old-fashioned custom of marriage, urged northerners to look backward, to an earlier moral standard of domestic harmony and familial integrity. In fact, more than just reintroducing marriage, the reunion culture enshrined the institution and endowed it with wondrous social powers. For northerners who were anxious about a moral decline in their own society, the culture of conciliation thus reinvigorated their commitment to a more traditional moral standard and encouraged middle-class Yankees to further idealize the marriage bond.[36]

Ultimately, the whole reconciliation scheme offered northerners a way to reconceptualize and rearticulate their image of Victorian morality. Through their culture, they revived a vision of domestic harmony, familial integrity, and strictly demarcated gender spheres. This last point was particularly important because many northerners feared that as men and women violated traditional gender norms, society in turn would lose its moral fiber. In the end, the marriage of reconciliation returned women to their more traditional and Victorian role of submission. Yet, significantly, that Victorian role was now played by the southern belle, the woman who was once a political outcast and who now came closest to the true ideals of womanhood.

Indeed, as a number of cultural pundits proclaimed, southern women approximated the ideals of simplicity, self-sacrifice, and domesticity more closely than their northern sisters. Thomas Nelson Page told *Harper's* readers in 1893 that northern women could not hold a candle to their southern sisters. To the northern traveler, he explained, the southern "women will appear less expensively dressed. A man will probably not notice this; for they will be generally prettier than those he left the other side of the bridge [over the Potomac], and they will have something about them . . . which will be more attractive." Postwar southern women, Page believed, came closest to northern men's view of ideal womanhood, now that the war had removed idleness and luxury from their lives. Nor was it only southerners like Page who promoted these notions. Rebecca Harding Davis, a Philadelphia author who had at one time written some very unsentimental and realistic Civil War fiction, now joined in the sentimental chorus in praise of southern womanhood. She described her own version of the ideal southern woman, who "receives you with a grave, modest simplicity and innocent dignity which her northern sister might envy." Northern women, who writers and dramatists claimed were obsessed with the money and social connections of their business-oriented society, now paled in comparison to these simple and impoverished southern women. As one critic, surveying the women's roles in *Alabama*, explained, "Southern women are expected to look pretty, and be modest and dignified. The autonomous adventuress and the aggressive society woman has no part in the 'pastorals' of Dixie."[37]

In short, southern women became the domestic and morally refined exemplars of true womanhood. Even their devoted sectionalism confirmed their womanly nature, as it showed them to be women with a narrow and limited vision, committed above all to home, to family, and to neighborhood. In one *Ladies' Home Journal* short story, an old southern colonel proclaimed that "our Southern ladies . . . thoroughly understand the art of housekeeping" and "never dreamed of anything but politeness or consideration." Unlike northern women, who were constantly in search of worldly pursuits like politics or money, southern women were believed to be more content with their domestic limitations. Praising a fictionalized southern woman she created for a story in *Scribner's*, Rebecca Davis explained: "While she may not instruct her daughters in either science or art, she will teach them to love God and honor their husbands." Men, in contrast, especially the northern men who wooed the southern belles, were accepted as creatures of the world, as beings whose sights moved far beyond the home and embraced business, travel, and a wide range of national concerns. Ultimately, the marriage of southern women and northern men represented a very traditional union, one which seemed less possible up North, in which the homebound female joined with the more worldly, and clearly more dominant, male.[38]

The South, then, had produced a feminine ideal while northern women, in many cases, had violated all sense of moral and gender propriety. Perhaps no northern author made this point more strongly than Henry James. While *The Bostonians* does not follow the standard formula for reconciliation, James's preference for a passionate South, here embodied in Basil Ransom, a southern man, and his fear of the gender-disorienting, even masculine, northern women's movement echoes themes found elsewhere in northern culture of the late nineteenth century. Published in 1886, *The Bostonians* reversed the basic reunion plot by romantically pairing a southern man, Basil, with a northern woman, Verena Tarrant. But James also set the emotional and virile Basil against the cold, crusading Olive Chancellor, a Boston spinster and advocate for the rights of women. Olive's cohorts in reform have a dispassionate, unfeeling, almost masculine demeanor. The sole exception is Verena, the object of both Olive's and Basil's affections, who is only a naive pawn in Olive's reform crusade. The only northern woman whom Basil respects is the somewhat impetuous Mrs. Burrage, a wealthy matron who "had a brisk, familiar, slightly impatient way, and if she had not spoken so fast, and had more of the softness of the southern matron, she would have reminded him of a certain type of woman he had seen of old," the plantation mistress. Basil rants against the "damnable feminization" of the North, but it is clearly not a very womanly or romantic transformation; it is, rather, a feminization led by unsexed and domineering "old maids" like Olive Chancellor.[39]

James's selection of the virile and masculine Basil for the romantic lead set his novel outside the standard conciliatory format of the late nineteenth century. Nonetheless, James's views of gender and sectional distinctions sounded a cry of concern that could be heard throughout the culture of conciliation. As James and other writers implied, the postwar period had thrown formerly recognized boundaries of gender into a state of confusion, making cultural observers wonder if men were more manly and women more womanly in the North or in the South. "It is greatly to be feared," remarked the Atlanta *Constitution*, "that woman's complete independence has made her very much like a man in her temper, judgment and taste." The paper went on to report, somewhat relieved, that "the strong-minded woman flourishes only in communities here and there in the North and West." In 1892 the New York *Herald*, fearful of women's growing political voice, found itself asking the question, "Will the coming man be a woman?" Certainly by the early 1890s, as northern, mainly middle-class, women took up a "manly" defense of their rights, while southern women were believed to have quietly and submissively taken up their "womanly" responsibilities, it seemed as if the South had scored a victory for femininity. Perhaps of equal importance, it was also the southern woman who could make the northern man feel more secure in his masculinity, as she did not threaten his familiar gender preserve.[40]

While northern and southern authors praised the superior femininity of southern women, and despite the occasional appearance of characters like Basil Ransom, most conciliatory literature was loathe to look approvingly on southern masculinity. Convinced that northern men had attained the masculine ideal in their heroic duty during the Civil War, many northerners continued to portray Billy Yank as the manly superior of Johnny Reb. This certainly seemed to be the implication behind the frequent pairing of southern women with northern men; taking it even further, several works of fiction made a young Confederate soldier, often one with a long-standing engagement to the southern belle, the chief villain of the story. Yet, conscious of deepening the healing metaphor in the reunion culture, some northerners, by the 1890s, toned down their critique of southern men. Russ Whytal, in his play *For Fair Virginia* (1895), struck a note of compromise by making the evil Confederate villain a foreigner, a tactic also employed by H. P. Mawson in *A Fair Rebel* (1891). A reviewer of the Whytal play found that the retreat from the assault on southern manhood struck a note for theatrical reconciliation. According to the critic in *Godey's Magazine*, while the play hardly justified the "Lost Cause," "it must prove pleasing to Southern audiences, for its villain was, after all, only a transplanted foreigner."[41]

Most novels and plays of the reconciliation era, however, kept up a somewhat humorous assault on southern manliness through their depictions of elderly southern gentlemen, the anachronistic "befo' the wah" types who lacked the industriousness and business sense required of men in the modern world. In their rejection of northern society's constant money-grubbing, these characters revealed moral characteristics which Gilded Age Yankees found appealing; yet they also displayed the unfortunate habit of being unable to forget the past and were thus condemned to a fate of historical irrelevancy, which made them often humorous but seldom noble. In *Down in Dixie* (1894), the old planter was Squire Hasbin Lounds, anachronistic even in name. "The only reminiscences of the dark days introduced," one reviewer explained, "are the oft expressed laments of Squire Hasbin Lounds, who imagines that even the sun doesn't act quite right 'since the war.'" In one of the most well-known portraits of the old southern gentleman, Francis Hopkinson Smith's *Colonel Carter of Cartersville* (1891), the colonel was an unreconstructed but "high-toned Southern gentleman," "happy as a boy" in his simple dedication to the old way of life. In the dramatic version of Smith's novel, the kind but incompetent Carter lives with his aunt Nancy, who, a reviewer explained, "has a clearer view of life than he, and . . . patiently watches and cares for him as though he was still a small boy." As helpless, time-warped individuals,

Carter and Lounds epitomized the northern critique of southern men who still wallowed in the distant past. Although northerners may have recognized something noble and charming in these figures, they ultimately found them lacking the practical and realistic vision which forward-looking northern men possessed.[42]

Such weak, helpless, and unreconstructed southern gentlemen humorously derided many of the anachronistic features of the South's antebellum code of honor and manliness. For northerners in the 1880s and 1890s, however, this may have been less important than the message that these characters implicitly conveyed regarding the South's celebration of the lost cause. After all, these old Confederates tended to be cantankerous types, quick to defend the honor of the South and the high-minded, although vaguely stated, nature of its cause. In a sense, these ancient patricians became the embodiments of the South's continued devotion to that cause. By personifying the lost cause in these somewhat humorous and hot-tempered old men, as well as in the flirtatious coquettes and the devoted black servants, northerners undoubtedly relieved some of their own anxiety about the South's continued celebration of its role in the Civil War.

Not surprisingly, these reunion-oriented plays and novels appeared precisely when the lost cause cult reached new heights in the South, with thousands of southerners turning out for the dedication of each new Confederate monument. These grand and ritualized dedications to the old Confederacy made even the most sentimental of reunionists uneasy about the South's commitment to conciliation, and northerners often pointed with wariness to the elaborate monuments being built for the South's Civil War dead. In a typical expression of such concern, a Philadelphia Memorial Day speaker in 1890 voiced alarm regarding the southerners' tendency to "unite with enthusiastic zeal to warm into life the . . . angry elements which ruled their judgements in 1861." But on the stage and in the novels there was no "enthusiastic zeal" and no widespread invigoration of "angry elements"; there were only weak and helpless men like Hasbin Lounds and Colonel Carter—characters who undoubtedly soothed northern concerns about southern sectionalism. "Had the hot words of prejudice been put in the mouth of any but an old man," explained one actor in *Alabama*, "the piece would have been hissed from the boards north of Mason and Dixon's line."[43]

Thus, the images of reunion smoothed over tensions which still pervaded sectional relations in the 1880s and 1890s and affected the ways in which northerners and southerners dealt with each other in political, economic, and social settings. Indeed, when life imitated art and inter-sectional romance bloomed, regional antagonisms could often be seen in their most bitter manifestation. Not surprisingly, the real-life love affair seldom inspired the same sentimental ecstasy as the fictional one. A number of northerners and southerners, for example, offered their own irate reactions to one of the most celebrated of inter-sectional liaisons, the engagement of Alfred Wilkinson, grandson of abolitionist Samuel May, to Jefferson Davis's daughter Winnie. Having met during Winnie's 1886 visit to Syracuse, Davis and Wilkinson soon fell in love and in 1890 publicly announced their engagement. Unfortunately, many southerners were far from overjoyed at the news. "The very sleeping dead Southern soldiers would rise from their graves," wrote one Confederate veteran to Wilkinson soon after the engagement, "and hustle you back to Yankeedom ere they would see the daughter of Jefferson Davis ruined, and shame-covered forever." Apparently, southern soldiers were especially disgusted by the prospect of this union and interpreted Wilkinson's advances as an intense rebuke to southern manhood. The Davis-Wilkinson engagement was eventually broken off, perhaps less because of the irate remarks, however, than because of the failure of the Wilkinson family business; even true, heartfelt sympathies could not mask the legacy of sectional bitterness or the economic considerations which influenced people in their real-life interactions.[44]

Thirty years after Appomattox, then, reunion, in both the North and the South, could only go so far. The cultural offerings of the period revealed the ambiguities encountered on this route to reconciliation. In the plays and novels of the 1880s and 1890s, the specifically southern roles, those which embodied the full spirit of southern sectionalism, were usually played by the least threatening characters. The culture minimized the specter of southern sectionalism for northern audiences by equating the spirit of the Confederacy, and, perhaps more important, the continued influence of the lost cause, with the rantings of old men, the feisty flirtatiousness of southern belles, and the simplistic devotion of black servants. At the same time, these dramas of reunion presented Gilded Age Yankees with a soothing moral counterpoint to their own society. In the economic hardship of the southern elite, the class loyalty of black domestics, and the superior womanliness of southern females, northerners found an alternative to the materialistic and conflict-ridden components of their own lives. But even while they celebrated Dixie's moral attributes, northerners still expressed faith in the Union victory by envisioning a gendered relationship of power in which the young and energetic northern hero always won the heart of the compliant southern belle.

The reform movements of the period, especially the Populists and the WCTU, were interested less in messages of sectional power and more in championing the unique moral insights of their specific constituencies. They highlighted the moral imperative behind the reuniting of common, hardworking farmers or righteous, sentimental women. Both groups adjusted the reunion message to fit their own demands and enjoyed some genuine success in bringing people together across sectional lines. Yet both groups sacrificed something in the process, for both found it impossible to maintain an equitable alliance with southern blacks and southern whites. More and more northerners—within and without the reform circles—were discovering ways and rationales which allowed them to abandon their concerns for and commitment to the African American population altogether. As the following chapters will explain, the reunion process was increasingly becoming a whitewashed affair.

5 MINSTRELS AND MOUNTAINEERS

THE WHITEWASHED ROAD TO REUNION

One of the most noteworthy features of the reunion process was the transformation in white northerners' racial outlook. Never known for racial enlightenment, northern opinion, nonetheless, underwent a noticeable change from the 1860s, a period characterized by a certain optimism regarding the position of African Americans, to the 1890s, when northerners seemed uninterested, pessimistic, and derisive regarding the status of southern blacks. Increasingly, northern whites bowed to the racial pressures of reunion, to a process that depoliticized the legacy of sectionalism, overlooked the history of American slavery, and came to view southern blacks as a strange and foreign population. At the same time, northerners began to view southern white people in a more sympathetic vein, adopting a more exalted opinion not only of southern white womanhood but also, by the 1890s, of certain "manly" features among some sectors of southern white society. This new orientation paved the way for northern acceptance of some of the most virulent forms of racism which American society had ever produced.

In contrast to the extreme prejudice of the fin de siècle, discussions of race in the late 1860s and early 1870s often took on a more compassionate tone. After the Civil War, northern whites of all social classes manifested an increasing interest in southern black folk, now freed from the traumas of slavery and ostensibly brought under greater northern care. Northern teachers and reformers headed South with a missionary zeal in their efforts to uplift this downtrodden people. Social observers wrote with curiosity and optimism about the freedpeople's adjustment to the new labor conditions. Philanthropists contributed to newly created funds which supported southern black education. In general, middle-class northerners revealed the continued influence of the "romantic racialism" that had guided them in the antebellum period, asserting the innate racial differences between blacks and whites but finding the African American race to be closer to nature and potentially more spiritual.[1]

More than this, northerners in the immediate postwar years also embraced a more inclusive and far-reaching view of American nationalism that sought to broaden the scope of who was included within the confines of American citizenship. In part, this new nationalism was a product of postwar optimism, a recognition that the nation had been saved and that the future beckoned with promises of growth and expansion. Northerners acknowledged the contributions made by different ethnic groups to the Union cause and thus restrained many of the nativist impulses from the 1850s. For a brief and elusive moment, northern whites trespassed over racial boundaries and viewed the men of the ex-slave class not as national outcasts but as loyal, hardworking Americans, a group that must surely be embraced by the bonds of reunion. "Upon what good grounds," queried the editors of *Harper's Weekly* in 1865, ". . . can the ballot be refused to the loyal black citizens of the Southern States? They are the sturdy workingclass." Reconstruction legislation reflected this more broadly defined nationalism and the sense that southern blacks would be part of the coming economic expansion. In general, the former slaves received not only the legalistic sanctions of nationhood, but also a certain cultural acceptance from sectors of northern white society.[2]

Few episodes better reveal this new sense of inclusiveness than northern interest in the music of the southern black "jubilee" singers. First sent North in the early 1870s from southern black colleges such as Fisk and Hampton, these jubilee groups were used by school administrators to appeal to the hearts and pocketbooks of the northern middle class. Well-to-do northerners flocked to the concerts of these southern singers, often held in northern churches and sponsored by northern religious leaders, because they offered a more refined cultural contact with southern African Americans than could be found elsewhere in northern culture, especially in the crass and vulgar entertainments of the minstrels. To a great extent the jubilee singers, who sang the hymns and spirituals of both white and black churches, provided something comfortably middle class—they came as well-mannered students carefully trained in northern values who hoped to build schools in the South based on "the model of New England colleges and universities." They epitomized, in other words, many of the ideals of Reconstruction, especially the desire of many to "northernize" the southern states.[3]

Middle-class northerners also hailed the jubilee performers as the representatives of a thoroughly American cultural form. In these laments from the historic and tragic period of slavery, northerners heard the songs of a truly American experience. "At last the American school of music has been discovered," one 1873 reviewer of the Hampton singers proclaimed. Throughout the North, the jubilee songs were celebrated as native American music, more genuine than many other musical forms. Of course, middle-class Yankees were able to celebrate the American dimensions of this music precisely because whatever signs of slavery the jubilee singers had retained had been softened to suit northern audiences. Northerners embraced these performers as true representatives of the slave experience, overlooking the way the jubilee format had altered slave culture. "Allow me to bespeak a universal welcome through the North," exclaimed the Reverend Mr. Cuyler of New York upon greeting the Fisk Jubilee Singers, "for these living representatives of the only true native school of American music. We have long enough had its coarse caricatures in corked faces; our people can now listen to the genuine soul-music of the slave cabins, before the Lord led his children out of . . . 'the house of bondage.'"[4]

Thus, in this very direct way, northern antislavery activists sought to embrace the former slaves in a national bond while vindicating their own righteous path in the antebellum struggle. Moreover, as Americans scrutinized the differences between American and European nationalism, they demonstrated a growing interest in expressions of national "folk" culture. The jubilee singers seemed to reflect one of the few truly indigenous forms of American culture, a cultural strain that was firmly embedded in American history. "American music," explained New England writer Constance Woolson, "is at present but a pot-pourri," with "no original national airs save the negro melodies."[5]

Still, relatively few Yankees ever had much exposure to the refined and uplifting performances of the jubilee singers. In the 1870s most white northerners had one main source of contact with the southern black experience—the minstrel show, which few would have described as either refined or uplifting. Yet, in many respects, the message of the postwar minstrel show did not differ all that much from the jubilee performances. Both forms of entertainment, if only for a brief period of time, lent the southern black experience an aura of national inclusiveness. The minstrel shows, performed mainly by white entertainers in blackface, continued to present their contrived view of southern black life to mostly working-class audiences in the North. At the same time, the minstrel image of the 1870s revealed subtle but important changes since the antebellum period. For one, emancipation made it easier for minstrels to lament the cruelties of a system that had finally been obliterated. More than they had before, minstrels called forth a certain sympathy for this downtrodden race and elicited some of the same sentiments which drew middle-class audiences to the jubilee groups. Minstrel songs, for example, often recalled the agony of family separation or celebrated the happiness and joyousness of freedom.[6]

In addition, many postwar minstrel shows depicted the former slaves as excited and willing participants in the new free labor arrangements, as workers who sought respect for their laboring abilities. Minstrels stressed an identity and affinity with their working-class audiences and also extended a degree of cultural acceptance to the black people of the South. *The Great Republic*, an allegorical drama presented at the 1876 centennial celebration, included a few minstrel numbers to be sung by the "black" characters in the performance. "I'm looking now for somfin dat will pay," sang one performer, "somfin 'spectable—terms—two dollars a day." "Happy Little Sam" repeated these sentiments in a show done by the Dockstader minstrel troupe. Sam sang of running away from the white folks "to be a contraband" and of enjoying a new sense of self-respect as a free-laboring individual. "An' when I does my work," he explained, "why dey pays me like a man."[7]

Yet, even within the same minstrel song, the burnt-cork characters often seemed torn between their desire to leave the cruel old plantation and their longing for homes and families once they had left. "Ain't I glad I got out de wilderness, and left old Alabam?" one minstrel tune began and then concluded, "I neber will leab de old plantation, Down in Alabam."

These ambivalent views of the old plantation revealed more than just the minstrel show's perpetual indecision about slavery. In effect, minstrels in the postwar period embodied the conflicts of working people in northern cities, many of whom had left behind homes and families in the country and stepped into strange and unfamiliar urban settings. Minstrels, like recently arrived migrants, recalled their old country homes with nostalgia yet maintained a certain optimism about their new lives in the city. "We just came here from sunny Alabam," sang "Slippery Dick" and "Careless Sam" in one minstrel tune. Now the two looked forward to bright futures but had to adjust to new circumstances. "In the morning when we rise," they sang, "we feel so gay / That we both commence to dancing right away / When the people underneath / They commence to grit their teeth / But they hate to tell us for—To go away." Dick and Sam humorously addressed a problem that many rural migrants to the city faced: sharing their floors and ceilings with neighbors above and below in the strange, urban apartment houses. Taking a less cheerful view of the problem, other minstrel tunes stressed the pain of the moment when the migrant took his leave from his rural home. "I've packed up my satchel and I soon will have to leave you," one of the Haverly troupe minstrels cried. "Tell all de children good-bye." Indeed, perhaps the most pervasive theme in the minstrel tunes of the 1870s and early 1880s was the minstrel migrant's painful separation from loved ones and family on the old plantation, an image which could certainly arouse the sympathies of white, working-class migrants in the North.[8]

Through laments for the old homestead, minstrels stirred the emotions not only of native migrant workers but of immigrant laborers as well. Arriving in increasing numbers during the 1870s and 1880s from Germany, Ireland, Canada, and England, immigrants often attended the northern minstrel shows and undoubtedly empathized with the sentimental appeals to a faraway homeland. Because a majority of minstrel performers were themselves the descendants of recent European immigrants, the appeal was probably even stronger. "I've wandered very far away / From the clime where I was born," sang one performer. "And my poor heart has been so sad / Dejected and forlorn." Jonathan Baxter Harrison, a Massachusetts cleric surveying life in New England factory towns in 1880, saw evidence of the sympathy which the minstrel songs could arouse in immigrant workers. Harrison found that many factory laborers, including some foreign employees, sought a respite from their daily drudgery in the minstrel shows. In one town he visited a music hall bar where the crowd listened closely while a "young colored man," who had traveled with various minstrel companies, sang a few selections. "When he sang 'I got a mammy in the promised land,'" Harrison recalled, " . . . the English waiter-girl, who was sitting at my table, wiped her eyes with her apron, and everybody was very quiet." While the minstrel's "promised land" may have been the South, the immigrants in the audience were reminded of their own birthplaces in distant lands.[9]

Postbellum minstrel troupes recognized the ethnic diversity in their audiences and made efforts to appeal to the changing crowd. Burnt-cork performers in the postwar period thus increasingly portrayed—in blackface—members of the new immigrant groups. Often depicted with more complexity than southern blacks, blackfaced German and Irish characters on the minstrel stage could be distinguished by the ethnic dialect the performer adopted. In this way, the minstrel with the blackened face came to represent the ubiquitous immigrant, and southern blacks became, in effect, just another part of the growing ethnic mix that sought inclusion within the bounds of American nationalism. The quasi-minstrel show at the 1876 centennial played on this theme of interchangeable ethnic groups, all of whom were welcomed by the spirit of "Liberty" to American shores. At one point in the performance, a German character in whiteface expressed surprise at seeing a blackfaced performer who pretended to be his countryman. "Dis am sunburn," the blackface character explained. "I did left Yarmany swansy year ago. All Yarmans did got dis way when dey am vas in dis country finif year." An Irishman laughed at the blackfaced man's joke but warned him not to "be claimin' to be a countryman of mine, blast your smutty countenance."[10]

The centennial performance implied that southern blacks shared a certain ethnic distinction with the new immigrant groups. The show also bespoke the climate of national inclusiveness that existed in the 1870s, a climate that extended to European ethnic groups and, at least to some degree, to southern blacks. Still, as the Irishman's warning to the blackfaced impostor suggested, these black migrants could not simply melt into a common pot of cultural similitude. Minstrel songs made clear what southern blacks did and did not share with other ethnic populations. The laments for long-lost homes could be heard as metaphors for immigrant displacement, but they also stressed themes that specified how southern blacks differed from white ethnic groups. Numerous songs mourned the departure not only from the old home but from the kindly old master and mistress as well. The minstrel who moaned about being far from home also cried that he now had "no master kind to treat me well, to cheer me when in pain." One tune even took this point to the extreme of proclaiming, "Dey can talk about the free man / But I'd rather be a slave / In my old home in Carolina 'for de war." Minstrel songs and sketches thus held a twofold significance: they voiced a universal lamentation for homeland and birthplace while they also accentuated the old South mythology, with its celebration of the antebellum plantation lifestyle, that had taken root in popular culture. So, while they drew a parallel between the immigrant's and the former slave's feelings of displacement, most minstrel songs stressed the southern black's specific attachment to a southern home, with all the trappings of the old South environment—the master, the mistress, and the good old plantation. In the minstrel shows, African Americans were not simply immigrants who longed to go home; they were also former slaves who fondly recalled their former days of servitude.[11]

In the end, the longing for the old southern environment overcame the migrating impulse in many minstrel songs, sending the wandering freed-man back to his Dixie home where he allegedly belonged. Telling of their return to Kentucky, two minstrels sang, "We've been to see our birth-place / We couldn't stay away." Or, as two others proclaimed:

> We belong away down South,
>   Down in Alabama. . . .
> Nebber mind whar you be,
>   On this great wide earth,
> A darkie's heart can never lose
>   The spot that gave him birth.

More than other migrant groups, southern blacks seemed to be bound to their homelands, regardless of the compulsions that may have taken them away. The minstrel shows and other cultural forms kept black people con-fined and connected to a southern locality, unable to move on and possibly blend into other surroundings. Working-class audiences, already confront-ing cramped and competitive conditions, must have derived some comfort from this message that one less ethnic group would be competing with them for jobs and dwellings in the industrial cities of the North. When the Irish character in the centennial performance cautioned the blackfaced minstrel against passing himself off as an Irishman, he probably echoed the sentiments of many northern workers who saw the performance.[12]

So, despite some of the inclusive and welcoming tendencies of the 1870s, the minstrel show increasingly stressed the difference and, ultimately, the "southernness" of the black experience. By the 1880s this emphasis had become an all-consuming component of the minstrel presentation. Indeed, virtually every northern depiction of black life began to advertise its "authentic" southern setting or its "real" plantation melodies, and each new show promised a more genuinely southern experience than all others. Frequently this took the form of a crude attempt to re-create some aspect of slave or plantation life. In other cases, black minstrels, as opposed to white delineators, responded to the demand for authenticity and assumed the main responsibility for depicting the "genuine" southern black to northern audiences. "Dar has been a great deal ob talk and abbertising 'bout de plantation scenes and real brack minstrels at different periods of American history since de warh," explained one of the "genuine" black Callender minstrels, but the public was "offen doomed to disappoint- ment." The Callender troupe, however, presented "de real old-time plan- tation nigger waranted to tote pure brack blood in his beins and a certifi- cate ob his peddygree, dating clean back to de cannibals." Here was the real southern "darkey," this minstrel proclaimed, seen in his natural environment and with all his strange and distinct peculiarities which the white minstrel lacked. "De darkies ob de Souf," he concluded, "hab jess been waiting to get into a rale genuine show, what aint got no sawdust, nor cheers, nor none of dem white tomfooleries, and we will jess hab de naturallist show you eber seed."[13]

Stage productions of Harriet Beecher Stowe's *Uncle Tom's Cabin*, one of the most popular forms of entertainment in northern postwar commu- nities, likewise found it necessary to stress a distinctively southern com- ponent. The "Tom shows" adopted a number of elements from the min- strel stage, including the depiction of the "genuine" plantation black. A Boston production of the play, for example, introduced a "crowd of 'cullud pussons' . . . for the performance of hymns, 'plantation' melodies, break- down and banjo performances, just like the people down South 'befo de wa' used to do." One actor who appeared in the Tom shows of this period recalled what seemed to be a highly self-conscious effort to invoke the themes and images of Dixie. "We gave what is called a 'Southern version' of the play," the actor recollected in the 1920s. "We stressed the 'Southern' dialect and costumes and all that."[14]

This is not to suggest that these performances presented anything that even remotely resembled southern black life. But many found it necessary to make some sort of an attempt. Indeed, by the 1880s performers and troupe managers found themselves subjected to growing criticism—from both northern and southern reviewers—if they failed to present a more authentic view of Dixie. Perhaps because it was derived from a northern view of the southern experience, *Uncle Tom's Cabin* came under special pressure to produce something that was genuinely "southern." "As a reproduction of scenes in the South during the ante-bellum days," remarked one New York reviewer about the Tom show, "it cannot be depended upon." The black characters, in particular, were criticized if they failed to conform to the plantation image. One New York critic thus attacked "the psalm singing of the Thompson Street slaves, who never saw a plantation beyond the one they play in." Such comments echoed the remarks of southern white critics, who often faulted the whole minstrel enterprise for failing to present the real southern black experience. Responding to such critiques, the managers of Tom shows and minstrel shows felt compelled to introduce into their performances "genuine Southern colored folks—men, women, and children—most of whom were slaves . . . prior to the war."[15]

What accounted for this sudden and overwhelming interest in re-creating a more "authentic" southern black experience? One factor must have been northerners' increased contact, albeit from a narrow and limited perspective, with the South and with southern black people. As northerners traveled in and read more about the South, they were struck by the difference between the minstrel performer and the "genuine article." The members of the 71st New York Infantry, visiting the South on a reunion trip in 1881, expressed their interest in seeing a "genuine plantation dance." The group formed a ring around a "diminutive darkey" who, as one member explained it, danced in a way that would "make our 'variety specialists' turn green with envy." Thus, as northern audiences had more exposure to the South, they began to suspect that the black experience was not adequately captured by northern white delineators. In turn, minstrel shows probably found it necessary to address this more direct, although narrow-minded, contact with southern black people.[16]

Such attitudes dovetailed with northern white suspicions about the benefits of Reconstruction legislation. By the late 1870s northerners expressed a growing skepticism about the ability to reestablish the nation on wholly legalistic grounds. The sentimental viewpoint stressed that laws alone could not change the way people felt and that southern blacks, by extension, could not be forced into the national mainstream simply as the result of laws and amendments. They were bound by custom, by nature, and by feelings to a style of life that was closer to the ways of the old South. Consequently, it seemed only proper for the entertainer of the 1880s to be a "genuine Southern negro," as opposed to a northern black man or blackfaced imitator, both of whom seemed to defy the logic of nature and the sentimental view of national culture.

In addition to this northern desire for a more authentic cultural representation of southern blacks, there was a growing sense that the "real negro" was more likable and beguiling in a southern setting. Despite the lip service paid to notions of black progress and middle-class success, northerners apparently became convinced that the black person's most "natural" setting was not just in the South but in a context that closely resembled the old plantation conditions. "The general inclination of the negroes to leave the plantations and congregate in the towns," wrote one northern observer in 1882, "is injuring the race seriously, in many ways." Among many Yankees there existed an underlying fear that southern blacks would add to the already disturbing problems of industrial strife and urban decay, especially in the North. By the 1880s it was not uncommon for middle-class, and even some working-class, northerners to make an explicit connection between the social problems of the Gilded Age and the growing tide of immigration and ethnic diversity. Many believed that black migrants would only compound the social problems of industrialization, especially in light of their poor preparation for industrial labor. In this context, then, it is not surprising to find northern culture placing a special emphasis on the rural and southern setting of black Americans, and describing this as the most "natural" setting of all.[17]

Middle-class northerners, including some former abolitionists, generally affirmed these sentiments during their own travels in the South. They found that the former slaves, and their children, seemed to be content, even well off, in their southern clime. Young white southerners, explained the Reverend A. D. Mayo at an 1890 conference on "the Negro question," were more and more like young white Americans everywhere, interested in success and less rooted to their states and birthplaces. In contrast, "the

Negro loves the sacred soil, the old home, the climate, and its surroundings." Some observers even stressed the congenial nature of southern race relations, perhaps because it confirmed their own view of the unqualified benefits of emancipation. They overlooked southern white antagonisms as they envisioned a bright road of progress from slavery to freedom. Former abolitionist Thomas W. Higginson may have been guided by such thoughts during his own tour of the South in 1878, an experience which encouraged him to see enormous progress for southern blacks and to embrace members of the old plantation class as coworkers for social and racial harmony. "One sees a marked, though moderate progress," wrote Higginson, "in all the comforts of life" for southern blacks. Moreover, even though a number of observers claimed otherwise, Higginson remarked that he "did not hear a single charge of laziness made against the freed colored people in the States I visited." Edward Atkinson, anxious to see improvement in the southern economy, also found cause for optimism. In his view, the days of Klan violence and intimidation had "nearly gone by" throughout the South.[18]

Such observers were not simply blinded by the hue of their rose-colored glasses. As C. Vann Woodward has explained, southern race relations in the 1880s often were characterized by a good deal of tolerance and fluidity, a condition which undoubtedly encouraged northerners to accept the idea that black people would do well by remaining in the South. Republican politician Carl Schurz, traveling in the South in 1885, found that there was no consistent pattern of intolerance in southern race relations. In some states he saw black people traveling with whites in first-class railroad cars. In general, he concluded that the South showed "more kindness" to blacks than the North. Indeed, as the decade progressed, and as evidence mounted of northern intolerance toward immigrants and blacks, some observers suspected that the South might be a more agreeable place than the North for interracial living. Writer Henry Field, for example, maintained that one should "not ascribe what we call race prejudice to the peculiar perversity of our Southern brethren." By 1890 it was apparent to many that northerners had their own difficulties in coping with a nonwhite population and that southern blacks were probably better off where they were.[19]

During the 1890s, and especially after the depression of 1893, the industrial crisis that had seized the nation in the 1880s deepened profoundly. Labor unrest and urban decay increased, as did the number of newcomers who came to American shores. In the eyes of native-born workers who were desperate for work, as well as many middle-class Americans, it had become more and more difficult to absorb new elements into an increasingly restless labor pool and a severely depressed economy. Moreover, according to many northern observers, southern blacks seemed totally unprepared to accept a modern and industrial way of life. Now, more than ever, their most "natural" setting was apparently in the old South. Confirming this viewpoint was one of the most spectacular renderings of the "authentic" southern black experience, the 1895 traveling production known as "Black America." Produced by Nate Salisbury, former manager of the Buffalo Bill and Wild West show, "Black America" was part minstrel show and part exhibition. Salisbury created a southern black "village" which featured performances of "typical" plantation music, cake walks, buck and wing dancing, and military drills of "colored troops." First produced in Brooklyn, the show in its initial run attracted 200,000 spectators. Eventually, it also played in Boston, Philadelphia, Baltimore, Washington, D.C., and, by the end of 1895, in London.[20]

"Black America," like other minstrel presentations of the era, advertised its "natural" southern setting, an environment that was clearly beneficial for the region's blacks. "The lovable bright side of the true Southern Negro" was "presented in a series of animated scenes of rural simplicity." Salisbury himself took pains to emphasize the authentic origins of his performers. "All these negroes came from the South," he told an interviewer. "They are not show people, but are the genuinely southern negro in all his types." And reviewers agreed that the show oozed with authenticity and a natural feel of the black South, something which standard white minstrelsy could not achieve. "One of the chief charms of the exhibition is its naturalness," a reviewer claimed. "The North went wild over the production of 'Uncle Tom's Cabin' yet it was produced by counterfeit representatives of the characters portrayed while 'Black America' produces the genuine article, surrounded by the people, scenes and habits of their lives and they cannot be imitated even by the blacks of the North, much less by the negro dilineators [*sic*] of modern minstrelsy." Southern blacks, this reviewer explained and others agreed, had their own distinctive features which set them apart from northern blacks and white imitators. More important, it was in this authentic southern setting that blacks seemed most "natural" and least threatening to northern audiences.[21]

By stressing the "southernness" of the "genuine negro" performer, these presentations helped to reposition the boundaries of American nationalism. The authentic black performer was often viewed as unusual and exotic, a creature who embodied all that was strange and distinctive about the old South. Unlike some white southerners, who revealed a certain drive and determination that was consistent with the new sense of national will, black southerners now seemed to share little by way of national characteristics. No longer compared with immigrants, like the blackfaced minstrels of the 1870s, performers depicting southern blacks in the 1880s and 1890s increasingly called up comparisons with the "primitive" people of "backward" countries around the world. Ironically, as the minstrels aimed for a more genuine representation of the South, they stressed characteristics which seemed to make southern blacks more foreign. The Callender minstrel interviewed by the New York *Clipper* thus stressed the "cannibal" roots of his troupe and described his own family home in Africa where the tribes "nebber took no prisoners, kase dey eat dem up as fast det kotch dem." Some Uncle Tom shows likewise introduced scenes that stressed the "savage" and African origins of African Americans. One 1888 performance in Boston inserted a "voodoo" scene into the plot. At the same time that American culture was discovering the "inferior" and "uncivilized" people of other lands, these performances in the North highlighted similar ideas and themes, encouraging northern whites to view southern blacks as if they were representatives of a foreign and barbaric country.[22]

By the turn of the century, the stereotype of southern blacks shared many similarities with the stereotyped depictions of nonwhite people from foreign lands. Influenced by the popularity of Darwinian thought, many northern whites were inclined to believe in the overwhelming racial degeneracy of all nonwhite people, situating southern blacks along with other people of color on the lower rungs of the racial hierarchy. More significantly, as white Americans began to confront issues of world power and influence, they tended to conceive of this international power in racial terms. Racial superiority, many believed, and not just good ideas or economic leadership, would make America a dominant and civilizing world leader. In this context, a cult of Anglo-Saxonism developed, stressing the unique Anglo-Saxon traits that would make for national and international greatness. Drawing on ideas being advanced in Europe, a number of Americans applied the notions of Anglo-Saxon supremacy to their own developing view of American nationalism. As many racial theorists explained, Anglo-Saxons had already demonstrated their fitness for democracy and self-government in history; in the nineteenth century, they likewise proved their readiness to expand across and govern much of the globe. By the 1890s white Americans often defined their sense of national will, no longer seen as a legalistic entity, as the working out of the Anglo-Saxon destiny. This equation of nationalism and international greatness with Anglo-Saxonism thus made it difficult to define any nonwhite group, whether Filipino or Mexican or southern black, as anything but "foreign."[23]

In the realm of popular culture, this tendency to group southern blacks with other "lower" foreign races could be seen most blatantly in the exhibits at turn-of-the-century world's fairs and expositions. On the one hand, when it came to celebrations of national progress and achievement, blacks were virtually invisible at the fairs. Implicitly, fair organizers broadcast the message that black people had failed to make any significant contribution to the workings of American history. At the Chicago World's Fair in 1893, African Americans received almost no representation, despite the heroic efforts of black leaders to secure a place in the "White City." The fair's managers, however, did arrange for a Colored Jubilee Day in August 1893. During this celebration Frederick Douglass spoke, Paul Laurence Dunbar recited a poem, and two black concert singers provided the musical entertainment. Yet, despite an emphasis on "refined" culture during the actual celebration, northern white publications ridiculed Colored Jubilee Day as a gathering of savages and buffoons, describing it as a grouping of primitive black people from around the world. *World's Fair Puck*, a northern magazine devoted to news of the fair, ran the following poem in honor of "Darkies Day at the Fair":

> The events of the Great World's Fair
> Impressive went their way.
> Time rolled around; at last it was
> The Colored Peoples Day!
> The sons of Ham from far Soudan
> And Congo's sable kings
> Came to the Fair with all their hosts,
> Their wives, their plumes, their rings.
> From distant Nubia's torrid sands,
> From far-famed Zanguebar,

Together with their Yankee friends
The Darkies all were dar!

The accompanying illustration crudely depicted black people from America and from Africa frolicking with watermelons at the fair.[24]

When southern black exhibits appeared at world's fairs, fair managers usually arranged these presentations on the midways, the popularly oriented sections of the fair where the "primitive" peoples of the world were placed on display. Set alongside "villages" of Filipino or Fijian natives, the "Old Plantation" cabins became simply another depiction of a foreign way of life. "There are two complete innovations in the exhibition of foreign life on the Midway," wrote Richard Barry in his guide to the 1901 exposition in Buffalo, New York, "and both are quite essential to a Pan-American Exposition. . . . They are the picturesque and sunnily ecstatic people of modern Mexico, and the remnants of the jocular, careless serfs, who in the South before the war gave slavery the deceptive hue of contented and ofttimes happy dependence."[25]

Southern blacks, Barry insisted, were like a strange people from a foreign and feudal land. Moreover, because the presentation was so authentic, the "Old Plantation" offered an uplifting and educational type of entertainment, one that could instruct as well as amuse. Middle-class critics appreciated presentations such as "Black America" and the "Old Plantation" because they saw them as pedagogical tools for the unrefined masses, preferable to the crass amusements which might otherwise occupy working peoples' time. "It is easy to pick up the colored people of the North and draught them into the show business," explained Barry, "but the darkies of the South do not take as kindly to the public rouge box. . . . [the southern black] is a more valuable acquisition than the somewhat machine-made coon of the variety stage, has more of the real ginger of genuine enjoyment and gives more correctly a picture of real southern life. Negroes of this kind are those that the Old Plantation has." These were the authentic "natives" of an unknown land, as genuine as the Mexican peasants on the "Streets of Mexico" or the tribespeople in the "African village," all of whom offered entertainment, coupled with education, to white Americans of all social classes.[26]

While some observers applauded the instructive value of the midway show, many northern whites continued to shun such cheap amusements and sought a more sophisticated cultural contact with southern black people. But even in more "refined" settings, northern whites received messages that were similar to those broadcast by the minstrel shows and the midway exhibits. Contributing to the sense of distance between northern whites and southern blacks, many white authors, both northern and southern, turned in the 1880s and 1890s to the composition of "dialect stories." These tales recounted fictional incidents in the lives of southern blacks and compelled readers to wend their way through dialogue and narrative supposedly written in the peculiar idiom of African Americans. Joel Chandler Harris, undoubtedly the most popular and successful of the dialect delineators, created one of the most enduring characters in this literary genre. In Uncle Remus, Harris constructed a vehicle for conveying the folktales of southern blacks and for presenting northerners with the southern white view of harmonious race relations. Harris explicitly set out to challenge northern misconceptions and to establish the authority of the southern white voice; he proclaimed his tales to be a more accurate presentation of southern blacks than anything else that northerners had been exposed to, especially the crude imitations of the minstrel stage. "To all who have any knowledge of the negro," wrote Harris in an obvious slight against northern ignorance and fakery, "the Plantation darkey, as he was, is a very attractive figure. It is a silly trick of the clowns to give him over to burlesque."[27]

Yet, according to Harris and his supporters, the best indication of Uncle Remus's authenticity was Harris's "genuine" rendition of African American dialect. Reviewing the Uncle Remus collection, the *Nation*'s critic concurred that the stories gave "Mr. Harris an opportunity to display still further his mastery of the negro dialect, of which probably no better representation has ever been given." Other reviewers agreed. Harris's dialect "is the only true negro dialect I ever saw printed," wrote critic James Davidson. "After so many dead failures by a hundred authors to write thus," including the poor imitations "of the so-called negro minstrels, 'Uncle Remus' is a revelation."[28]

Joel Chandler Harris apparently offered yet another refined and instructive view of the southern black experience by presenting African American dialect in a more "genuine" and "realistic" manner. In claiming to have mastered the dialect of southern blacks, he also cast himself in the role of expert analyst, as the leading interpreter of what was perceived to be a strange and foreign language. Lengthy and pseudoscientific explanations often accompanied stories which used black dialect, suggesting the need to study and scrutinize the language as if it were a foreign tongue which only educated experts could decipher. Moreover, the constant use of dialect seemed to suggest that southern blacks remained at a more primitive level of language development, using their own peculiar spoken idiom to convey what a more civilized people would put down in writing. Yet, as an educated white man, Harris had managed to capture this peculiar black tongue in written form, a linguistic triumph which his reviewers never tired of trumpeting. "The North noted the strange fact that the South was reading a Southern book," explained Virginia writer Thomas Nelson Page in a review of the first Uncle Remus collection. "It studied the unknown dialect, and recognized through its difficulties the unmistakable hand of the master." Harris himself gave the impression of having conquered the linguistic challenge to understand black dialect as if he had lived abroad and learned a native tongue. "I have Mr. Harris' own word for it," wrote Walter Hines Page, "that he can think in the negro dialect. He could translate even Emerson, perhaps Bronson Alcott, in it, as well as he can tell the adventures of Brer Rabbit." Apparently Harris had become so expert at the black dialect that he could use the language even better than the native people themselves.[29]

Harris's expertise in learning, writing, and speaking the dialect of southern blacks helped to establish not only the foreignness of the dialect, but also the unique ability of southern whites to act as the educated interpreters and intermediaries of black culture. Northern whites increasingly suspected that they had to see either real southern blacks or southern white interpretations in order to understand the actual experience. They accepted the idea that southern white people, simply because of their southern birthplace, possessed a unique understanding of blacks and race relations. "No Northern man ever journeys far into the South," wrote northern travel writer Julian Ralph, "without hearing that his people do not understand the negro. . . . I never went South without being impressed by the fact that no Northern man who has not been South can even faintly appreciate the relation there between the whites and the colored people." Another traveler agreed that "the Southern people have even now more kindly feeling instinctively to the negroes than the people of the North, for they know them better, are accustomed to them, and understand them." Thus, as northern whites began to cast African Americans outside the boundaries of their Anglo-Saxon nation, they likewise became convinced that a certain mystery surrounded black people and everything about their race, something that was foreign and ultimately unknowable except to a few southern whites. "I'm afraid," an Iowa newspaper reporter explained in a piece on the good relations that prevailed between former masters and their slaves, that "we Yankees don't understand the 'nigger' question yet." This attitude gave northern whites a justification for ignoring southern blacks altogether, at least in terms of the South's racial problems, as they believed they would never really grasp the workings of this strange relationship. In the end, northern whites clung to this cover of ignorance, using it to deemphasize the place of blacks in the American past and to overlook the racial troubles in the American present.[30]

As ethnic tensions and immigration problems swelled in the northern states, especially in the 1890s, northerners were more inclined than ever to admit their own ignorance and to accept the authority of southern whites on racial matters. Apparently, many saw white southerners as models of etiquette, and of control, in managing a non–Anglo-Saxon population. Northerners looked with a certain nostalgia on features of the master-slave relationship, finding a degree of harmony and cooperation that was lacking in the turbulent world of northern class conflict. In the 1890s historians reassessed the history of slavery and found a system characterized by intimacy and loyalty. Even more, as middle-class northerners confronted the political challenge of accepting new immigrants, and perhaps even overseas colonials, as voters and citizens, they showed greater sympathy for the South's problem and for southern whites' professed interest in uplifting and educating the black electorate, and even, in some cases, for limiting black suffrage. One northern participant at the 1890 Mohonk Conference on the Negro Question thus agreed with "the idea that it would be well if the South would establish an educational test for suffrage. . . . I believe that the results of such a course would be so good that it would eventually spread to most, if not all, of the Northern states."[31]

Finally, as northern whites showed increasing respect for the southern white view of the race problem, they also adopted a tone of growing admiration and regard for southern white people in their own right, as a people capable of offering guidance on race matters but also possessing their own admirable racial and national characteristics. Indeed, many of the speakers at the Mohonk conference, including a number of former Union officers and abolitionists, explicitly advanced this view. "I want this Conference and these Northern people," explained Ohio banker and former Union general Roeliff Brinkerhoff, "somehow . . . to look at this [Negro] question from the standpoint of the white men of the South. Let us remember that the white people of the South are a noble people, that there is nowhere in the United States a purer strain of American blood than in the Old South."[32]

Brinkerhoff stressed one point which became increasingly significant in northerners' new racial discourse: the recognition of southern racial purity and homogeneity. Southern white people, northerners found, stood in sharp contrast to their own motley mixture of ethnic groups. "The South," explained Charles Dudley Warner in 1889, had always been "more homogeneous than the North, and perhaps more distinctly American in its characteristics." Under the title "The South Is American," a writer for the *Arena* magazine, Joshua Caldwell, explained that "the Anglo-Saxon supremacy in the South has never been overcome. . . . The white population has always been American and homogenous." The emphasis on homogeneity is striking; if nothing else, it confirms the growing tendency of northerners to ignore the black population altogether. Southern blacks, like various immigrant groups, stood outside this more exclusive view of the nation and thus became invisible in the overall picture of the South.[33]

The Anglo-Saxonism of the southern white people gave added significance to northerners' conciliatory efforts at the turn of the century. As many writers explained, northerners could no longer reject the South, steeped in its proud Anglo-Saxon heritage, while opening their gates to the strange foreign immigrants who flooded into northern cities. After tabulating the percentage of foreign-born people in the total population of various southern states, Caldwell found that it would be difficult to find a population more American, that is, Anglo-Saxon, than in the South. Because of their racial heritage, the southern white people, he believed, could better protect the principles of freedom and Union, certainly better than those who descended from alien cultures. For the Anglo-Saxons of the South, Caldwell explained, "no life but one of freedom is possible, and I can never believe that the hybrid population of Russians, Poles, Italians, Hungarians, which fills so many Northern cities and states, has the same love for our country, the same love of liberty, as have the Anglo-Saxon southerners, whose fathers have always been free." Others implicitly agreed with this contention that the racial purity of the white South undercut the region's earlier rebellion against the Union, making the move toward conciliation more critical than ever before.[34]

The 1890s cult of Anglo-Saxonism encouraged northerners to reevaluate all southern white people in a more approving light. Even poor whites attained a slightly elevated stature in certain northern circles. But one group, in particular, became northern culture's cause célèbre. By the end of the nineteenth century, northerners had "discovered" the white people of the southern mountains: they celebrated their picturesque qualities in numerous short stories and novels, described their sturdy American characteristics in countless articles, and devoted considerable time and energy to drawing these formerly outcast white people more completely into the national fold. Initially stressing the strange and alien qualities of this isolated population, northerners by the 1890s wrote of, read about, and helped to cultivate the truly American qualities of these people. More than the rest of the poor white population, the mountaineers revealed the South's racial purity and Anglo-Saxon heritage and could promote the economic progress of the entire region. And, as the purest and most patriotic of all the South's Anglo-Saxons, they formed a crucial link in the reconciliation chain.[35]

Beginning in the 1880s, the railroad opened up the southern mountains to northern investment, bringing in tourist promoters who set up new mountain resorts and speculators interested in the mining and timber capabilities of the region. As economic optimism surged, observers became increasingly enthusiastic about the region and its inhabitants. Although outsiders still found much that was odd, peculiar, and even degraded about the mountaineers, they also stressed the positive features which made this group deserving of northern assistance. The mountaineers may have displayed many "primitive" characteristics, northerners believed, but they also possessed qualities which made them capable of uplift and improvement. For one, they seemed to be adaptable to economic change. Perhaps even more important, they retained a wholesome and desirable racial demeanor. William Goodell Frost, the northern-born president of Berea College in Kentucky and a leading interpreter of Appalachian culture, spent much of his career lauding the economic, and racial, potential of the mountaineers. They are, wrote Frost, "a glorious national asset. They are the unspoiled and vigorous reserve forces. They will offset the undesirable foreign elements, and give the South what it has always lacked, a sturdy middle class."[36]

The mountain whites thus possessed a quality which observers had discovered in other white people of the South, but the mountaineers seemed to be an even purer embodiment of the American Anglo-Saxon heritage. In the last years of the nineteenth century it was this feature that northern whites cherished most about Appalachia's inhabitants. Having established their racial wholesomeness, northern whites could embrace the southern mountaineers, bringing them into their national heritage at precisely the same moment that northern culture had cast southern black people aside as savage foreigners. While northerners may never have recognized the mountain folk as their equals, by stressing the racial purity of Appalachia, they established a bond through which the mountaineers became worthy of northern attention. "Nowhere will be found purer Anglo-Saxon blood," claimed William Brewer, writing about Georgia's mountaineers in the pages of *Cosmopolitan*. Other writers agreed that the southern mountaineers epitomized racial purity, largely because the mountains had kept these people isolated from the waves of immigration that had polluted the racial stock of the rest of the nation. The mountaineers, in effect, embodied the same racial makeup as the early settlers in America and the hardy pioneers who had pushed their way up the mountain range one hundred years earlier. "These people have not changed in any essential respect," one writer explained in 1902, "since the days of the pioneer."[37]

Impressed by the racial purity of Appalachia, observers, travelers, and folklorists in the 1890s and early 1900s reexamined the mountaineers and found much to be admired. The newly established American Folklore Society (1889) became enthralled with the study of the Appalachian people, finding in the mountains a guide to the traditions and values of the American past and, indeed, some of that indigenous American culture which northerners had at one time seen in the jubilee performances of southern blacks. In time the ideas of the folklorists influenced other educators, missionaries, and travelers, who turned with a new interest to the southern mountains. Although many objected to some of the "primitive" characteristics of the region, such as feuding and moonshining, they found that even these features embodied distinctively American and Anglo-Saxon qualities. In effect, because they were primitive, the mountaineers demanded uplift, but, because their primitiveness revealed their early

Anglo-Saxon roots, they were also especially deserving of all the assistance they could get. "The mountaineer is to be regarded as a survival," explained William Frost. "In his speech you will soon detect the flavor of Chaucer. . . . his very homicides are an honest survival of Saxon temper."[38]

Significantly, the "primitivism" of the mountaineers was nothing like the "barbarity" of southern blacks. The mountain people were primitive in the sense of being less civilized Anglo-Saxons; they were Americans-in-the-making. Southern blacks, in contrast, were strange and barbaric creatures who revealed little in the way of national Anglo-Saxon characteristics. In light of the late-nineteenth-century celebration of the primitive, Appalachian primitivism could even present an attractive, antimodern counterpoint to the overcivilized society of the North. Primitive peoples, like those of Appalachia, were seen to possess a childlike intensity and simplicity, characteristics which modern, overworked, and overcivilized Americans might do well to emulate. The Appalachian primitive offered a graphic, and appealing, depiction of the childhood stage of the Anglo-Saxon race, exuding the innocence and racial vigor of a youthful white America.[39]

In the eyes of many northern observers, the white mountaineers held the key to the North's reconciliation with the South. Here, after all, was a group of southerners that, in their pioneer and Anglo-Saxon ways, seemed to reveal the essence of American nationalism. Moreover, the history of the Appalachian people revealed a tendency toward patriotism, and an explicit commitment to the nation, which seemed to be lacking in other southern whites. William Frost, for example, linked the mountaineers' racial nature with their love of country. They were, he explained, a "simple, primitive people, showing the strong traits of their race—independence, respect for religion, family affection, patriotism." Apparently mountain whites excelled where other southern whites had failed. Northerners also found that, among white southerners, the Appalachian people had been some of the most consistent supporters of the Union side in the Civil War. As early as the Reconstruction period, northerners had asserted the Unionist strength of the mountain region. During the 1880s and 1890s other publicists and reformers expanded on this theme of the patriotic, and therefore deserving, mountain people in scores of fictional and nonfictional accounts of Appalachia. Missionary writer Thomas Hume presented one of the classic arguments for Appalachian unionism in his work, *The Loyal Mountaineers of Tennessee* (1888). "It is certain," Hume wrote, ". . . that the steadfast attachment of East Tennessee to the Union and the efficient aid it gave to its preservation, formed an important factor in the war and contributed in no small degree to its final result." William Frost agreed that "the greater part [of the mountain population] were steadfast in loyalty to the old flag."[40]

Crucial to the mountaineers' pro-Union stance was their isolation from the system of slavery. The mountaineers, claimed missionary writer Mrs. S. M. Davis, "would have no complicity with slavery, and hence the slaveocracy would have nothing to do with them." According to the historical accounts, the slave system left many poor whites with little choice but to escape the control and domination of the slaveholders' economy by retreating to the isolated mountain regions. Here, explained Harvard geology professor Nathaniel Shaler, they "formed independent and singularly isolated communities, in which no negroes were ever seen." Distance from the degradations and sectionalism engendered by the slave system made the mountaineer unreceptive to the Confederate cause and more sympathetic to the boys in blue.[41]

Perhaps of even greater significance, this separation from slavery highlighted the mountain people's racial isolation, their dissociation from a racial institution and from the slaves themselves. Northern observers, missionaries, and educators, actively looking for "the white side" of southern race relations and for Anglo-Saxon purity, needed to look no further than this racially unadulterated and definitively nonblack population. Here, amazingly, was a group of southern white people who, it could be argued, had had virtually no contact with the unwholesome influences of slavery— the devaluation of free labor, the extremes of wealth and impoverishment within the white population, and the racial hostility that beset many poor whites, not to mention familiarity with the degraded characteristics of southern blacks. Indeed, what began as an explanation of the mountaineers' isolation from the sectional politics of slavery and the slaveholder became a tribute to their detachment from the black people. "The landless, luckless 'poor white,'" argued William Frost, "degraded by actual competition with slave labor, is far removed in spirit from the narrow-horizoned but proud owner of a mountain 'boundary.' The 'poor white' is actually degraded; the mountain man is a person not yet graded up."[42]

Suddenly, the southern mountaineers had become a people defined by their distance from African Americans, a point of considerable significance in a period when northern culture had begun to cast the black population aside as foreign and to embrace Anglo-Saxonism as pure Americanism. "Men and women would ride twenty miles to see the black men and stare them out of countenance," explained Nathaniel Shaler, thereby suggesting that the mountaineers had virtually no contact with, and no understanding of, this strange population. Whereas writers had, at one time, described the mountaineers as suffering from depravities similar to those of southern blacks, turn-of-the-century observers commented on the noteworthy absence of African peculiarities, something which could not be said of other poor whites. "These mountaineers," explained Frank Waldo, "are by no means as superstitious as the people of the southern lowlands who have been brought up surrounded by a negro population." In many ways, then, the southern mountain folk captured the imagination of northern observers precisely because of their ignorance of black people. Like many northern whites, the mountaineers did not understand the workings of race relations or the features of slavery; their ignorance was viewed as a wholesome attribute which enhanced their patriotism as well as their racial purity.[43]

Turn-of-the-century fiction writers championed the proud and patriotic mountain people and made a virtue out of their racial ignorance. One author became the preeminent exponent of the wonders of Anglo-Saxon mountain culture. A Kentucky native, born during the Civil War into a southern middle-class family, John Fox found compelling material for his fiction in the people of the Cumberland Mountains. Although not a product of the mountain society, Fox did come from a culture which, in the late nineteenth century, showed an interest in poor southern white people, and mountain people in particular. Like his friend Thomas Nelson Page, Fox was also a southern writer who was acutely aware of northern literary interests. He received a Harvard education and later secured a job as a tutor for a well-to-do northern family, a position which he believed he got mainly because of the apparent prestige of his southern birth. Fox wrote with a northern audience in mind, and many of his novels and short stories first appeared in northern magazines. In the white people of Appalachia Fox found, to a great extent, the ideal blend of northern and southern interests, as well as the perfect vehicle for a reunion novel through which he could convey certain pro-South sympathies. Fox tied these various threads together in *The Little Shepherd of Kingdom Come*, the most successful novel of his career and a book that became a best-seller soon after its 1903 publication.[44]

The Little Shepherd of Kingdom Come chronicled the adventures of a Kentucky mountain boy, Chad Buford, who, at the outset, was left without a home and family when cholera killed his aunt and uncle. In the midst of this initial tragedy, Fox described Chad's noble American heritage. Resolving to depart from his forlorn surroundings, Chad was moved by that "restless spirit that had led his unknown ancestor into those mountain wilds after the Revolution." Leaving his isolated mountain home for the somewhat more civilized valley, Chad met the Turner family, who promised to nurture and care for the orphaned boy. But, as he approached the settlement in the valley, Chad also met two black slaves, a strange and unusual sight for the naive mountaineer. His newfound companions from the valley expressed amusement at Chad's racial ignorance. "Lot's o' folks from yo' side o' the mountains nuver have seed a nigger," explained one of his new friends, apparently as much for the reader's understanding as for Chad's. "Sometimes," the friend said, "hit skeers 'em." Chad, however, lacked any clear-cut racial code or philosophy and replied, "Hit don't skeer me." Like many other mountaineers, Chad was a blank slate when faced with questions of race relations.[45]

Eventually Chad traveled with the Turners to the aristocratic bluegrass region, where he met old Maj. Calvin Buford. When the major invited Chad to live with him, the mountain boy agreed. Here he slowly won the respect and friendship of his new bluegrass friends and family, even the black servants, who were at first bemused by his appearance but gradually came to revere him. Acting in part out of his own unfamiliarity with race relations, as well as his unswerving commitment to justice, Chad even defended a helpless black "pickaninny" who had been tormented by his young master.[46]

Predictably, Chad's personal turning point coincided with that of the nation. Resisting the Confederate sympathies of both the Turners and Major Buford, Chad enlisted on the side of the Union in the Civil War, thus responding to the sentiments and traditions that he had learned—or, more precisely, that he had remained ignorant of—in the mountains. In the Kentucky hills, John Fox explained, "unionism was free from prejudice as nowhere else on the continent save elsewhere throughout the southern mountains. Those southern Yankees knew nothing about the valley aristocrat, nothing about his slaves, and cared as little for one as for the other." This much Fox had drawn from long-standing tales of southern mountain unionism, but he added a new twist to the story. Explaining the mountaineers' stand in the Civil War, Fox noted that Chad's ignorance of slavery made his commitment to the Union cause noble and pure, untainted by extraneous causes and issues. Fox implicitly compared Chad's unionism to that of the abolitionist who was fired, and presumably sidetracked, by a vision of cruelty and oppression. Chad, who saw the slaves as "sleek, well-fed, well-housed," remained untouched by "the appeal of the slave." He was moved by the cause of nationalism itself, making him, and his mountain compatriots, "the embodiment of pure Americanism."[47]

Fox's book stood on the side of the Union, although its position was thoroughly infused with the southern white view of the kindly conditions of slavery. As Fox suggested, the isolation from slavery not only made the mountaineers dedicated Unionists, it also made their Union spirit more lofty and noble than that of the abolitionists, who apparently had been dragged down by a more mundane concern for the slaves. Nationalism, at least in the case of Chad, and increasingly for many northern white readers, rested on ignorance of the history of slavery and of the present circumstances of southern race relations. Instead, nationalism became more abstract and bound up with intangible and vaguely understood principles. Chadwick Buford, the Anglo-Saxon boy of the southern mountains, who rejected the extremism of the abolitionist and embraced the Union cause without condemning southern slavery, became the embodiment of the national spirit.

In contrast, the women in Chad's life often posed obstacles to national progress. Both Melissa in the mountains and Margaret in the bluegrass stood by the Confederacy and its ideals of sectionalism. Both embodied that fierce rebel spirit so common, at least in fiction, among the women of the South. Nonetheless, with the end of the war and Melissa's eventual death, romantic reconciliation reigned once again as the bluegrass woman surrendered her ideals and her love to Chad and the Union victory. Fox strayed slightly from the standard conciliatory formula that brought northern men and southern women together, but Chad, a southern mountaineer guided by a pure and noble sense of patriotism, was the perfect hero for this southern-oriented tale of national celebration and reunion. Indeed, as Fox suggested, the mountaineer, who remained wholly ignorant of the nation's racial troubles, may have been the best hero of all.[48]

While the turn-of-the-century celebration of Appalachia stressed the racial purity and patriotic, pioneer spirit of the mountain people, mountain culture also garnered praise for its supposedly manly and virile qualities.

In this age of "the strenuous life," when war and adventure and sports were the pinnacle of manly activity, every facet of American culture had to be measured on a scale of vigor and virility. By all calculations, Appalachia seemed to measure up; certainly the potential for manliness and virility were present. John Fox was himself on friendly terms with that most ardent advocate of masculinity, Theodore Roosevelt, and he gave his fictional hero some of the virility of the age. Indeed, much of the novel showed Chad's quest for and attainment of manhood. After defending the beleaguered servant who was abused by his young white master, Chad received the commendations of the white boy's father. "My papa," the boy told Chad, "says you are a man." In the bluegrass region, where there are "manly virtues" and "manly vices," Chad imbibed both, becoming a courageous fighter and stopping, albeit briefly, to sow his wild oats. As Fox's book suggested, the "real" men who lived "the strenuous life" seemed to embody a new spirit of manliness, one that would not have been condoned by northerners in the early postwar years. This new masculinity continued to respect the northern work ethic but now gave some room to what had formerly been condemned as the illicit practices of unrestrained southern men. As a "southern gentleman," Chad Buford was a hard-working and patriotic man who also had to indulge, momentarily, his urge for drinking and card playing. But even this bout with vice only underscored Chad's progress on his successful journey to virile and vigorous manhood.[49]

Chad, of course, was not the only real man of the mountains. Others confirmed this notion of mountaineer manliness, often connecting it explicitly to the racial sturdiness and purity of the Appalachian people. In the racial vitality of the mountaineers, some writers and observers suggested, one could find the essence of Anglo-Saxon manliness, a manliness that recaptured noble, albeit "primitive," values of courage and action. In many ways, the primitive nature of the mountaineer proved a fertile breeding ground for many of the qualities of the "strenuous life," for certain "basic" and "natural" male instincts which rejected the over-breeding and refinement of modern society. Discussing the feuding tradition among southern mountain people, William Frost maintained that "the fighting tendency in our own race indicates at least some vigor," a characteristic which had been reinforced in the peculiar conditions of the mountains. Indeed, although he deplored the lawlessness of the mountain feuds, Frost respected the seemingly masculine purpose that lay behind these illegal contests. They revealed, he explained, "a code of honor and a moral standard" under which women were "never molested." This latter point took on an added significance in a period when many non–Anglo-Saxons, especially southern blacks, were castigated and condemned for their unmanly abuse of white women.[50]

Late-nineteenth-century depictions of the southern mountains encouraged northerners to envision a world of strenuous manliness and virility. Perhaps nothing is more illustrative of this point than the curious reception accorded another writer of mountain fiction, the Tennessee author, Mary Murfree, who perplexed her readers by writing successfully, as a woman, in an apparently male domain. Mary Noailles Murfree was born in 1850 on her parents' plantation near Murfreesboro, Tennessee. During the 1860s and 1870s, when she vacationed with her family in the Cumberland Mountains, Murfree became familiar with the people and the terrain of southern Appalachia. She began composing fiction in the 1870s and received notice in the 1880s, when her writing appeared often in the *Atlantic Monthly* and later in book form. Until 1885, however, Murfree had written under a man's name, Charles Egbert Craddock. In that year she disclosed to the *Atlantic* editor, and to an astonished reading public, her true, feminine identity. Significantly, the revelation prompted, at least in some quarters, a certain discomfort.[51]

Nineteenth-century American readers were not unfamiliar with women writers who assumed male pseudonyms. In the 1880s and 1890s, however, literary critics were particularly perplexed by Murfree's gender, especially in light of the specific subject matter about which she chose to write. "Her work," explained one critic, "is so strong, so vivid, so intense, and the power is so steadfastly maintained throughout . . . that it is not easy to credit a woman with having produced it." *Century* editor Richard Watson Gilder confirmed the sense of gender confusion in Murfree's work. "The public," he wrote in 1890, "is only lately over its surprise in the discovery that Charles Egbert Craddock's vigorous pen was wielded by a quiet, hard-working young woman of Tennessee." To a great extent, the vigor and intensity of Murfree's writing stemmed from her subjects—the virile and adventuresome people of the southern mountains. "The startlingly vigorous and robust style," explained critic William Baskerville in 1897, "and the intimate knowledge of the mountain folk in their almost inaccessible homes, suggestive of the sturdy climber and bold adventurer, gave no hint of femininity, while certain portions of her writings, both in thought and treatment, were peculiarly masculine." Well into the 1890s, and past Murfree's popularity as a writer, the ability of a female author to write convincingly in this domain of fiction continued to confound literary critics, suggesting a growing tendency to view this subject as a field not for sentimental scribbling but for masculine veneration.[52]

The racial characteristics of the Appalachian people, especially their pioneer sturdiness, their hardy adaptation to their environment, and, as one historian explained, their ability to resist "slave encroachments quite strenuously," all suggested a virile and vigorous population of southerners. And yet, during the 1890s, northern whites found that Appalachian men did not have an exclusive franchise on southern masculinity. If Chad Buford, the nationalist hero who remained indifferent to the problem of slavery, represented one brand of southern manliness, northerners gradually found another model of manhood among the leading, and refined, white men of the South. In particular, as northerners gained a growing respect for the ability of southern white people to handle their mysterious and complex race relations, they showed increasing admiration for southern white men's stern and forthright confrontation of their region's racial problems. Although they could empathize with the white mountaineer, like Chad, who was ignorant of race relations, they also admired those who were allegedly knowledgeable and skillful in questions concerning race. In recognizing the white southerner's unique skill in racial matters, northerners found themselves acknowledging the southern white man's ability to stand up to the "Negro problem," to control the unruly behavior of savage blacks, and, especially in the 1890s, to come to the defense of white womanhood when, as many fantasized, it seemed to be under such dire attack.[53]

Northerners' recognition of a "Negro problem," at least in the 1890s, did not in any way detract from their appreciation of southern white superiority in handling racial matters. The problem, as many saw it, was one of preparing the black race for modern civilization, educating them to be proper citizens and intelligent voters, training them to be steady and conscientious workers, and controlling the impetuousness and immorality that were thought to be a holdover from slavery. Northern whites recognized in southern white men, in part based on the historic legacy of the master-slave relationship, a degree of authority in confronting these matters. Northerner Henry Field, for example, saw the former slave masters as the ultimate model for solving the race problems of the present. Where should the black people, he queried, "get moral stamina but from you, their former masters, who are still in their eyes the highest types of manhood, their heroes and examples?" Discussing the problem of the uneducated black voter, Field again believed that the solution lay with southern white men. The South's leaders, he maintained, were "old soldiers, trained to military discipline, and they know that the only way to meet danger is to look it squarely in the face." A historian of the early twentieth century likewise trusted the old southern leaders to take the race matter in hand. He looked, in particular, to that "group of noble Southern gentlemen who realize that neither cruelty nor repression is going to make a good citizen of the negro . . . and, that, while the races must always be kept distinct socially, the dominance of the white man" must continue like that of an older brother. These were the superior men of the South, who had been raised with a peculiarly insightful understanding of race relations.[54]

Not everything that southern white men did in the 1890s garnered northern approval. In particular, Yankees revealed a good deal of ambivalence on the most vexing manifestation of the race problem in the late nineteenth century—the violence and brutality of lynching. Sometime in the 1890s lynching became a common and much-publicized practice throughout the South, often perpetrated in response to the fears of the "black beast rapist" and his alleged assault against innocent southern white women. In part, as historian Edward Ayers explains, lynching loomed large on the nation's agenda because a more comprehensive media apparatus was able to spread the news about lynchings more thoroughly and more quickly. In many northern circles, especially in "respectable" journals and among middle-class reformers, lynching sparked sharp recriminations. "Lynching," explained the *New York Times* in an 1898 editorial, "is an exact measure of the ratio of barbarism lingering in any community." Even "Uncle Hank's" guidebook to the 1901 World's Fair had something to say about southern lynching. After seeing the "Old Plantation" exhibit on the Buffalo midway, Uncle Hank reflected on race relations in Dixie. "'Pears ter me," Uncle Hank explained, "them darkies is good-natured and peaceful like; they don't look ez ef they needed Lynch Law keep 'em straight, an' I reckon ef ther people down South didn't break ther law by lynchin', th' blacks would hev more 'spect fer ther law, too."[55]

Many of these northern observers offered fairly lukewarm condemnations of lynchings, however. Northern whites saw lynching as uncivilized and barbaric, but most seemed to agree that blacks committed horrendous crimes, often against white women. They agreed with the idea that a class of criminals had grown up within the South and that the southern justice system had proven to be ineffectual in this crisis. And many, although they condemned the final act of lynching, sympathized with the sentiments of protecting the sanctity of white womanhood. As northerners came to look upon southern white women as a sort of feminine ideal, they were almost compelled to go along with the message that demanded their protection and that honored the men who sought to protect them. "Let us cease this criticism of our Southern brethren," wrote Reverend J. E. Gilbert of Washington, D.C. "While we deplore their method, we must admire their purpose to avenge the wrongs of woman." White northerners and south-erners agreed that the southern man's defense of his womenfolk proved his manly fortitude. Walter Hines Page, a southern-born editor of north-ern magazines, offered this idea to northern readers of the *Forum.* "Noth-ing else," wrote Page in regard to the alleged sexual assaults, "could so arouse all the white man's race feeling," especially given the "old-fashioned gallantry" and "knightly" disposition of southern men. [56]

In 1898 *Harper's Magazine* dramatized these arguments in a short story entitled "An Incident." The story, focusing on the disappearance of a "strange negro" named Abram and a married white woman, revealed the dilemma of the law-abiding sheriff who sympathized with the husband's desire to hang Abram for what was assumed to be the sexual assault and murder of his wife. "Poor Mr. Morris!" lamented the sheriff, referring to the white husband. "In his place I'd do just what he's doin'." Summing up his own personal philosophy about lynching, and undoubtedly echoing the views of many northern whites, the sheriff sighed, "It may be wrong to lynch, but in a case like this it's the rightest wrong that ever was." In the end, Mrs. Morris returned, explaining that Abram did not rape her, although he attempted to, and prompting the judge to send Abram to prison for the rest of his life. The rule of law was vindicated, but only half-heartedly, and support for the southern white man's chivalrous defense of women was duly registered. [57]

Whether they condemned or condoned the lynchings, northern whites clearly responded to the South's attempt to resurrect a more traditional standard of gender behavior. They empathized with the image of sexual chaos which racial extremists depicted, in which white women's sexuality was publicly displayed and white men were no longer in complete control. In some northern circles, these concerns encouraged a more enthusiastic support for the South's racial fanaticism. Lynching advocates like South Carolina's Ben Tillman and Georgia's Rebecca Felton frequently spoke before large and receptive northern gatherings at the turn of the century. These audiences seemed to concur with the extremists' view that a break-down in sexual order had occurred, in the South and in their own society as well. Native-born Yankees often looked with horror at the gross immor-ality which seemed to prevail in closely confined immigrant quarters. Many were also disturbed by the more public sexuality of working-class women who now frequented dance-halls, amusement parks, and movie houses—all places that seemed to foster greater sexual contact between men and women. White women now seemed more vulnerable to sexual assaults, although whether this was the result of women's own assertive-ness, misguided notions of "negro equality," or men's failure to do their protective duty remained unclear. Whatever the cause, northern whites seemed to agree with at least part of the South's message that the old virtues of womanhood were no longer respected, that sexuality seemed to be flaunted more openly, and that the old boundaries of women's sphere were no longer so secure. "It is a common occurrence in this city," wrote one Indianapolis resident to Rebecca Felton, "to see white girls flirting with young negro bucks." The Indianapolis man attributed this sorry state of affairs to his society's liberal views on "social equality," yet he seemed equally alarmed by the more open sexual behavior of white women, something which, perhaps, needed to be restrained just as much as black assertiveness.[58]

Some northern white women also feared the loosening bonds of sexual behavior, especially as it seemed to demean the status of refined white womanhood. They suspected that women no longer occupied the same distinctive and sanctified space that they once did. In this regard, the so-called black menace was only one manifestation of a larger problem. "When the people of the South," one Philadelphia woman explained in her letter to Rebecca Felton, " . . . learn to curb the education of the negro, they will then learn the value of the purity of our sex." And Fannie Guilliams feared that white men were not doing their part to preserve women's proper, and previously protected, place. "It is the duty of white men," she wrote, "to those whom God has given them, their greatest blessing, to put a stop to this awful state [of black rape]." It seems that many northerners responded to the South's racial hysteria not because of a deep and abiding fear of black rape, but because the southern message about sexual and gender disorder, and the need for white men to play a greater role in reasserting the old boundaries, resonated with their view of the sexual changes they saw occurring in their own society.[59]

By the turn of the century, as Paul Buck explained, "a tremendous reversal of opinion had materialized" in the northern white view of southern race relations. Having already shown an empathy and understanding for the fallen southern elite, northern whites now looked to the white men of the South, sometimes even to the most virulent racists, to solve the region's racial troubles. Moreover, as they confronted their own vision of unruly immigrant workers and an uneducated ethnic electorate, they became more sympathetic to the ordered and hierarchical vision of race relations created by white southerners. But, ultimately, the northern reunion with the South demanded a degree of ignorance when it came to issues of slavery and race: ignorance of the way slavery had worked in the past, of the role it played in the nation's history, and of the present state of race relations. This ignorance, many assumed, would clear the table of "unimportant" and "extraneous" issues and pave the way toward a more complete reconciliation. In particular, it would allow the new sense of nationalism to emerge from genuine, heartfelt sympathies, unencumbered by other concerns. This, in part, explains the appeal of Chad Buford, a neophyte in southern race relations, to the northern reading public. It also explains why northerners often depicted Dixie's racial matters in terms that were shrouded in mystery, hidden under a cloud of inexplicable history that northern whites would never really know.

Indeed, many northerners tried to reexamine the past by downplaying the subject of race altogether. Those who did analyze slavery often did so in vague and impersonal terms, portraying it as a problem that was abstract and disconnected from human agency. Professional historians concurred with this basic message: slavery may have been part of American history, but it was not significant enough to demand too much attention in the present. A true sense of nationalism, they claimed, one which rested on Anglo-Saxon unity, could more quickly be restored if such issues were overlooked.[60]

In this atmosphere of historical amnesia, only a few lone voices called out in protest. Some abolitionists, and their children, did not ignore the southern past or the present reality of southern racial oppression. A number of them continued to engage in reform work for southern blacks. In their rhetoric, they also stressed remembrance, especially the need to remember the scourge of slavery and the reasons why the Civil War had been fought. Former abolitionist orator Anna Dickinson, for example, took to the campaign stump for the Republicans in the 1888 elections and emphasized this theme. "The fashion of the day has been, and is," sneered Dickinson, "to talk of the love feast that is spread between old foes, till at last we of the North and they of the South are doing what our forefathers did thirty years ago—grasping hands across the prostrate body of the negro." Most of all, Dickinson feared that the new generation of young men would be ignorant of history and their fathers' legacy. "Young men just voting," she urged, "remember it is your father that lies buried on a Southern field. . . . Teach these boys of to-day what the boys of twenty five years ago were who stood ready to die for them." Dickinson used the memory of slavery to ennoble the legacy of the Union veteran, a legacy that continued to demand political support. Many northerners, of course, condemned Dickinson's preaching as tired-out "bloody shirt waving" which needlessly revived the old wounds of war.[61]

A number of northern blacks also sought to counteract the ignorance and forgetfulness of the reunion process, as well as the demeaning cultural trends of the late nineteenth century. Frederick Douglass continuously urged his listeners, especially audiences of younger African Americans, to remember the war and the history of race relations and to use that past to challenge present injustices. "Well the nation may forget," he remarked in 1888, "it may shut its eyes to the past, and frown upon any who may do otherwise, but the colored people of this country are bound to keep the past in lively memory till justice shall be done them." Others in the black community also objected to the ignorance which racial reunion seemed to foster. For many, it was especially important to remember the real history and the real lessons on Memorial Day, and not to get swept up in the conciliatory sentiment. The Kansas *State Ledger*, a weekly black newspaper, published the following poem in honor of "Decoration Day" in 1893:

> Why should we praise the gray, and blue,
> And honor them alike?
> The one was false, the other true—
> One wrong, the other right.[62]

In the realm of culture, some African Americans tried to respond to the degrading and stereotyped depictions which had become so prevalent by the 1890s. Although they did not press the political message as forcefully as Douglass, a number of writers, musicians, and artists tried to counter the tendency to remove black people from American culture altogether and to turn them into something foreign and barbaric. The black poet Paul Laurence Dunbar, tried, albeit unsuccessfully, to make his literary mark without relying exclusively on dialect verse; he longed to produce something "higher" and more refined, something that would make his work more acceptable in elite cultural circles. In a similar vein, the black musician Will Marion Cook wanted to place the music of southern blacks firmly within the nation's boundaries. Recalling the earlier attitudes of northern whites toward the jubilee performers, Cook in 1901 urged Booker T. Washington to support the formation of a troupe of Tuskegee singers. Their music, Cook explained, "may form a basis for the growth of a music which shall be called truly American."[63]

Ultimately, although for different reasons, Cook, Douglass, and Anna Dickinson desired a similar objective: to restore African Americans to the national consciousness and to recall the black presence in the American past. And yet, by the turn of the century, very few Americans were prepared to think along these lines. The new nationalism rested on the unity of Anglo-Saxons, namely, the bonds between southern whites, including the people of the mountains, and northern whites. That which was "truly American" was increasingly defined in racial terms, as the destiny of a race of striving, active, vigorous—and white—individuals. In contrast, black people were cast outside these national boundaries. Many people saw their character traits as completely inconsistent with those of the typical hardworking American. In popular culture they were depicted as strange and barbaric foreigners. In historical consciousness, they became invisible, especially as the legacy of slavery and emancipation became merely incidental in the history of national formation. In the final years of the nineteenth century, as Americans embarked on a crusade of patriotism and imperialism, these tendencies would become even more pronounced in northern culture and consciousness.

6

NEW PATRIOTISM AND NEW MEN IN THE NEW SOUTH

Between 1865 and 1900, American society underwent a series of profound transformations destined to make life in the twentieth century fundamentally different from what it had been in the nineteenth. A wave of immigration swept over the American continent, bringing thousands of sojourners and settlers from distant European and Asian countries into the United States. These migrants from foreign lands, and also from rural America, poured into cities that grew ever larger and ever more strained by their increasing, and often impoverished, populations. The gulf between rich and poor widened as the rich reaped the benefits of corporate conglomeration and the poor suffered the consequences of the periodic panics that shook the American economy in the late nineteenth century. Yet those in the lower classes did not quietly accept their economic hardships; throughout the 1890s American workers took to the streets, striking at Homestead and Pullman and marching with Coxey's Army, to voice their concerns and frustrations with the intensified social and economic exploitation. Farmers, too, revealed a new level of activism in their protests against the excesses of monopoly and industrialization. Finally, amidst all this social upheaval, and in part because of it, American society began to turn outward. Businessmen and policymakers showed new economic and political interests in spreading American influence into remote regions in North America, South America, and the Pacific. The Spanish-American War, initially begun as a battle for Cuban indepen- dence in 1898, signaled the new spirit of imperialism that would bring the United States into the twentieth century.

By and large, these fundamental changes in American society affected northerners more than southerners. Industrial and urban development moved at a quicker pace in northern states, and immigrants flocked to northern cities in much greater numbers than to the South. The North also bore the brunt of industrial upheaval and became the geographic locus for unemployment, strikes, and political radicalism. But, in varying degrees, all Americans were touched by the transforming power of industrial cap- italism and the spirit of imperialism. Many Americans, according to histo- rian Robert Wiebe, experienced these changes as a crisis in their local communities. They became, Wiebe explains, a people under siege from seemingly hostile outside forces, especially from an invisible national market and an intangible national government. Initially, a wide array of Gilded Age reformers fought to maintain the integrity and the values of the community structure. By the 1890s, however, it had become clear that national influence—in the form of corporate control as well as federal legal power—had achieved a new stability and permanency. To those who attained positions of command in the 1890s, the reformers of the 1880s were no longer harmless crusaders for the community but dangerous agitators who threatened American civilization at every turn.[1]

Faced with an apparent multitude of social and cultural divisions—be- tween state and community, workers and bosses, immigrants and native- born, urban and rural—Americans confronted the question of their na- tional identity, often in explicit and self-conscious ways. What, after all, defined someone as "American" in these years of conflict and stress? Moreover, as a shift occurred from community to nationally based experi- ence, where was the locus for this Americanism? This, says Alan Trach- tenberg, was the principal dilemma of American society in the late nine- teenth century, especially in the 1890s: whether the nation was defined by a shared culture of "the people" or by a political apparatus that promoted the interests of a few more than the interests of all. Of course, not many people, whether they were Populists, presidents, or even corporate lead- ers, chose explicitly to advocate the rule of the few. Instead, most Ameri- cans devoted considerable attention to understanding and articulating those common values or principles which seemed to capture the distinctive role and identity of the American nation. In a period when the older values of the community and the church had begun to wane, many hoped to construct a new, secular, and tangible focus for American national loyalty. In the 1890s this took the form of a variety of self-conscious ruminations about nationalism and patriotism.[2]

The last decade of the nineteenth century, then, generated a burst of nationalistic inquiry and enthusiasm. New hereditary societies—such as the Sons and the Daughters of the American Revolution—focused their attention on the elite national legacy that was passed down through the descendants of revolutionary leaders. Under the auspices of these and other patriotic organizations, schoolchildren, as well as the public at large, were encouraged to reflect on the meaning and the lessons of the American past. Older nationalistic organizations, especially the Grand Army of the Republic, also joined in the fray and called attention to the symbols and rituals of the national experience. In 1897 the American Flag Association formed to promote the celebration of the flag and a new holiday, Flag Day. Many of these groups reflected, in particular, on the need to hoist high the banner of American loyalty in the face of massive immigration. "Among no class [more] than that born under other climes and with widely different conditions of society," commented one GAR man in 1892, "should the effort be made to instill the highest ideals of American loyalty."[3]

In an increasingly heterogeneous society, many Americans found it difficult to pinpoint the precise nature of their national identity. Journalists, politicians, and intellectuals brooded over the question of "Americanism," but many, perhaps, found it easier to talk about patriotism, which assumed that a tangible national presence already existed and only required that people profess their loyalty to it. Indeed, in the last years of the century, a variety of religious, political, and economic leaders began speaking about a "new patriotism" that had swept the land. This new patriotism shifted attention away from specific values and principles and focused instead on the expression of national loyalty, on the commitment to a cause more than on the cause itself. Speaking on Memorial Day in 1895, Oliver Wendell Holmes gave what was perhaps the most well-known articulation of the new patriotic ideology. "The faith is true and adorable," Holmes explained, "which leads a soldier to throw away his life in obedience to a blindly accepted duty, in a cause which he little understands." Despite the apparent emptiness of such patriotic rhetoric, many were drawn to this Holmesian discourse because it implied a willingness to commit oneself to high ideals, no minor accomplishment in an epoch that had bred an intense preoccupation with materialistic objectives. The president of the New York Sons of the American Revolution thus defined patriotism not only in terms of the legacy of 1776, but also as a willingness "to spring to arms and sacrifice all material interests for the preservation of the country." The true patriot placed the country first, certainly before any international obligations and before personal economic self-interest, and did not stop to worry about the values or the culture which the country embodied.[4]

The new patriotic rhetoric not only stressed commitment and determination, it also placed a premium on unity. Again, it was not always apparent what the unifying force was, but it was clear that the health and well-being of the nation demanded the coming together of seemingly fractured forces throughout the society. In this regard, the specter of class division appeared just as threatening as the ogre of sectionalism. "West against East, North against South," commented one author in the *North American Review*, "class legislation, agitations of labour to depress capital or of capitalists to oppress the labourer, all antagonisms of citizen against citizen, sectional, local, or of different classes and conditions, are unpatriotic because they hurt the country." As many saw it, failure to maintain social and regional consolidation would call into question the whole notion of a shared culture, of common national values in which all Americans partook. "The man who would foment strife between East or West, North or South, between labor and capital, or any section of our life," claimed the Reverend Charles Kloss, "is the universal enemy."[5]

Yet castigating the sectional agitator did not automatically make the southern states, or the southern people, patriotic. It was one thing, after all, to speak in sentimental terms about reunion, to reflect on the femininity of southern women or even the leadership qualities of southern men, and it was one thing to be noble and forgiving toward southern transgressions, but it was another thing altogether to wrap the South, especially the southern past, in the mantle of patriotism. *Harper's Weekly* editor George William Curtis, for example, had his doubts. "Whatever view we may take of that [lost] cause," Curtis wrote to a southern correspondent, " . . . and whatever titles of honor may be justly due to its official leader, I cannot admit that patriot is one of them, except in some sense as yet unknown to me." GAR members, not surprisingly, also remained wary of pronouncements of southern patriotism. Indeed, their skepticism increased in the late 1880s and early 1890s as they witnessed a resurgence in southern communities of lost cause celebrations. Berating the new Lee memorial in Richmond and the lack of memorials to Union leaders up North, one Philadelphia speaker challenged the notion that the Confederate cause could be reinterpreted in more righteous terms. "Keep alive the truth that secession was treason, and eternally wrong," Lemuel McMichael exhorted his listeners. "It is a noticeable fact that, as years roll by, we are apt to forget our trials and hardships, and the persistence of the enemy that he was right and that his cause was holy is already accepted by many well-meaning people who made no sacrifices in war times." In McMichael's view, the GAR's own sense of integrity demanded a condemnation of the notion of southern patriotism.[6]

So troubling was the problem that the GAR embarked on a campaign to instill patriotic teachings in school history textbooks throughout the country. The veterans, now men of fifty years and older, showed a growing concern to influence the next generation regarding the principles for which they had fought. In the interest of educating the young about their fathers' noble legacy, GAR members put aside some of the conciliatory sentiments they had shown in the 1880s and adopted a more strident determination to expose the evils of the Confederate past. The "use of United States Histories in some of the common schools of this state," remarked a Nebraska GAR committee, "that palliate, and in some cases emulate the doctrine of States Rights . . . has a tendency to poison the mind of those who are to follow in the administration of the offices of state." As late as 1896 the GAR remained vigilant in its textbook campaign and explicitly promoted those interpretations that condemned the Confederacy. John McMaster, a historian at the University of Pennsylvania, was one textbook writer who won GAR approval and expressed his agreement with the GAR objective to define loyalty and patriotism solely in terms of the Union cause. "I want it understood beyond doubt," McMaster explained, "that in this history the great Southern generals . . . are not condoned."[7]

There were many, however, who were not troubled by the idea of southern patriotism. The emphasis that had been placed on forgetting, or on selectively remembering, the past allowed a number of northerners to reintegrate the South into a patriotic view of the nation, and even into national history. Indeed, for many of the patriotic societies of the 1890s, sectional reunion was a crucial part of their raison d'être. The Sons of the American Revolution made a point of stressing southern patriotism, claiming that a revolutionary legacy made southerners just as loyal as northerners. A recollection of the revolution, they suggested, could erase the memory of the Civil War. "It is the memory of the Jeffersons, the Madisons, the Pinckneys, the Marions," observed Chauncey Depew of the New York SAR, "of Charleston, of Cowpens and of King's Mountain, which, when slavery is gone, makes the Southern people of to-day as loyal to the flag . . . as the people of the North." The reference to slavery is noteworthy, but Depew was apparently paying lip service; the SAR certainly never made the issue a litmus test for patriotism. Rather, in keeping with the new mentality of blind obedience, it seems that a willingness to declare oneself a patriot was all that was really necessary. In the case of the SAR, this meant little more than a desire to join the organization. William McDowell, a New Jersey businessman who helped to found the SAR, apparently sought few other credentials. The organization, McDowell believed, would give the southern man "the chance to assert his patriotism, and . . . you would be surprised how enthusiastic [he is] and hungry for the opportunity."[8]

Like the SAR, the Daughters of the American Revolution, founded in 1890, also made a point of playing up the patriotic unity of northern and southern women. They, too, believed that a recollection of the heroic deeds in the American Revolution would "bring back the brotherly love that once existed in our union before the terrible war that severed our great family." Yet, unlike the SAR, the DAR was also driven to find a uniquely feminine angle in the promotion of patriotism, to establish the idea that women were not just assistants in the revolutionary struggles of the past but were also active contributors to the patriotic consensus of the present. In this respect, the DAR occasionally echoed some of the sentiments of the Woman's Christian Temperance Union, maintaining that women's healing capacities might do more than male posturing in restoring sectional harmony. The reunion spirit, explained one DAR member from Georgia, would not arise from "man's eloquence alone, or diplomatic subtleties, but rather by the gentler influences of women."[9]

Even outside of the self-consciously patriotic societies, northerners showed a growing willingness to acknowledge a sense of patriotism among the southern people. "Certainly as far as honoring Washington's birthday is concerned," observed a northern tourist in the South in 1897, "the people of New Orleans are more patriotic than [the people in] many Northern cities." Yet, even among those who accepted the notion of southern patriotism, there was still a recognition that something distinctive lingered in the mind of the white South, a certain commitment to state and section which was not so characteristic of the northern mind-set. Although he was pleased to find that the people of New Orleans celebrated Washington's birthday, the same northern tourist wondered about that city's display of Confederate relics. "It may be a good thing to have some place to keep such mementoes [*sic*]," this traveler noted, "but does [this] . . . serve to obliterate the feeling between the North and the South in the Southerner's breast?" Northerners continued to acknowledge a distinctive southern tradition that was rooted in the Confederate legacy and believed that southern whites maintained a more vivid sense of their past than northerners. One northern traveler found that in Savannah "the old party feeling still lingers," while in Charleston "the lost cause still survive[s]."[10]

When Yankees detected these lingering Confederate feelings, they often held southern women responsible for maintaining this vision of hindsight. The now elderly ladies of the Civil War generation, the southern grandes dames of the 1890s, it was believed, clung most fervently to the old South's legacy. Northerners no longer viewed them with hostility or disgust, yet they suspected that, in various and subtle ways, these women prevented the full blossoming of the South's patriotic spirit. Implicitly, they believed that the southern women possessed a more constricted world view which clung to family, neighborhood, and state and could not make the more abstract leap to nationhood. One northern traveler, for example, was struck by the feminine spirit that reigned during a Memorial Day celebration in Atlanta. "How women's hearts," he observed, "are ever true to departed memories." Another northern author, writing in 1903, found that southern women, "even of today, have [not] lost their sectional prejudices. They are still not quite so much American women as they are Virginians or South Carolinians." Thus, the image that had emerged in the 1860s—of southern women's intense commitment to their section—remained at the turn of the century. In political terms, the image offered northerners, as well as some southerners, a way to analyze and qualify southern patriotism. The man's vision, associated with progress and the future of the nation, was viewed as the patriotic norm; the woman's vision, associated with the past and with the more narrow confines of home and family, might be viewed as a deviation from total patriotism, yet slight enough and harmless enough to be tolerated. As many northerners came to see it, the extent to which the South strayed from the patriotic fold could mostly be attributed to this narrow but harmless viewpoint of its women.[11]

Apparently, then, a critical component of the new patriotic ideology rested on the traditional Victorian view of gender, a view that placed women by hearth and home while men moved in a wider and more complicated world of national allegiances. Many flag-waving societies of the 1890s bemoaned what they saw as a decline in earlier gender standards and sexual mores and implied that a thoroughgoing patriotic renewal would reinvigorate a proper respect for gender distinctions. Indeed, traditional notions of masculine and feminine behavior assumed a special significance in the context of this patriotic upsurge as many saw gender providing a unifying thread, as well as a necessary sense of order, for the country's diverse population. Implicitly, many people believed that patriotism would unify the population around basic and time-honored values of manhood and womanhood, that workers and bosses, natives and immigrants would all come together as loyal American men and women. According to the Woman's Relief Corps, a female auxiliary of the GAR, the introduction of the flag into the public schools would have precisely this effect. Not only did the flag help to make immigrant children "enthusiastic Americans," claimed the WRC, but it also "has been a grand step toward making brave, manly boys and womanly girls."[12]

But, ultimately, as many patriots saw it, the real will and vitality of the nation depended on the manliness of its men and their willingness to commit themselves to an abstract national entity. This, of course, was not an unfamiliar refrain. In the aftermath of the Civil War, northerners had stressed the role of Union men in saving and protecting the nation while women, especially southern women, tried to tear it apart. Likewise, the GAR and the Populists had connected the higher principles of patriotism and nationalism with a sense of manly and moral integrity. In the 1890s a growing body of politicians and intellectuals also highlighted the connection between masculinity and the nation. The enormous avarice of many Gilded Age leaders, especially noteworthy during the economic hardships of the 1890s, encouraged others to echo the idea of masculine selflessness and to identify the commitment to the higher principles of patriotism as a specifically manly ideal. In this way, manhood became more than just an individual expression of gendered characteristics; it also came to symbolize something noble, abstract, and principled. The nation, many leaders explained, was not about business concerns or technicalities, but about the loftier beliefs of manhood. "The true glory of our country," explained Charles Kloss in preaching on the "New Patriotism," "consists in her type of manhood. . . . We are talking less about our machines and more about our men."[13]

Many, however, conflated a gendered view of masculinity with this abstract and philosophical understanding of manhood. Patriotism, in other words, not only reflected the nation's commitment to something noble and high-minded, it also revealed the vigor and fortitude of men. Theodore Roosevelt, who infused all of his rhetoric with references to manhood, frequently connected the will of the nation with the virility of its men. His view of manhood thus stressed a gendered notion of courage and bravery, as well as a commitment to higher principles. Roosevelt often berated the overcivilized fop, the decadent individual who abandoned America, hungered for European culture, and "lost the hardihood and manly courage by which alone he can conquer in the keen struggle of our national life." Putting the issue even more directly, Roosevelt explained, "No nation can achieve real greatness if its people are not both essentially moral and essentially manly."[14]

In part, then, these homages to manhood reflected Americans' attempts to pinpoint the noble, yet abstract, qualities of nationalism. But these references to manliness were also shaped by the shifting cultural and intellectual climate of the 1890s, a period which a number of historians have described in terms of a "masculinity" crisis in America. Feeling increasingly alienated from economic and social productivity, American men at the turn of the century searched relentlessly for images and activities that might restore their depleted reserves of power and virility. As early as the 1870s, farmers and working-class men had spoken of the need to restore their sense of manhood in the face of eroding economic independence. By the 1890s, men of the older middle and upper classes also felt compelled to join in the refrain. Seeing their power and prestige under siege by new corporate leaders and by working-class and immigrant unruliness, many of these men hoped to recapture a sense of masculine authority. In many cases, they tried to resurrect a sense of sexual order, which was assumed to be natural and immutable, as a way to counteract what seemed to be a decaying social hierarchy and their own loss of control. Theodore Roosevelt, with his exhortation of "the strenuous life," was only the most obvious representative of the new cultural trend. In the

South, as Joel Williamson has explained, white men responded to their own crisis of authority most acutely after the depression of 1893. With their preeminent place as breadwinners now in jeopardy, southern white men emphasized their role as the protectors of white womanhood, especially against the alleged threat of black rapists.[15]

The men of the 1890s also took up the masculinity refrain in response to the social and political activism of the "New Woman." As women moved into career and educational circles formerly deemed the province of men, American males hoped to reestablish seemingly natural gender demarcations that would affirm a basic sense of male virility and female weakness. Indeed, to a great extent, middle- and upper-class men tried to appropriate notions of vigor and virility which workers and women had both attempted to assume for themselves. Hence, male college students in the 1890s became obsessed with a rough and aggressive athleticism, perhaps hoping to challenge the "model of vigorous femininity" that had emerged in female colleges in the 1880s where women's physical well-being had been emphasized. Likewise, these men also became fascinated with violent sports, such as prizefighting, previously considered to be a working-class activity. In symbolic ways, middle-class leaders vied with workers and women in constructing for themselves a distinctive model of vigorous authority. In doing so, they often reinterpreted the whole concept of manhood, focusing on aggressiveness and athleticism more than the earlier qualities of restraint and self-control.[16]

The connection between manliness and patriotism also helped to transform the reunion rhetoric of the late nineteenth century. A supplication to the manhood (or, less frequently, to the womanhood) of the nation blurred the reality of class, ethnic, and sectional division. The appeal to a common manhood thus became a critical component of the reunion mentality in the 1890s. As many explained it, the future of American nationalism and the present spirit of patriotism rested on the cultivation of certain fundamental gender attributes, recognized by "civilized" southerners as well as northerners. In a truly civilized, and democratic, society, all men could share in the common recognition of their strength and virility, and all women could benefit from the protection they would receive from manly endeavors. Most notably, the Civil War veteran, both northern and southern, revealed the nation's common and now-unified legacy of manliness. "The great fatherhood of our country," explained orator Theodore Bean in 1888, " . . . left a progeny North and South, whose loyalty to leaders,

whose bravery in battle, whose industry and indurance [*sic*], demon-
strates the glory of our enheritance [*sic*], and in the grand battles fought
between ourselves, however unfortunate in some respects, reveals a manhood of the Republic, as now reunited, capable and willing to protect and
defend the Union against the political powers of the earth." It may not
have been Bean's intention to obscure sectional (or any other) differences
in his appeal to a common manhood, but the emphasis on masculine bravery, loyalty, and industry did speak to traditional notions of manliness in
which it was hoped all American men could share.[17]

For many men in the 1890s—veterans and sons of veterans as well as
noncombatants—the Civil War represented the pinnacle of manliness. In
this age of greed and materialism, there was a sense that the veteran of
both regions, who supposedly had fought for principles and not for money,
offered a truly masculine ideal. Rejecting the enslavement and the depen-
dency of the pocketbook, the former soldier demonstrated that courageous and manly independence which now seemed sorely lacking in American society. Paying tribute to the old soldiers at an 1892 Memorial Day
ceremony in Dubuque, Iowa, one speaker called particular attention to
their manhood. "They remind us," he explained, "that with all the greed
there is in this world, the holy leaven of manliness, true manliness may yet
be found." The generation that came of age in the 1890s, and only knew of
the Civil War through its romanticized legacy, undoubtedly felt a particular concern to live up to the masculine tradition established by their
forebears. "Make us who are younger," exhorted the Reverend N. M.
Walters in an 1894 ceremony, "worthy of such sires; and America worthy
of such a past." The Sons of Veterans, a GAR offshoot that was founded in
the 1880s, often stressed the idea of military preparedness as a way to live
up to their fathers' manly legacy. And Theodore Roosevelt, who experienced the war as a very young child, frequently paid tribute to the virility
of the veterans, both northern and southern. "The children of a reunited
country," he explained, "have a right to glory in the countless deeds of
valor done alike by the men of the North and the men of the South."
Significantly, Roosevelt's veneration of the active and aggressive veteran
led him to castigate the apparently emasculated abolitionist. As he praised
the soldiers, he condemned foolish reformers like Wendell Phillips, men
who were "swept aside" by actual combat.[18]

Nonetheless, behind this seemingly unified, and unifying, celebration of
masculinity, there was not complete agreement on just what was glorious

Poster for Bearing's Decoration Day cycle races. Characteristically for the 1890s, it shows both the reunion motif and the new emphasis on leisure on Memorial Day. Courtesy of the Library of Congress.

about the veterans' manhood, or about manhood in general. Although American men seemed to agree on the need to reinvigorate the nation with a proper sense of manliness, they differed on the question of what made a proper man. The GAR, for example, resisted the tendency to glamorize the athletic and aggressive components of wartime valor. It criticized those who depicted the war "as a contest simply between two sections of our country, as an athletic contest, if you please, to determine the question of whether the north or the south was the biggest or which had the best men." The GAR also showed an increasing reluctance to acknowledge the manliness of former enemies, despite some tentative steps taken in this direction during the 1880s. Having experienced firsthand the horrors of war, many veterans showed little patience for the celebration of the purely physical features of martial activity. In addition, Union veterans seemed unreceptive to a thoroughly apolitical perspective which would equate bravery with manhood and thus bestow on former enemies an equal degree of manliness. "The fact that [a Confederate soldier] fought like a bull-dog to sustain a bad cause," observed one GAR publication, "does not make him a hero." Rejecting the strenuous view of manhood, the GAR continued to draw on an older model of manliness, one which stressed restraint, self-control, selflessness, and loyalty to leaders and to country, as well as loyalty to a specific political orientation.[19]

Many who came of age and assumed power in the 1890s found the GAR model outmoded. Aggressive athleticism now seemed manlier than self-control and offered a necessary counterpoint to the vigor being demonstrated both by "new women" and angry workers. Even more, the notions of Union loyalty and Confederate treason no longer seemed vital or urgent, certainly not as urgent as a willingness to commit oneself to some type of high ideals. Indeed, in light of the Union veterans' current pension prattling, there were those who wondered if the Confederate veterans had not proven to be more manly than the GAR men. The former, explained *Nation* editor E. L. Godkin, had "built up a new prosperity on the ruins of the old by working hard and depending upon themselves," while the Union veterans had become hopelessly dependent on federal support. And Brander Matthews, writing in the *Century*, pictured the GAR veteran as one who cavorted with "professional politicians of the baser sort" and as "a soldier who had never fired a shot." "As though to make up for his delinquencies during the struggle," Matthews wrote, "he was now untiring in his abuse of the Southern people."[20]

Thus, as GAR historian Stuart McConnell has explained, while many people in the late nineteenth century were drawn to the notion of manly independence and self-sacrifice, the GAR stressed their sacrifices of the past, but contemporary observers stressed a man's present status and behavior. Even if they celebrated a man's earlier accomplishments, many Americans objected to the image of the veteran who wallowed in the past and did not contribute toward the future. In this context, many non-GAR men were drawn to a southern model of manhood, one that was personified in Confederate soldiers and veterans and in many of the present leaders of the southern states. This was especially true of the period during and after the Spanish-American War, but it was also apparent in the years before the war commenced. Because the new patriotic ethos stressed commitment and a willingness to fight, more than the cause for which one fought, it was easier now to celebrate the manly course of action which the Confederate soldier had adopted. He had proven himself a man, even a patriot, by his willingness to fight, and it did not matter that he had fought against the Union. "A man," explained northern writer Henry Field as early as 1886, "may have been opposed to us in the field, and yet acted with a heart as honest and a purpose (to him) as patriotic as ours; and when he has shown the courage of his convictions . . . he has shown great qualities which we can not but admire." Speaking some years later, Theodore Roosevelt apparently agreed. "As a nation," he claimed at the unveiling of the Sherman monument in Washington, D.C., "we are the greater not only for the valor and devotion to duty displayed by the men in blue . . . , but also for the valor, and the loyalty toward what they regarded as right, of the men in gray."[21]

All of this, not surprisingly, encouraged northerners to revive a heroic and militaristic view of southern men—to recognize the bravery of the southern soldier in battles of the past and, especially, to anticipate his bravery in contests of the future. In 1895 a number of wealthy Chicago businessmen donated the funds for constructing a memorial to the Confederate prisoners-of-war who were buried in their city. Some of the contributors were former southerners, like A. O. Slaughter, now a prominent Chicago banker. Others were northern men, like Philip Armour, Cyrus McCormick, and the former president of the Columbian Exposition, Harlow Higinbotham. At the various dedication ceremonies, numerous speakers, both northern and southern, repeatedly touched on the theme of the unified patriotism and manliness of the nation, noting in particular the martial heroism and manly valor of the Confederate veteran. By and large, the speakers shunned the prevailing sentiments of romantic reunion and instead took a more practical and militaristic approach to sectional cooperation. They emphasized the present and future capabilities of southern manhood, not past achievements or transgressions. They especially stressed the martial ties that would bring northern and southern soldiers together to confront a foreign foe. The solicitor-general of the United States thus praised the southern soldiers' present-day military preparedness. "Let but some hostile invader from a foreign shore," he said, "insult our coasts and the citizen soldiers of the north will be swift indeed if they anticipate those who will gather from the South to the defense of our common country." Gen. Michael Ryan of Cincinnati explored a similar theme. "What foreign foe," he queried, "could withstand us when united, as we are to-day?"[22]

In some respects, the southern man might have presented an even more appealing image of the martial hero than the northern man. Having been enshrined in their lost cause, southern men seemed to be permanently cast in a military mold. Describing a Kentucky gentleman she met at the Chicago World's Fair, author Octave Thanet explained that, because of his military bearing, "it seemed natural to address him as Colonel." Southern men undoubtedly appeared as warriors who had failed, or perhaps refused, to adapt to a modern industrial society and thus would be forever linked to a soldierly, and masculine, past. Of course, this image did not always confer respect on southern manhood. In some circles, northerners continued to subscribe to an image of weak, old, and impotent Confederates who chattered, harmlessly and humorously, about the lost cause. But northern men's anxieties about their own masculinity helped to put that image, and the Confederate veteran, in a more positive light.[23]

In effect, the southern soldier became a more noble warrior precisely because his cause had been lost and because he had not been able to share in the fruits of victory. His loss, in other words, insured his manly independence from the state and from the all-pervasive money powers. Unlike the victorious Union soldier, the Confederate veteran had spent the years since Appomattox in learning to cope, manfully, with defeat. In this context, Robert E. Lee increasingly garnered the respect of northern pundits. Clearly, Lee had been uninterested in his own self-aggrandizement, a fact that was borne out by his willingness to surrender. Even some GAR men were willing to give Lee a little manly credit on this score and occasionally reflected on "the simple, earnest, manly manner in which he accepted final defeat." In a more celebratory vein, Henry Field praised Lee not only for fighting for his "cause" and for his "country," but also for his postwar retirement. He lived, Field explained, a life of "quiet dignity" and "gave an example of moderation and self-restraint" which helped restore the nation. Indeed, as the subdued and sober president of Washington College, Lee, according to Field, offered the nation an "education in manliness."[24]

Yet many northerners also wanted a model of manliness that was not quite so restrained and might, when occasion called for it, reveal a more aggressive demeanor. In this respect, the southern man offered the image of a racially commanding presence, one who intimately understood his region's racial hierarchy and could present a model of leadership that would maintain the racial balance. As we have seen, northerners spoke approvingly of the southern white man's ability to control the black vote, his handling of labor problems, and, perhaps most notably, his desire to protect the purity of southern white womanhood. It was in this regard that the southern man's whiteness seemed to make him a most manly being. Even if one condemned the practice of lynching, as many northerners did, they nonetheless saw in the rape-and-lynch scenario an affirmation of the southern white man's racially motivated desire to prove himself a man. Driven, or so it was assumed, by a long-standing legacy of chivalry and gallantry toward white women, the southern white man revealed a manly passion to protect his females and to conquer his enemies, especially the "black beast rapist." Walter Hines Page, the southern-born editor of several northern publications, probably voiced the ideas of many northern readers when he condemned southern lynching but defended the southern white man's chivalric posture toward women. The crime of black rape, he explained, brought the southern white man's racial and sexual instincts together; as he was moved to defend his race, so was he also moved to prove himself a man. "The race tiger and the romantic tiger," Page explained, "both leap to life."[25]

Anglo-Saxonism thus made the southern white man an especially masculine and more aggressive figure. This idea was consistent with notions of "race" and "civilization" that gained currency in the late nineteenth century. The white race, explained racial theorists in the 1890s, had advanced to the most civilized stage yet known to exist. Whites, in fact, seemed to be the only race truly capable of promoting an advanced "civilization," one that had progressed beyond the savagery and barbarism of other peoples. One way in which that advanced civilization was supposedly measured was by the clear demarcation of sexual spheres, by a clear sense of order and hierarchy between men and women. If nothing else, southern white men were keenly attuned to that sense of sexual order and demarcation. A long and romantic legacy of chivalry made the southern white man very much aware of the weaknesses and frailties of the feminine sex. More than many northerners, they recognized the true manliness of men and the womanliness of women, and they were prepared to act to insure that these strict boundaries were maintained.[26]

Throughout the 1890s, northerners praised the southern man's chivalry and his keen recognition of women's submissive nature. Although there were few explicit references to race, the issue of the southern white man's chivalric protection of weaker beings was built upon a racial subtext, upon a recognition of his position at the top of the social order. Everything about the southern man's bearing and etiquette revealed his finely tuned (and apparently racial) sensitivity to gender difference. "When he talks with a lady," explained Octave Thanet, "he addresses her as 'madam,' using the word oftener, and with more of a flourish of respect than would a Northerner." A popular song of the early twentieth century put these sentiments to music:

> I am a Southern gentleman, with gracious mien and air;
> I love to serve my mistress sweet, with manners debonair.
> I doff my hat and wait on her, Obedient to her will,
> For I'm a Southern gentleman, Yes, I'm a Southern still.[27]

Yet, in some respects, this idea of the southern white man as knightly and chivalrous is not completely consistent with the notion of the white man as the ultimate personification of modern civilization. In part, the southern white man appealed to the antimodernist strain in northern middle-class culture, to the desire to escape the decadence of the modern world and to live a life of greater personal intensity. As northerners became enamored with notions of medieval simplicity and knightly fortitude, they imposed this feudal framework on their image of the southern white man. "The days of knighthood now are past," went the musical tribute to southern gentlemen, "yet still the knight am I." Middle-class northerners, explains historian Jackson Lears, were drawn to the vitality and fervor which seemed to characterize feudalism, to its martial experience in particular. Yet, as Lears notes, among many late-nineteenth-century medievalists there was also a tendency to seek out modern character traits in their feudal heroes, to impose on the medieval knight a late-nineteenth-century sensibility which continued to stress restraint and self-control. Thus, in their medieval constructions, middle-class Americans found a counterpoint for some of their frustrations with bourgeois society, but they also found a way to venerate certain bourgeois character traits. Nathaniel Shaler, a southern-born professor at Harvard, found the southern man to be an excellent model for combining feudal courage with more modern attributes. "It is to be hoped," wrote Shaler, "that the better part of those inheritances from the age of chivalry may survive and mingle with the essential good of modern life: the keen sense of personal honor, the respect for women, the belief in the dignity of courage and external manners." The southern man, in other words, offered an extremely pliable and useful model in this age of the masculinity crisis. He was especially useful at a time when American men searched for masculine characteristics but were not entirely certain as to what, precisely, they were searching for. To those who craved the "strenuous life," he presented a model of martial activism. To those who sought a vital counterpoint to modern materialism, he presented a model of lost cause idealism. And to those who were skeptical of too much fervor and who continued to emphasize notions of manly self-control, he possessed enough bourgeois character to be a model of restraint.[28]

No northerner worked harder to manipulate the character of southern manhood than the historian and intellectual Charles Francis Adams. Adams, who turned sixty-five in the last year of the nineteenth century, had fought as a cavalry officer during the Civil War. As a soldier, he had come to accept a hard-edged and pragmatic view of war, one that differed sharply from the humanitarian outlook of the antebellum reformers with whom he had been familiar in his youth. Soldiering, in short, had made Adams disdainful of high-minded abolitionism, but it also made him skeptical of the blustering talk about war and strenuousness that characterized the 1890s, a discourse which seemed to be more prevalent among those who had been too young to do the fighting. At the turn of the century, Adams made the celebration of Robert E. Lee one of his professional preoccupations. In October 1901 he began his historical odyssey with Lee in a speech delivered before the American Antiquarian Society. Six years later Adams traveled to Washington and Lee University in Virginia to deliver a centennial address on the occasion of Lee's birth. This speech, in its effusive and unrestrained praise of the Confederate commander, has been hailed as a culminating point in the reconciliation of North and South. As a tribute to Lee's manhood, it also reveals Adams's own attempts to understand the meaning of masculinity in late-nineteenth-century America.[29]

In the 1907 address, Adams repeated many of the standard Lee doctrines, stressing his tortuous decision to leave the Union and his honorable commitment to defend his state. Moreover, Adams discovered in Lee the personal embodiment of masculine restraint and inner control, notions which Adams believed had fallen out of fashion in the current athletic cult. Adams praised Lee for his reserve at Appomattox and tied it to his racial instinct. "There is not in our whole history as a people," Adams wrote of Lee's surrender, "any incident so creditable to our manhood,—so indicative of our racial possession of Character. Marked throughout by a straightforward dignity of personal bearing and propriety in action, it was marred by no touch of the theatrical, no effort at posturing. . . . Lee, dignified in defeat, carried himself with that sense of absolute fitness which compelled respect." After Appomattox, Adams explained, Lee maintained a dignified and controlled manner which enhanced his masculinity. Adhering to the principle of "abnegation of self," Lee's "record and appearance during those final years . . . reflect honor on our American manhood." Discussing Lee's influence on the student body at Washington College in the last five years of his life, Adams made his dislike for the strenuous life even more explicit. Lee, Adams explained, imposed a sense of order on the university students which was "sorely needed . . . for the young men of the South were wild, and resented efforts at restraint." Lee also advised one student to "attend more to . . . studies and less to athletics," a lesson which Adams suggested had considerable applicability for "the modern university spirit." Lee thus became Adams's historical spokesman against college athletics, against the strenuous life, and against Roosevelt-style imperialism—and the representative of his own image of masculine statesmanship.[30]

Despite his dislike of the athletic approach to manliness, Adams had nonetheless accepted key components of the new masculine ethos. Like Roosevelt, Adams found it necessary to return to the Civil War to recapture the golden age of masculinity. In this context, he honored Lee as a man of action, as a soldier who proved his masculinity by his willingness to fight for his commitment, irrespective of the cause. Moreover, Lee's "abnegation of self" revealed a refreshing counterpoint to the late nineteenth century's spirit of greed, in which men had lost their sense of will and independence as they became slaves to materialistic excess. In a manner reminiscent of Roosevelt and other northern speakers, Adams also gave Lee's manliness a racial component: he posed Lee's masculine action and demeanor in war against the feminine abolitionist and antislavery mentality, attributing Lee's defeat to the work of Harriet Beecher Stowe and "that female and sentimentalist portrayal . . . that the only difference between the Ethiopian and the Caucasian is epidermal." Such romantic nonsense, Adams suggested, was the work of women; Lee, on the other hand, adhered to the more sensible, and presumably masculine, doctrine of Anglo-Saxon superiority. In this way, Adams, like Roosevelt and other statesmen and novelists of the period, connected Lee's masculinity not only to his commitment and courageous actions, but also to his belief in white supremacy.[31]

To a great extent, the Spanish-American War made northerners of different ideological persuasions recognize and accept the manliness and martial heroism of southern white men. The war, as a number of historians have noted, provided a culminating point for much of the patriotic and reunion-oriented ideology that had been building in the preceding years. In the first few months of 1898, before the war was officially declared, southerners sought to establish their patriotic credentials in northern circles, frequently calling attention to their manly military dedication. On February 17, one day after the explosion of the *Maine*, the New York *World* ran an article on the heightened military spirit engulfing New York City. The *World* reporter described "a man with gray hair and an empty sleeve" who explained, "I was a Johnny Reb but that was thirty years ago. I wish they'd fight us. Then we'd put the Northern and Southern regiments in the same brigades, and . . . how the boys'd fight." Southern writers frequently used the pages of the *World* to reveal Dixie's dedication to the defense of the nation. In an article suggestively entitled "Against a Foreign Foe the Nation Is as One Man," Jefferson Davis's widow explained that "the Southern men can never cease to be Americans, and are for Americans against the world in arms."[32]

By April 1898 Varina Davis's pronouncement was being put to the test. When war against Spain was declared, both "Dixie" and "The Battle Hymn of the Republic" were the musical accompaniments to the congres-

Tableau depicting the reunion of Union and Confederate veterans in defense of "Little Cuba," by Capt. Fritz Guerin. Courtesy of the Library of Congress.

sional pronouncement. Moreover, the patriotic symbolism which accompanied the Spanish-American War was thoroughly imbued with the symbolism of reunion. Countless songs composed for the war praised the joint participation of Union and Confederate soldiers in the new war effort. Even President McKinley, who at first resisted the military impulse, claimed that this new war would be welcome for its healing effect on sectional divisions. Most of the wartime symbolism, not surprisingly, stressed a militaristic bonding. Northern theater audiences in 1898 cheered the Civil War dramas which paid tribute to northern and southern martial heroism, especially the revivals of Bronson Howard's *Shenandoah*. "The war against Spain engendered a new spirit," explained one advertisement for this play, "and the old familiar glories of 'Shenandoah' seemed to be precisely what the people wanted to place them in touch with the military spirit that prevailed." *Shenandoah* highlighted the wartime bravery that brought the sections together, revealing, as one critic explained, "a rough patriotism neither mawkish nor anti-Southern." Finally, the play also revealed how patriotic commitment elevated the common ties of gender above the divisive issues of sectionalism. In *Shenandoah*, a Boston reviewer observed, "the manliness and womanliness of the Gray as well as of the Blue are [the] constant themes."[33]

The ideological tone of the Spanish-American War helped to popularize the new understanding of patriotism. American culture now stressed unquestioning devotion to vague and unspecified causes, suggesting that a true patriot shunned all notions of material gain and worked only for abstract and noble principles. Southerners again won the praise of writers and speakers who acknowledged the strong, though ill-defined, commitment that had guided the Confederacy and now motivated the South to fight the Spanish. In a 1900 editorial entitled "Patriotic Confederate Veterans," the *Independent*, a one-time abolitionist publication, succinctly summarized the new understanding. "Patriotism fought patriotism with a splendid courage on every field from Bull Run to Appomattox," explained the editor, "for the Southern soldiers loved the South as their country, its flag as their flag, its honor as their honor, and what is patriotism but love of country." Moreover, the article continued, if that experience did not prove southern patriotism, then we had only to look at the recent conflicts in Cuba and the Philippines, "a splendid outburst of Americanism in which the South equaled the North."[34]

The war with Spain accentuated other features of the new patriotic consensus as well. For one, both northern and southern whites understood their patriotic reconciliation as the cohesion of the Anglo-Saxon race. The Spanish-American War seemed to confirm the natural unity of southern and northern white people. Even imperialists and anti-imperialists, who often subscribed to different racial philosophies, similarly envisioned the war as a victory for white American unity. Southern writer and racist Thomas Dixon, for example, saw the war as the culmination of patriotic recommitment and racial cohesion. Dixon linked white control of the South to Anglo-Saxon control of the globe in his best-selling novel, *The Leopard's Spots* (1902), which he subtitled *A Romance of the White Man's Burden*. "Most marvellous of all," wrote Dixon of the Spanish-American conflict, "this hundred days of war had reunited the Anglo-Saxon race . . . [and] confirmed the Anglo-Saxon in his title to the primacy of racial sway." In this book, which focused on eliminating the African American influence in southern life, the analogy which Dixon hoped to establish was obvious.[35]

But even those who did not subscribe to Dixon's extreme racism, nor to his ultra-imperialist platform, drew out the racial parallels between white control in the South and the new position of the United States as a world power. In April 1899 the Progressive-minded journal *Arena* ran a symposium on "The Race Problem," a series of articles written from different perspectives which examined the black question in the South in the context of a heightened international race consciousness. "As through fire and blood, poverty and struggle," the *Arena* editor explained in the introduction to the symposium, the former "slave owners of the south have come into broader understanding of the evils of slavery and the blessings of freedom for white and black alike, so this dominant Anglo-Celtic race of ours is preparing for its grand mission of human enlightenment and redemption." Whereas Dixon's racial hysteria demanded the total subordination of all nonwhite peoples to Anglo-Saxon hegemony, the *Arena* editor counseled racial enlightenment and uplift, but also from the perspective of white control. Another writer found that American involvement in the Philippines offered a unique opportunity to bring all of the primitive races together under white supervision. Was it a coincidence, asked John T. Bramhall in his article for the *Overland Monthly*, that Rudyard Kipling composed his poem on "The White Man's Burden" when "the Americans were just going into the Philippines, and . . . were confronted at the same time with the necessity of furnishing employment to our red men, and of solving the negro problem in the South?" Through the experience of war and colonial expansion, northern and southern whites internationalized the race problem, identifying the common, backward characteristics of all nonwhite peoples, as well as the common superiority of Anglo-Saxons, around the world. In the process, especially as analogies were drawn between the southern and international race problems, northerners gained a new appreciation for the southern white man's ability to provide racial leadership.[36]

The patriotic cohesion of North and South through international conquest thus revealed more than just unified Anglo-Saxon strength. Because of the much-needed boost which the conflict in 1898 gave to the nation's virility, the Spanish-American War, at least in the eyes of many leading men in the North, could not have come at a better time. In keeping with their new appreciation of the southern soldier's manliness, and of manliness in general, northerners celebrated the unique masculine contribution that southern men could and did make to the war effort. Theodore Roosevelt, not surprisingly, often took the lead in garnering and cultivating the South's virile support. With men from all parts of the nation, Roosevelt built his regiment of Rough Riders, which he led in battle on the Cuban island. Roosevelt formed the Rough Riders in the interest of promoting nationalism over sectionalism, giving special prominence to western men who came from an environment which was supposedly conducive to a virile and athletic constitution. But on the way to Cuba Roosevelt led his battalion through the South, where he found men possessed of a similar patriotic, masculine spirit. "We were travelling through a region," Roosevelt later recalled of his southern tour with the Rough Riders, "where practically all the older men had served in the Confederate Army, and where the younger men had all their lives long drunk in the endless tales told by their elders. . . . The blood of the old men stirred in the distant breath of battle; the blood of the young men leaped hot with eager desire to accompany us." By building a regiment of strong western men that was led by virile easterners and had won the support of manly southerners, Roosevelt created in the Rough Riders a genuine vehicle of reunited masculine patriotism.[37]

There were other ways, too, in which the war with Spain encouraged northerners to appreciate the distinctive masculine contributions of the South. Both northerners and southerners evaluated the sacrifices which men made for their country from the perspective of a peculiarly southern code of masculine behavior. Now that the United States had achieved a greater international presence, many claimed that the question of national honor assumed paramount importance. In this context, the manly man did not stop to negotiate or arbitrate; when the nation faced a foreign challenge, he jumped without hesitation to defend his country's reputation. Implicitly, patriots in the 1890s invoked the image of the fiery southern white man who knew when his reputation had been challenged, or when his women had been threatened, and quickly and forcefully met the insult. In this way, the notion of total and blind obedience to country was reminiscent of the southern man's unquestioning defense of personal and family honor. The real man, Roosevelt explained in 1896, is able "to stand up manfully for [his country] when her honor and influence are at stake in a dispute with a foreign power." Two years later, war allowed Roosevelt's desire to become manifest. The insult to honor came in February 1898 when a letter by Spanish ambassador Enrique Dupuy de Lôme was publicized in the New York press. Referring to the heightening tensions between the United States and Spain, the letter characterized President McKinley as a "weak" man, a "bidder for the admiration of the crowd." According to the New York *World*, the minister had even, in an earlier missive, "slurred" the character of American womanhood. Thus the de Lôme letter, needless to say, ignited hostilities and squarely raised the issue of honor. American congressmen, the New York *World* explained, were now calling on McKinley "to take such a stand as would uphold the honor and dignity of the United States." Spanish atrocities against light-skinned Cuban women received prominent attention in the press, thereby playing up the need for a chivalric response. When war was declared in April, the northern and southern man's defense of honor was praised. "The reunited sections of the Union," proclaimed Kentucky journalist Henry Watterson, "stand [as] a wall of iron between the Nation's honor and, if need be, all the world."[38]

Reinforcing that wall of iron were the specific southern commanders who, imbued with the South's knightly legacy, could lead in this protection of the nation's reputation. Many took note of the uniquely southern efforts of Gen. Fitzhugh Lee, former Confederate, relation of Robert E. Lee, and now the United States consul at Havana, who was noted for his defense of American "honor" in the face of Spanish insults. Lee embodied the southern tradition of honor and chivalry, now brought to the defense of the nation as a whole. "Fitzhugh Lee," explained one letter writer to the New York *World*, "has illustrated the dominant characteristic of all the Lees, which is to do the duty that lies before them, absolutely irrespective of consequences." A Memorial Day speaker in Iowa called Lee "a magnificent type of American manhood" and found that he presented "an ideal figure of a knightly 'man on horseback.'" In a musical vein, patriotic tunes often paid a special tribute to Lee. The lyrics to "The Re-United States"

"The Blue and Gray Together," words and music by C. H. Addison (Danville, Virginia, 1898). A typical patriotic song of the Spanish-American War, it exemplifies the new respect conferred on southern commanders such as Fitzhugh Lee and the renewed emphasis on reunion in militaristic terms. Courtesy of the Library of Congress, Music Division.

claimed that "on to Cuba Lee will lead us," leading the charge against the Spanish who "make war on women, children." In another patriotic air composed for the war, "the blue and gray together . . . only ask one man to lead, that man is Fitzhugh Lee."[39]

The southern man thus emerged in an invigorated light after the conflict with Spain, assuming a new and prominent position in American culture. White southern men who for years had been conscious of trying to reignite their sense of virility, lost little time in helping to promote their regional manliness to both southern and national audiences. In an unpublished preface to his novel *The Leopard's Spots* (1902), Thomas Dixon expressed his intention to reinvigorate the image of southern manhood. "A voice is given to the Silent South," Dixon wrote, "that scorns public opinion, defies proper laws, and lives his own life—a life brave, kindly, chivalrous yet with bursts of volcanic passion. . . . The hero is an athletic son of a lion brood of men." For Dixon's men, manliness and racial instinct were inextricably linked: the true test of manhood lay in their response to the black "menace." Toward this end, Dixon showed his southern heroes relinquishing the notions of controlled and self-restrained manhood and assuming a more active, indeed violent, demeanor. Charlie Gaston, Dixon's main protagonist in *The Leopard's Spots*, turned his chivalric defense of white womanhood into a brave and manly defense of the Anglo-Saxon race. "We have been congratulated on our self-restraint under the awful provocation of the past four years," Gaston remarked. "There is a limit beyond which we dare not go, for at this point self-restraint becomes pusillanimous and means the loss of manhood." Having finally discovered his manly impatience with black rule in the 1890s, Gaston declared in a climactic, impassioned speech that black domination of southern politics and abuse of white womanhood must come to an end. "Let the manhood of the Aryan race," Gaston shouted, "with its four thousand years of authentic history," solve this problem once and for all.[40]

But as Dixon invigorated the sons of the South, he also emasculated the men of the North. In *The Leopard's Spots* as well as in his 1905 novel, *The Clansman*, Dixon portrayed northern men, especially those who defended Radical Reconstruction and the rights of southern blacks, as weak and feminine. Simon Legree, Harriet Beecher Stowe's vicious northern slave owner, reappeared in *The Leopard's Spots* as an opportunistic supporter of Reconstruction. But, because of his cowardice during the Civil War, Legree had "shaved clean and dressed as a German emigrant woman." And Austin Stoneman, the northern Republican politician in *The Clansman*, "was as susceptible to flattery as a woman." With northern men frequently wallowing in feminine ineptitude, Dixon reversed the standard formula of romantic conciliation and made southern men the heroes of his novels, the conquerors of the northern woman's heart. Whereas northern romantic fiction had made southern women succumb to Yankee men, and eventually to their belief in the Union, Dixon's work showed southern men converting northern women to their white supremacist philosophies. Hence, in *The Clansman*, Austin Stoneman's daughter, Elsie, gradually relinquished her sentimental concerns for blacks, partially as the result of her love for the southern hero. "Love," Dixon explained, "had given her his point of view."[41]

Objecting to the violence and barbarity of lynching, not all northerners were avid fans of Dixon's extreme racial hysteria. Many, however, were enthusiastic supporters of Thomas Nelson Page, a southern writer of more moderate racial views who employed many of the same themes as Dixon. Page, at one point in his career, had been conscious of presenting a more soothing picture of reunion to his northern audiences and had helped to popularize the image of marital reconciliation. By the 1890s, however, Page apparently realized that a more strident approach could be adopted. In *Red Rock* (1898), a novel that was extremely popular among northerners, Page presaged Dixon's formula of courageous southern manhood triumphing over the black menace and over northern women's sentimental attachment to black equality. Northern reviewers responded readily to books such as *Red Rock*, voicing their appreciation of the new emphasis on southern virility. A critic for the *Forum* observed, and welcomed, a gendered shift in southern literature. Immediately after the war, observed Benjamin Wells, southern literature had been "dominated by imagination" and had been "largely the work of women." But now, Wells noted, "of recent years there has been a change. Literature has widened its scope in the South." The implication seemed to be that as southern literature matured and became more realistic, it had become the creation of southern men.[42]

Northern authors likewise found that southern men offered new models for literary heroism. As early as 1886, Henry James had celebrated southern strength and chivalry in the figure of Basil Ransom, the virile hero from Mississippi who fought against the feminine impotence which pervaded the world of *The Bostonians*. In the last years of the nineteenth century, a number of northern writers began to fashion a new type of southern hero, a strong and virile character who was very much a southerner by birth but whose masculinity had often been enhanced by a set of conditions that lay outside the South. In many ways, he was a product of the "new nationalism" and "new patriotism," a figure who unified essential, masculine character traits that could be called "American." In short, he represented the merging of two distinct cultural tendencies: on the one hand, the new veneration of southern manhood, and on the other, the growing appreciation for the masculine and nationalist features of the American West.

In the imagination, and sometimes in the actions, of late-nineteenth-century Americans, the West had become a splendid and mystical place for the development and enhancement of national character. According to Theodore Roosevelt, the West helped to forge an Anglo-Saxon mix of "the English-speaking peoples," motivated to carry out their objectives of national greatness. To many people, the West provided that unifying force that seemed to be absent from Gilded Age society. The settling and expansion of the frontier offered a way to bring northerners and southerners, workers and bosses, and many different strands in American society together. Moreover, in its raw and unsettled state, the West offered a hopeful alternative to the decadent and overcivilized society of eastern, urban America. In the constant struggle between Indian savagery and white civilization, it also provided a model for national development and national character. Countless tourists, adventurers, and health-seekers headed west in the late nineteenth century, hoping to soak up some of the energy and excitement which seemed to emanate from this region.[43]

The historian Frederick Jackson Turner gave many of these imaginative longings a scholarly focus, most notably in his famous essay on "The Significance of the Frontier in American History," presented in Chicago in 1893. Responding to the Census Bureau report on the 1890 "closing" of the western border, Turner examined the frontier, and its various stages of exploration and development, as the source for American character. Yet Turner's point was not so much to bemoan the frontier's passing as to extract from the frontier experience a sense of what unified and defined the American nation. Significantly, Turner found that the western frontier negated the problems of sectionalism in the Civil War era. "When American history comes to be rightly viewed," he observed, "it will be seen that the slavery question is an incident." More important were the land and development policies that emanated from the West; more important still were the unifying, American characteristics which the people of this region displayed. In the West, observed Turner, "North and South met and mingled into a nation." More specifically, they developed a common set of characteristics—individualism, democracy, inventiveness—which revealed American distinctiveness. In an age when people often seemed at a loss to define a common basis of American nationalism, indeed, in an age when conflict seemed more pervasive than commonality, the Turnerian West offered a reassuring alternative. Out of the western experience, claimed Turner, came those national features which could combat the debilitating influences of class and sectional division.[44]

The cultural celebration of the American West encouraged, in turn, a veneration of western individuals, especially the men who embodied those hardy and nationalistic character traits which the frontier had produced. Roosevelt, as we have seen, paid particular attention to the virile men of the West who would fight with his Rough Riders. Likewise, writers produced scores of cowboy novels in the latter half of the nineteenth century, all of which celebrated the unique manliness of the western hero. As the new century began, one writer in particular gave voice to both the tradition of virile western literature and the celebration of the West as the locus of sectional unity. In 1902 Owen Wister created in *The Virginian* one of the most enduring models of manliness and one of the most popular novels in American literary history. Indeed, Wister's Virginian seemed to set a new standard for manliness in literature. "Mr. Owen Wister's 'Virginian,'" explained the reviewer for the *Nation*, "is a 'sure-enough' man, a male being, whom the most earnest female advocates of equality of the sexes could never convert into a thing like unto themselves." Significantly, he was a man who not only put "female advocates of equality" in their place but also combined the most manly characteristics of the West and of the South.[45]

Wister's own history undoubtedly contributed to his ability to create this remarkable literary hero. His maternal grandfather was Pierce Butler, the scion of a prominent Philadelphia family and the owner of an extensive cotton and rice plantation in the Georgia Sea Islands. Butler was also the husband of English actress Fanny Kemble, a woman of fierce convictions who wrote a scathing account of slave life on her husband's plantation. Soon after Fanny Kemble's stay in Georgia, the Butler-Kemble marriage dissolved, but not before two daughters, Sarah and Fanny, had been born. Owen Wister, born in Philadelphia in 1860, was the son of Sarah. He was too young to understand the politics of the war that began soon after his birth, but his extended family was torn in two by the sectional conflict. His mother, father, and maternal grandmother were ardent Unionists; his aunt and grandfather, however, persisted in their pro-South sympathies. Nonetheless, in the postwar period the bloody chasm that divided the Wister-Butler clan began to heal. Dismayed with the corruption and greed attributed to the reigning political powers, Owen's father abandoned the Republican party in the 1876 election. Moreover, all of the Wisters revealed a growing sympathy for the hardships now faced by Sarah's sister in trying to maintain the old plantation properties. Influenced more by the postwar healing than by wartime animosities, the young Wister was thus acutely aware of the close affinity between national reconciliation and the reunion of his kinfolk. More than many young men his age, he was probably conscious of his own personal responsibility in trying to effect both a national and a familial unification. One of Wister's first literary offerings, a poem written in 1877, was a plea for the fraternal unity of northern and southern soldiers.[46]

Wister enrolled at Harvard in the fall of 1878. As a college student, he became immersed in upper-crust Boston society and the pursuit of elite and refined culture. He devoted particular attention to his writing and his music. But Wister never seemed completely comfortable in the life of the cultivated gentleman. In the spring of 1879 he met the man who would be his lifelong friend and a source of inspiration for much of his literature. Wister first saw Theodore Roosevelt at a college boxing match. Roosevelt lost the match, but his sportsmanlike behavior enormously impressed the Philadelphia freshman. Wister would not forget the incident or the man; when he published *The Virginian* he dedicated the novel to the president. In 1911 Wister rededicated the novel to Roosevelt, a man he called "the greatest benefactor we people have known since Lincoln."[47]

In the summer of 1885, following a nervous collapse, Owen Wister set out for a "rest cure" in the West. The trip proved to be his salvation—and his inspiration. He was drawn to the primitive nature of western life and the simple and unrefined qualities of the men he met. Wister found the West personally rejuvenating. He also came to believe, like Frederick Turner and Theodore Roosevelt, that the West could be a source of national rejuvenation as well: its newness, its openness, and, perhaps especially, its whiteness, could erase the vestiges of sectional distinctiveness. "All of the patriotism of the war," Wister wrote in his journal during his first western sojourn, "doesn't make us an institution yet, but the West is going to do it." In particular, Wister became fascinated with the type of manhood the American West had produced, what he saw as a blend of northern, southern, and eastern types who were bound by a common racial instinct. In the West, Wister believed, their distinctive qualities had been blurred and they had been compelled by their conditions to develop that inner core of manliness which characterized the Anglo-Saxon people. The "bottom bond of race," he explained, "unified the divers young men, who came riding from various points of the compass." Thus, claimed Wister, was born that unique American type, the cowboy.[48]

In the context of the turbulence and dislocation of the 1890s, Wister came to imbue the cowboy with an enormous mystique. In that age of self-interest and working-class unruliness, Wister viewed the cowboys as ideal men. "They are," he explained, "of the manly, simple, humorous, American type which I hold to be the best and bravest we possess and our hope in the future. They work hard, they play hard, and they don't go on strike." While he continued to speak of the various regional strains that had merged in this western man, Wister revealed a particular attraction for the cowboy's southern origins. He believed that the West had drawn, most of all, on the fighting and courageous qualities of the southern man. The first cowboys, Wister maintained, had emerged in Texas in the 1860s, where "the adventurous sons of Kentucky and Tennessee, forever following the native bent to roam and having no longer a war to give them the life they preferred, came into a new country full of grass and cattle." As Wister saw it, the southern man's rebellious energy would be channeled in this new, productive direction in a way that would shape and direct the nation's future.[49]

Wister did not invent this formula on his own. There were plenty of southerners who had relocated to the West at the war's conclusion, especially to California, and Wister himself met cowboys of southern birth. Wister may have also been influenced by his friend and coworker, the artist and writer Frederic Remington. A year before Wister wrote about the cowboy's origins, Remington offered the suggestion that the American cowboy had emerged from the union of Kentucky and Tennessee men with those of Spanish descent. In fact, Remington created his own literary type based on this model of the ex-Confederate who went West; he appeared as Carter Johnson in Remington's story, "A Sergeant of Orphan Troop." Like Wister, Remington even called his character "the Virginian." Remington stressed the man's military past, as both a Confederate soldier and a former Indian fighter. He also, as Wister would do with his own Virginian, played up his character's sense of chivalry, a sensibility that revealed itself in the hero's interactions with women.[50]

Like Remington, Wister was interested in identifying that unique blend of regional qualities which produced a distinctive American character. He also saw that character in gendered terms. Owen Wister's Virginian first appeared in "Em'ly," a short story published in 1893. On one level, "Em'ly" is a quaint animal fable; it is also, however, a story of gender run amok, of a world where roosters are scared of hens, where female dogs become "unnatural, neglectful mother[s]," and where Em'ly is a hen who cannot lay eggs. At one point, she is even described, by the Virginian, as "manly-lookin'." The Virginian looks at this sexually disordered community with a certain bemusement, but also with concern. And it is concern for Em'ly's frustrated motherhood that brings the Virginian and Wister's narrator (the eastern traveler who would reappear in *The Virginian*) together for the first time. In "Em'ly" Wister clearly set out to identify something more than a barnyard dilemma. The Virginian, in fact, implies the existence of a larger problem of gender confusion in the modern world when he explains that Em'ly is "just one of them plumb parables." Significantly, the Virginian emerges as someone who has a more proper, albeit old-fashioned, view of appropriate gender behavior.[51]

Throughout Wister's writing, the Virginian appears as a somewhat mysterious character whose southern background remains rather vague and indistinct. Wister did, however, provide a few more clues about his hero's past when he made his appearance, nine years after "Em'ly," in *The Virginian*. Born in the hill country of Virginia and raised, presumably, among the poor white class, the hero took off for the West when he was fourteen years old. When the narrator meets him in the 1880s, he has become a cattle rancher in Wyoming. But despite his long apprenticeship outside of Dixie, the Virginian retains an unmistakably southern quality throughout the book. Indeed, Wister often identified the character as "the Southerner" and frequently reminded the reader of his slow and deliberate "drawl." But the hero's southernness, especially his southern masculinity, also presented itself in less tangible ways. The Virginian was not just a strong and athletic man, he was also a gentleman, embodying those innate qualities of chivalry and honor which characterized southern, feudal-style, manhood. He defended the reputation of the New England schoolteacher, Molly Wood, against the insults and insinuations of Trampas, the evil cow thief. In his first meeting with the eastern narrator of the novel, the Virginian came off "the better gentleman of the two," demonstrated by his superior sense of courtesy and his lack of patronizing pretense. "The creature we call a gentleman," the narrator concluded after this encounter, "lies deep in the hearts of thousands that are born without chance to master the outward graces of the type."[52]

At the root of the Virginian's male persona and his aura of masculine superiority is his distinctly southern belief in and embodiment of the aristocratic spirit. Wister, like many of his northern contemporaries, had been charmed by the aristocratic notions and lifestyle of the old South. In January 1902, while he was finishing his work on *The Virginian*, Wister and his family moved temporarily to Charleston, South Carolina, a city for which Wister had an unabashed fondness and devotion. Undoubtedly inspired by the southern wing of his mother's family, Wister especially loved the city's old-fashioned refinement and aristocratic ease and found it "an oasis in our great American desert of mongrel din and haste." Wister channeled his love of the southern aristocracy into his western hero, even though he provided the Virginian with apparently humble origins. Like the finest southern aristocrat, the Virginian had no innate love for the masses or the rabble and firmly believed in an inherent and natural elite. While Molly represented the feminine principle of "political equality," which apparently included her belief in women's rights, the Virginian proved that a natural aristocracy, including that of men over women, would ultimately prevail. The narrator elaborated on this fundamental premise. "All America is divided into two classes," the storyteller explained, "the quality and the equality." In decreeing that every man was equal, the Declaration of Independence merely "acknowledged and gave freedom to true aristocracy, saying, 'let the best man win, whoever he is.'" The Virginian, of course, became the ultimate winner, the natural, and clearly southern, aristocrat who proved the rule that the quality will rise from the equality. He not only proved his superiority over other men, like Trampas, but, by his final romantic victory over Molly, he also proved the superiority of manliness over femininity. "By love and her surrender to him," Wister explained at the novel's conclusion, "their positions had

been exchanged. . . . He was her worshipper still, but her master, too."
Significantly, Molly yielded to the Virginian, and to male supremacy, in
Wyoming, the first state which guaranteed women the right of suffrage.
Wister thus suggested that in this age of boisterous women, anxious men,
and gender subversion, in a world not unlike that of the hens and roosters
in "Em'ly," it was still possible to establish the basic and fundamental
superiority of the masculine over the feminine, although it helped to have
a southern man around to point the way.[53]

Wister provided one final ingredient that proved the Virginian to be a
true southern gentleman, at least in northern eyes. Although scrupulously
chivalrous and thoroughly devoted to white womanhood, the Virginian
knew when lynching was proper and when it was not. Speaking on behalf
of the Virginian, Judge Henry, his employer, explained to Molly the
necessity of lynching in the West and the evil of lynching in the South. "In
the South," the judge said, "they take a negro from jail where he was
waiting to be duly hung. The South has never claimed that the law would
let him go. But in Wyoming the law has been letting our cattle thieves go
for two years." Moreover, in the West, unlike the South, "we do not
torture our criminals when we lynch them. We do not invite spectators to
enjoy their death agony. We put no such hideous disgrace upon the United
States." Wister did not question the criminality of southern blacks; he
assumed their guilt in committing hideous crimes for which they must be
hanged. In this sense, he did not question the importance of southern
men's defense of white womanhood. But, like many northerners of the
turn of the century, he did assume that southern lynchings had become
dangerously uncivilized. It was possible, then, for the Virginian to condemn southern lynchings and still emerge with his sense of manhood
intact. As a lyncher of cattle thieves, as one who believed in swift justice
and not in sentimental principles, the Virginian managed to be both a man
of action and a gentleman of restraint. Mired in feminine and sentimental
philosophy, Molly opposed lynching on principle; but the Virginian, always
aware of the need for action, refuted this feminine abstraction and proved
himself to be manly and chivalrous at the same time.[54]

Although it would be hard to find a more perfect embodiment of the
turn-of-the-century masculine ideal than the Virginian, Wister's place-
ment of his southern hero in a western environment suggests a certain
ambivalence about southern manhood. Indeed, in a more general sense,
northerners at the turn of the century hesitated to offer a full endorsement

of Dixie's virility. As Yankees continued to connect the lost cause legacy with southern white women's sectional animus, they remained dubious of the South's masculinity. In their historical evaluations of the slave system, northerners still supposed that southern manhood had not always managed to keep itself free from feminine passions and sectional hostilities. The men and women of the old South, explained northern historian James Schouler, "strongly influenced one another, and here once more, in the reciprocal tendency to pair and live domestic lives, nature asserted itself powerfully . . . Southern women inspired the cause of Southern secession, and scarcely an order was seen emanating from Confederate generals for exciting hatred of the North that did not allude to the softer sex." Schouler confessed to being one of the more partisan historians in an age of "objective" historical analysis, yet his emphasis on the South's distinctive sectional and feminine legacy rang true for many northerners. To the extent that southerners continued to assert a distinctive sectional identity, northerners often attributed that distinctiveness to women.[55]

Owen Wister, too, feared that the feminine impulses of Dixie might smother the true spirit of southern masculinity. He hinted at these concerns in his second novel, a fictional tribute to his beloved city of Charleston, South Carolina. In *Lady Baltimore* (1906), Wister again gave prominence to the southern hero and defended the unique qualities of athleticism and chivalry which combined to produce a virile strain of southern masculinity. John Maryant, the southerner, explained to the northern narrator the qualities of southern manliness. "You'll find we're all men here," he remarked, "just as much as any men in the North you could pick out. South Carolina has never lacked sporting blood, sir." According to Maryant, southern manhood also possessed a gentlemanly refinement, a "moral elegance" which the northern narrator found especially attractive and unusual in this period of "fashionable idolatries." Here, then, was that chivalric and feudal quality of manhood which so many northern men, especially upper-class men like Owen Wister, were searching for in the late nineteenth and early twentieth centuries. As with the Virginian, Wister found in John Maryant a nearly perfect combination of gentlemanly refinement and manly athleticism. Still, Wister feared that southern men might well be smothered by southern femininity. "Was it much to the credit of such a young man," queried the narrator in regard to John Maryant, "to find himself . . . yet tied to the apron strings of Miss Josephine and Miss Eliza, and some thirty or forty other elderly female relatives?" Indeed, throughout the book the northern narrator confronts the female South's sectional spirit, still a force to be reckoned with forty years after the war's conclusion. And, even though Wister cherished the kindly old aristocratic ladies of Charleston, he nonetheless found it difficult, as did other northerners, to reconcile this adoration with his love for southern masculinity. The Virginian, in effect, offered the ultimate solution: to move the southern man out of his feminized environment and into the new territories of the West.[56]

Confronted by a changing and unsettling code of gender relations in the late nineteenth century, as well as a turbulent and chaotic social order, northern men sought anxiously for a new model of manhood which would offer elite white men a foundation for class, racial, and sexual authority. Southern manliness, rooted as it seemed to be in a firm military tradition and a heritage of gentlemanly chivalry, offered a potential symbol for the new man of the twentieth century, one that could even appeal to differing views of manhood. For men like Charles Francis Adams, who rejected both the money-making ethos of the Gilded Age and the model of the strenuous life, a southerner such as Robert E. Lee presented the perfect embodiment of lost manhood. Yet men like Theodore Roosevelt, Frederic Remington, and Owen Wister could also find in southern manhood a model of vigorous action, a man who would fight willingly and without hesitation for patriotic causes. Moreover, there was a widely shared admiration for the whiteness of the southern man, for the manly sense of race which made him noble and also respectful of proper gender distinctions. Many observers saw this cultivation of southern manliness, especially after the Spanish-American War, as a clear sign of the South's return to the patriotic fold. And yet, even in 1900, it was clear to many that there was still something different about the American South, something which seemed to feminize this region more than others. Hence, despite the new emphasis on southern literary heroes and the new positive assessments of southern soldiers, southern masculinity did not achieve a complete and unqualified victory in northern culture at the turn of the century.

Still, the various threads of reconciliation came together in the late nineteenth century to weave a very different picture of the South than had existed in the early years of the post–Civil War period. A new understanding of patriotism, which stressed the strength and not the content of one's commitment, allowed northerners to welcome the South, even the Confederacy, back into the patriotic fold. The patriotic propaganda of the Spanish-American War rested on the foundation of the reunited, military patriotism of northerners and southerners, especially the white people of the two regions. Moreover, the new symbolism of reunion also rested on the turn-of-the-century images of invigorated masculinity. As northern writers, speakers, and politicians fashioned the new patriotic ideology, they connected that patriotism to the unity of a common, although not always clearly defined, sense of manhood, one that could embrace the men of all regions. Women, in contrast, remained trapped in an outmoded point of view which ran counter to the new patriotism. Southern women, such as those in the novels of Owen Wister, John Fox, and countless other authors, continued to be the most virulent supporters of southern sectionalism. According to Wister, Charles Francis Adams, and Henry James, northern women also had been imprisoned, either by their own brand of sectionalism or some other foolish, and ultimately unpatriotic, philosophy. As abolitionists, northern women refused to accept the new patriotic ethos of Anglo-Saxonism, and as women's rights advocates, they revealed their hostility to the patriotic commitment to masculine superiority. The men of the North and the South, on the other hand, whether soldiers or cattle ranchers, epitomized the spirit of masculine, virile patriotism, the ideology that could finally bridge the bloody chasm of the Civil War.

NOTES

ABBREVIATIONS

AAS   American Antiquarian Society, Worcester, Mass.
HTC   Harvard Theater Collection, Harvard University, Cambridge, Mass.
LC   Library of Congress, Washington, D.C.
MHS   Massachusetts Historical Society, Boston, Mass.
NYPL   New York Public Library, Astor, Lenox, and Tilden Foundations, New York, N.Y.
NYPLPA   New York Public Library for the Performing Arts, New York, N.Y.
SHC   Southern Historical Collection, University of North Carolina at Chapel Hill, Chapel Hill, N.C.

INTRODUCTION

1. Charles Dudley Warner, *Studies in the South and West with Comments on Canada* (New York, 1889), 3.

2. Hampton quoted in John Cox Underwood, *Report of Proceedings Incidental to the Erection and Dedication of the Confederate Monument* (Chicago, 1896), 121.

3. For more on the economic motivations behind the New Orleans fair, see Robert W. Rydell, *All the World's a Fair: Visions of Empire at American International Expositions, 1876–1916* (Chicago, 1984), 72–80; for reference to the economic backing behind the Chicago event and an unusual reference to the financial motivations, see Underwood, *Proceedings*, 225, 33.

4. Paul Buck, *The Road to Reunion* (New York, 1937; reprint, New York, 1959). Clearly, C. Vann Woodward, especially in *Origins of the New South, 1877–1913* (Baton Rouge, 1971), has contributed to the study of reconciliation, particularly in his exploration of northern capital's interest in the New South. Still, his work mainly focuses on the southern side of the reconciliation process. Among the numerous books which have explored the southern attachment to the lost cause is Charles R. Wilson, *Baptized in Blood: The Religion of the Lost Cause, 1865–1920* (Athens, Ga., 1980). Countering this view of southerners' religious devotion to the lost cause and pointing to the region's commitment to reunion is Gaines Foster, *Ghosts of the Confederacy: Defeat, the Lost Cause, and the Emergence of the New South, 1865–1913* (New York, 1987). One of the most insightful examinations of the

southern legacy of defeat continues to be C. Vann Woodward, "The Search for Southern Identity," in *The Burden of Southern History* (Baton Rouge, 1968), 3–25.

5. David Thelen, "Memory and American History," *Journal of American History* 75 (Spring 1989): 1123.

6. Trenton *State Gazette* quoted in Louis C. Gosson, *Post-Bellum Campaigns of the Blue and Gray, 1881–1882* (Trenton, 1882), 181; David Blight, "'For Something beyond the Battlefield': Frederick Douglass and the Struggle for the Memory of the Civil War," *Journal of American History* 75 (March 1989): 1156–78. On Americans and historical memory, see also Michael Kammen, *Mystic Chords of Memory* (New York, 1991), especially the chapter on the Civil War, pp. 101–31.

7. Thelen, "Memory and American History," 1127. None of this, of course, is meant to suggest that the "southern myth" emerged full-blown in the postwar period. Several scholars have analyzed this myth and have found that it flourished, among both northerners and southerners, in the antebellum years. See, for example, William Taylor, *Cavalier and Yankee: The Old South and American National Character* (Garden City, N.Y., 1963); W. J. Cash, *The Mind of the South* (New York, 1941); Francis Pendleton Gaines, *The Southern Plantation: A Study in the Development and Accuracy of a Tradition* (New York, 1924); and George Tindall, "Mythology: A New Frontier in Southern History," in *The Idea of the South*, ed. Frank E. Vandiver (Chicago, 1964), 1–15.

Although the southern myth had strong antebellum roots, I would agree with the argument that the sectional conflict severely qualified and limited the impact of this myth in northern ideology. See, in this regard, Eric Foner, *Free Soil, Free Labor, Free Men* (New York, 1970), 69–70. For more on northern views of the southern myth, see Patrick Gerster and Nicholas Cords, "The Northern Origins of Southern Mythology," in *Myth and the American Experience*, 2 vols., ed. Patrick Gerster and Nicholas Cords (Encino, Calif., 1978), 2:320–34.

Among the books which have explored southerners' postwar creation of the southern myth are Rollin G. Osterweis, *The Myth of the Lost Cause, 1865–1900* (Hamden, Conn., 1973), and Wilson, *Baptized in Blood.*

8. Works which look at the postwar northern view of the southern myth include Joyce Appleby, "Reconciliation and the Northern Novelist, 1865–1880," *Civil War History* 10 (June 1964): 117–29; Jack Temple Kirby, *Media-Made Dixie: The South in the American Imagination* (Athens, Ga., 1986); and Anne Rowe, *The Enchanted Country: Northern Writers in the South, 1865–1910* (Baton Rouge, 1978). On northern and southern cooperation in building the New South and the South's "divided mind," see Woodward, *Origins of the New South*, 107–74. The definitive work on the New South ideology, as propagated by both northerners and southerners, is Paul M. Gaston, *The New South Creed: A Study in Southern Mythmaking* (New York, 1970).

9. Joan Scott, "Gender: A Useful Category of Historical Analysis," *American Historical Review* 91 (December 1986): 1053–75; Taylor, *Cavalier and Yankee*, 141–44; Carolyn Porter, "Social Discourse and Nonfictional Prose," in *Columbia*

Literary History of the United States, ed. Emory Elliot (New York, 1988), 345–63; Anne Norton, *Alternative Americas: A Reading of Antebellum Political Culture* (Chicago, 1986). While I agree with Norton, and with Taylor, that the feminine image of the South had roots in antebellum culture, I am not convinced that prewar southerners constructed a feminine self-image. Rather, I suspect that what Norton interprets as a feminine image was actually a distinctly southern view of masculinity, one that had very different attributes than the northern sense of manhood.

10. Elizabeth Fox-Genovese, *Within the Plantation Household: Black and White Women of the Old South* (Chapel Hill, 1988), 37–99, 192–241.

11. Bertram Wyatt-Brown, *Southern Honor: Ethics and Behavior in the Old South* (New York, 1982), 20, 35; Edward Ayers, *Vengeance and Justice: Crime and Punishment in the Nineteenth-Century American South* (New York, 1984), 19–25.

12. My assessment of the way northerners' views toward the South were shaped by Victorian ideology has been influenced by Joel Williamson, *The Crucible of Race* (New York, 1984). Williamson finds that white men's concerns about their loss of authority affected their attitudes about sex and race in the late-nineteenth-century South.

13. For an excellent examination of some of these twentieth-century southern images, see Kirby, *Media-Made Dixie*.

CHAPTER ONE

1. Allan Nevins and Milton H. Thomas, eds., *The Diary of George Templeton Strong*, 4 vols. (New York, 1952), 3:578.

2. Letter of Charlotte Holbrooke, April 11, 1865, Maurice Family Papers (Folder 26), SHC.

3. Chicago *Tribune*, April 11, 1865, 2; for more on early northern reactions to the end of the war, see J. Michael Quill, *Prelude to the Radicals: The North and Reconstruction during 1865* (Washington, D.C., 1980), 3–9.

4. Chase C. Mooney, ed., "A Union Chaplain's Diary," *Proceedings of the New Jersey Historical Society* 75 (January 1957): 9; diary of an unidentified Union soldier, August 12, 1864–June 12, 1865, transcript copy, Rare Books and Manuscripts Division, NYPL.

5. Boston *Post*, April 11, 1865, 1; Beecher quoted in Justus French, *The Trip of the Steamer Oceanus to Fort Sumter and Charleston, South Carolina. . . .* (Brooklyn, 1865), 37.

6. Boston *Daily Evening Voice*, April 10, 1865.

7. "George W. Julian's Journal—The Assassination of Lincoln," *Indiana Magazine of History* 2 (1915): 333.

8. Nevins and Thomas, *Diary of George Templeton Strong*, 3:579.

9. Elizabeth Botume, *First Days Amongst the Contrabands* (Boston, 1898;

reprint, New York, 1968), 175; letter of Rebecca Harding Davis, April 20, 1865, Richard Harding Davis Collection (#6109), Clifton Waller Barrett Library, Manuscripts Division, Special Collections Department, University of Virginia Library; Boston *Post*, April 19, 1865, 1.

10. Letter of Charlotte Holbrooke, April 17, 1865, Maurice Family Papers; James C. Mohr, ed., *The Cormany Diaries: A Northern Family in the Civil War* (Pittsburgh, 1982), 543.

11. Boston *Post*, April 17, 1865, 4; Nicholas B. Wainwright, ed., *A Philadelphia Perspective: The Diary of Sidney George Fisher Covering the Years 1834–1871* (Philadelphia, 1967), 492.

12. *Harper's Weekly* 9 (May 13, 1865): 290, and 9 (April 22, 1865): 242; Charles H. Lynch, *The Civil War Diary, 1862–1865, of Charles H. Lynch, 18th Connecticut Volunteers* (Hartford, 1915), 150; New York *Tribune*, April 18, 1865, 2.

13. Eric Foner, *Free Soil, Free Labor, Free Men* (New York, 1970), 69.

14. Michael Adams, *Our Masters the Rebels: A Speculation on Union Military Failure in the East, 1861–1865* (Cambridge, Mass., 1978).

15. Karen Halttunen, *Confidence Men and Painted Women: A Study of Middle-Class Culture in America, 1830–1870* (New Haven, 1982), 33–55; F. N. Boney, ed., *A Union Soldier in the Land of the Vanquished: The Diary of Sergeant Mathew Woodruff, June–December, 1865* (University, Ala., 1969), 11.

16. Whitelaw Reid, *After the War: A Southern Tour* (Cincinnati and New York, 1866), 63; Nevins and Thomas, *Diary of George Templeton Strong*, 4:11; Mark E. Neely, Jr., Harold Holzer, and Gabor S. Borritt, *The Confederate Image* (Chapel Hill, 1987), 70.

17. Bertram Wyatt-Brown, *Southern Honor: Ethics and Behavior in the Old South* (New York, 1982), 20. In this work, and in *Yankee Saints and Southern Sinners* (Baton Rouge, 1985), Wyatt-Brown develops his argument in much greater complexity than I am able to do here, noting especially the divergent moral and religious traditions of northern and southern upper-class men. Ultimately, I am not sure he would agree with the economic slant I have used to interpret his ideas. Also on this divergence, see Edward Ayers, *Vengeance and Justice: Crime and Punishment in the Nineteenth-Century American South* (New York, 1984), 9–33. Elizabeth Fox-Genovese does connect the distinctive gender codes of North and South to the different economic systems of the two regions. In this regard, see Elizabeth Fox-Genovese, *Within the Plantation Household: Black and White Women of the Old South* (Chapel Hill, 1988), 37–99.

18. Foner, *Free Soil*, 23–29. For more on the construction of middle-class masculinity in the antebellum North, see Charles Rosenberg, "Sexuality, Class and Role in Nineteenth Century America," *American Quarterly* 25 (May 1973): 131–53, and E. Anthony Rotundo, "Body and Soul: Changing Ideals of American Middle-Class Manhood, 1770–1920," *Journal of Social History* 16 (Fall 1983), 23–38.

19. Wyatt-Brown, *Yankee Saints and Southern Sinners*, 124–26.

20. William Taylor, *Cavalier and Yankee: The Old South and American National Character* (Garden City, N.Y., 1963), 123–55 and passim; Adams, *Our*

Masters the Rebels; Strong quoted in Phillip Paludan, *"A People's Contest": The Union and Civil War, 1861–1865* (New York, 1988), 5; Foner, *Free Soil,* 69–72.

21. John W. Phelps, Common Place Books, 7:87, John Walcott Phelps Papers, Rare Books and Manuscripts Division, NYPL; Chicago *Tribune,* May 25, 1865, 2.

22. Nevins and Thomas, *Diary of George Templeton Strong,* 3:583–84; letter of Edward Morley, April 18, 1865, Edward Morley Papers, LC; Chicago *Tribune,* May 25, 1865, 2.

23. On this postwar reorientation, see George Fredrickson, *The Inner Civil War: Northern Intellectuals and the Crisis of the Union* (New York, 1968), 166–98, in which he discusses an emerging interest in "the strenuous life" alongside "the twilight of humanitarianism."

24. On northern notions in the early phase of Reconstruction, see Eric Foner, *Reconstruction: America's Unfinished Revolution, 1863–1877* (New York, 1988), esp. chaps. 4 and 5.

25. New York *Tribune,* May 12, 1865, 4.

26. Governor Randall quoted in Foner, *Free Soil,* 290; on proving black manhood in the Civil War, see LeeAnn Whites, "The Civil War as a Crisis in Gender," in *Divided Houses: Gender and the Civil War,* ed. Catherine Clinton and Nina Silber (New York, 1992), 3–21; Sidney Andrews, *The South Since the War, as Shown by Fourteen Weeks of Travel and Observation in Georgia and the Carolinas* (Boston, 1866), 223–25, 396.

27. Andrews, *The South,* 318.

28. Benjamin F. Butler, *Butler's Book* (Boston, 1892), 418. Mary Ryan's unpublished paper, "Of Handkerchiefs and Brickbats: Women in the Public Sphere," has helped me to put the Butler incident in perspective. Reid, *After the War,* 46; John R. Dennett, *The South as It Is, 1865–66* (New York, 1965; reprint, Athens, Ga., 1986), 279; Andrews, *The South,* 9.

29. New York *Tribune,* April 18, 1865, 2; Andrews, *The South,* 320, 187.

30. Fox-Genovese, *Within the Plantation Household,* 334–71; Gaines Foster, *Ghosts of the Confederacy: Defeat, the Lost Cause, and the Emergence of the New South, 1865–1913* (New York, 1987), 29. Drew Faust, "Altars of Sacrifice: Confederate Women and the Narratives of War," in *Divided Houses: Gender and the Civil War,* ed. Catherine Clinton and Nina Silber (New York, 1992), 171–99, confirms the point that many southern white women's support for the Confederacy had begun to wane by the war's conclusion.

31. This notion of "northernizing" the South in the postwar period is presented in Richard N. Current, *Northernizing the South* (Athens, Ga., 1983).

32. Quoted in Chester D. Bradley, "Was Jefferson Davis Disguised as a Woman When Captured?," *Journal of Mississippi History* 36 (August 1974): 246; for more on the debate regarding Davis's disguise, see ibid.; for another interpretation of the event, and an excellent collection of capture cartoons, see Neely, Holzer, and Borritt, *Confederate Image,* 79–96; Natalie Davis in her seminal article "Women on Top," in Natalie Davis, *Society and Culture in Early Modern France* (Stanford, 1975), refers to a longstanding tradition of legends which tell of escaping men

in feminine disguise; C. Vann Woodward, *Mary Chesnut's Civil War* (New Haven, 1981), 172. Mary Chesnut also connected Jefferson Davis's capture to the Lincoln incident. "It is that escapade of their man Lincoln," she wrote, "that set them on making up the waterproof cloak story of Jefferson Davis." (Ibid., 819.)

33. "Jeff in Petticoats," words by Henry Tucker and music by George Cooper, in *Songs of the Civil War*, ed. Irwin Silber (New York, 1960), 345; Boston *Evening Journal*, May 27, 1865.

34. Chicago *Tribune*, May 31, 1865, 2; Neil Harris, *Humbug: The Art of P. T. Barnum* (Chicago, 1973), 169; Neely, Holzer, and Borritt, *Confederate Image*, 79–96.

35. Neely, Holzer, and Borritt, *Confederate Image*, 90; thanks to Bernard Reilly, head curator, Prints and Photographs Division, Library of Congress, for providing me with the information concerning the price and possible class audience for the Davis cartoons; Caroline Cowles Richards, *Village Life in America, 1852–1872, Including the Period of the American Civil War as Told in the Diary of a School-Girl*, with an introduction by Margaret E. Sangster (New York, 1913), 191.

36. New York *Independent*, May 18, 1865, 2; letter of Edward Morley, May 18, 1865, Edward Morley Papers, LC; *Harper's Weekly*, June 3, 1865, 347.

37. Dennett, *The South*, 17–18; Foster, *Ghosts of the Confederacy*, 26 and passim; Cleveland *Plain Dealer*, May 16, 1865.

38. New York *Herald*, May 16, 1865, quoted in *Public Opinion* 7 (June 3, 1865): 571–72.

39. Taylor, *Cavalier and Yankee*, 125–26; New York *Herald*, May 16, 1865, in *Public Opinion* 7 (June 3, 1865): 572.

40. Capt. G. W. Lawton, "Running at the Heads: Being an Authentic Account of the Capture of Jefferson Davis," *Atlantic Monthly* (September 1865): 342–47, copy found in James D. and David R. Barbee Papers, LC.

41. New York *Herald*, May 16, 1865, in *Public Opinion* 7 (June 3, 1865): 571–72.

42. William T. Adams [Oliver Optic], *Fighting Joe* (New York, 1865), 29, 30, 64, 73.

43. Joan Scott, "Gender: A Useful Category of Historical Analysis," *American Historical Review* 91 (December 1986): 1070; for more on European monarchs' use of gendered political discourse and the image of rape and marital subjugation, see Margaret D. Carroll, "The Erotics of Absolutism: Rubens and the Mystification of Sexual Violence," *Representations* 25 (Winter 1989): 3–30.

CHAPTER TWO

1. Russell Conwell, *Magnolia Journey: A Union Veteran Revisits the Former Confederate States* (Boston, 1869; reprint, University, Ala., 1974), 48.

2. Ibid., 49–52.

3. F. N. Boney, ed., *A Union Soldier in the Land of the Vanquished: The Diary of Sergeant Mathew Woodruff, June–December, 1865* (University, Ala., 1969), 49–

50; John Dennett, *The South as It Is, 1865–66* (New York, 1965; reprint, Athens, Ga., 1986), 348.

4. "Speech of Richard H. Dana, Jr. at a Meeting of Citizens Held in Faneuil Hall, June 21, 1865," and Henry B. Blackwell, "What the South Can Do" (New York, 1867), 1–2, Broadsides Collection, LC.

5. George C. Benham, *A Year of Wreck; a True Story by a Victim* (New York, 1880), 141; Lowell quoted in Jay B. Hubbell, *The South in American Literature, 1607–1900* (Durham, N.C., 1954), 697; letter of Oliver W. Holmes to Senator A. J. Beveridge quoted in Daniel Aaron, *The Unwritten War: American Writers and the Civil War* (New York, 1973), 166–67.

6. John W. Phelps, Common Place Books, 7:87, John Walcott Phelps Papers, Rare Books and Manuscripts Division, NYPL; Daniel Sutherland, *The Confederate Carpetbaggers* (Baton Rouge, 1988), 236.

7. Richard Morton, ed., "Life in Virginia by a 'Yankee Teacher,' Margaret Newbold Thorpe," *Virginia Magazine of History and Biography* 64 (April 1956): 192; letter of James Lawrence to Horace Greeley, December 16, 1866, Horace Greeley Papers, Rare Books and Manuscripts Division, NYPL.

8. Lawrence Powell, *New Masters: Northern Planters during the Civil War and Reconstruction* (New Haven, 1980), offers an excellent analysis of postwar northern interests in southern agriculture, including astute observations regarding Yankee views of the black labor force. Letter of Henry Lee Higginson quoted in Bliss Perry, *Life and Letters of Henry Lee Higginson* (New York, 1921), 253; Powell, *New Masters*, 29.

9. Allan Nevins and Milton H. Thomas, eds., *The Diary of George Templeton Strong*, 4 vols. (New York, 1952), 4:158; speech of Reverend George Hepworth in Boston *Daily Evening Voice*, July 5, 1867; for an example of northern views of nonslaveholding southern whites, see E. A. Seabrook, "The Poor Whites of the South," *Galaxy* 4 (October 1867): 681–90.

10. E. L. Godkin, "Lessons of the Campaign," *Nation* 15 (October 17, 1872): 244.

11. For more on changing conceptions of nationalism in the postwar period, see Merle Curti, *The Roots of American Loyalty* (New York, 1946), 173–80; Thompson quoted in ibid., 176; Gerrit Smith, "Let us Deal Impartially with the Sinning South and the Sinning North," March 20, 1867, Houghton Library, Harvard University. The notion of the nation as an "imagined community" is derived from Benedict Anderson, *Imagined Communities: Reflections on the Origin and Spread of Nationalism* (London, 1983), 14–19.

12. Robert Wiebe, *The Search for Order, 1877–1920* (New York, 1967), 5–6; Nevins and Thomas, *Diary of George Templeton Strong*, 4:538.

13. Edward King, *The Great South* (Baton Rouge, 1972), 793.

14. Mark Summers, *Railroads, Reconstruction, and the Gospel of Prosperity* (Princeton, N.J., 1984), 11; Whitelaw Reid quoted in Powell, *New Masters*, 66; Dennett, *The South*, 266.

15. Dennett, *The South*, 266; Herman Melville quoted in Hubbell, *The South in American Literature*, 698; Frederick B. Goddard, *Where to Emigrate and*

Why . . . (Philadelphia, 1869), 335; Conwell, *Magnolia Journey*, 105. Lawrence Powell suggests that, although many northerners feared southern insincerity, southerners were usually genuinely hospitable (see *New Masters*, 66).

16. Dennett, *The South*, 266; John W. Phelps, Common Place Books, vol. 8, Phelps Papers.

17. This analysis of the continued influence of sentimental concerns and the fear of market-induced hypocrisy comes from Karen Halttunen, *Confidence Men and Painted Women: A Study of Middle-Class Culture in America, 1830–1870* (New Haven, 1982), 1–55. Of course, it is important to note that the antebellum sentimental culture did not emerge from the Civil War completely intact. Halttunen points out that even before the war, middle-class northerners began to accept some level of social pretensions, and not just moral earnestness, as indicative of respectability. Moreover, the war itself went a long way toward destroying the sentimental mindset. Yet it does seem that the end of the war also saw a resurgence in sentimental concerns, perhaps a desire to recapture—in terms of home and emotional life—what had been lost during the conflict.

18. Letter of John Underwood to Horace Greeley, November 27, 1867, Greeley Papers.

19. Memorial Day address of Dr. Colyer quoted in Ernest Faehtz, *National Memorial Day* (Washington, D.C., 1870), 154; Harriet Beecher Stowe, *Men of Our Times; Or, Leading Patriots of the Day* (Hartford, Conn., 1868), 567.

20. ALS, Abigail Waters to James Waters, July 23, [186?], Waters Family Papers, James Duncan Phillips Library, Peabody and Essex Museum, Salem, Mass.; King, *Great South*, 32. Daniel Rodgers, *The Work Ethic in Industrial America, 1850–1920* (Chicago, 1974), 186, suggests that at around this time, middle-class northerners showed increasing sympathy for the ideal of idle womanhood.

21. Mary Abigail Dodge [Gail Hamilton], *Wool-Gathering* (Boston, 1867), 270.

22. Albert Webster, "Southern Home-Politics," *Atlantic Monthly* 36 (October 1875): 465.

23. On the ethic of suffering, see T. J. Jackson Lears, *No Place of Grace: Antimodernism and the Transformation of American Culture, 1880–1920* (New York, 1981), 221–22.

24. Elizabeth Hyde Botume, *First Days Amongst the Contrabands* (Boston, 1898; reprint, New York, 1968), 231; letter of W. Amory, February 6, 1867, quoted in Willie Lee Rose, *Rehearsal for Reconstruction: The Port Royal Experiment* (New York, 1964), 360; letter of Edwin Corning, August 10, 1867, Slack Family Papers, SHC.

25. As noted above, Halttunen observes the waning of sentimental culture and the increasing concern for social formalism as early as the 1850s. See Halttunen, *Confidence Men*, 157–67; John William DeForest, *A Union Officer in the Reconstruction*, ed. James H. Croushore and David M. Potter (New Haven, 1948), 186; for more on the northern elite's awareness of cultural stratification, see Lawrence Levine, *Highbrow/Lowbrow: The Emergence of Cultural Hierarchy in America*

(Cambridge, Mass., 1988), 85–168; Sutherland, *Confederate Carpetbaggers*, 227; Dodge, *Wool-Gathering*, 270.

26. Morton, "Life in Virginia," 190; letter of Whitelaw Reid, November 11, 1866, Anna E. Dickinson Papers, LC; letter of E[lizabeth] Devereux to James Waters, May 17, 1866, Waters Family Papers.

27. George Fredrickson, *The Inner Civil War: Northern Intellectuals and the Crisis of the Union* (New York, 1968), 192–96; letter of William Lloyd Garrison, Jr., February 22, 1875, Garrison Family Papers, Sophia Smith Collection, Smith College.

28. DeForest, *Union Officer*, 44; Dodge, *Wool-Gathering*, 271. As John Sproat points out, much of the dislike of Reconstruction rule stemmed from a class bias which likened Reconstruction politics to northern machine politics and blamed lower-class northerners, in particular, for political corruption. In contrast, many northerners preferred to promote the "best men" for political office. See John Sproat, *"The Best Men": Liberal Reformers in the Gilded Age* (Chicago, 1968).

29. Whitelaw Reid, *After the War: A Southern Tour* (Cincinnati and New York, 1866), 156; *New York Times*, October 13, 1870; letter of James R. Lowell to E. L. Godkin, November 20, 1868, quoted in Hubbell, *The South in American Literature*, 699.

30. Adams quoted in *New York Times*, June 17, 1875.

31. Theodore Romeyn quoted in Frederick Saunders, ed., *Our National Centennial Jubilee . . . on the Fourth of July, 1876, in the Several States of the Union* (New York, 1877), 645–46; William Lambert quoted in Grand Army of the Republic, *Memorial Ceremonies at Monument Cemetery, Philadelphia, Under the Auspices of Post No. 2, Department of Pennsylvania* (Philadelphia, 1879), 19; Dubuque *Daily Times*, May 30 and May 31, 1879.

32. Garrison and Whittier quoted in Larry Gara, "A Glorious Time: The 1874 Abolitionist Reunion in Chicago," *Journal of the Illinois State Historical Society* 65 (Autumn 1972): 290, 289. For more on the views of former abolitionists in the postwar period, see James McPherson, *The Abolitionist Legacy: From Reconstruction to the NAACP* (Princeton, N.J., 1975).

33. For more on the politics of the bloody shirt, see Stanley Hirshson, *Farewell to the Bloody Shirt: Northern Republicans and the Southern Negro, 1877–1893* (Chicago, 1968); for more on the veteran voting bloc in the Republican party, see Mary Dearing, *Veterans in Politics* (Baton Rouge, 1952).

34. Faehtz, *National Memorial Day*, 428.

35. Stuart Charles McConnell, "A Social History of the Grand Army of the Republic, 1867–1900" (Ph.D. dissertation, Johns Hopkins University, 1987), offers an interesting and insightful discussion of the Union veterans' concern for manhood. See esp. pp. 265–70.

36. John Logan, Memorial Day Resolution, Box 44, John Alexander Logan Papers, LC; for more on the origins of Memorial Day, see Paul Buck, *The Road to Reunion* (New York, 1937; reprint, New York, 1959), 120–26, and Gaines Foster,

Ghosts of the Confederacy: Defeat, the Lost Cause, and the Emergence of the New South, 1865–1913 (New York, 1987), 42–45.

37. Worcester *Daily Spy*, May 31, 1869; Horace Binney Sargent, *Address Delivered May 30, 1872 before Grand Army Post No. 11 at Charlestown, Mass.* (Boston, 1872), 9.

38. Hartford *Courant*, May 31, 1871; Illinois *State Journal*, May 30, 1871.

39. Grand Army of the Republic, *Memorial Ceremonies at Monument Cemetery, Philadelphia, Under the Auspices of Post No. 2, Department of Pennsylvania* (Philadelphia, 1877), 5; John Logan "Decoration Day Speech," n.d., John Alexander Logan Papers, Box 47; Worcester *Daily Spy*, May 30, 1868.

40. John Vanderslice quoted in Grand Army of the Republic, *Memorial Ceremonies at Monument Cemetery, Philadelphia, Under the Auspices of Post No. 2, Department of Pennsylvania* (Philadelphia, 1872), 17; Cincinnati *Daily Enquirer*, May 30, 1875; Worcester *Daily Spy*, May 31, 1875.

41. Providence *Daily Journal*, May 26, 1876; Worcester *Daily Spy*, May 28, 1877.

42. *New York Times*, January 27, 1878; speech of John O'Byrne, July 4, 1876, quoted in Saunders, *Our National Centennial Jubilee*, 90.

43. David Blight, "'For Something beyond the Battlefield': Frederick Douglass and the Struggle for the Memory of the Civil War," *Journal of American History* 75 (March 1989): 1172.

44. George Forgie, *Patricide in the House Divided: A Psychological Interpretation of Lincoln and His Age* (New York, 1979), discusses the significance of domestic and family imagery in the prewar period. Stevens quoted in Robert W. Rydell, *All the World's a Fair: Visions of Empire at American International Expositions, 1876–1916* (Chicago, 1984), 19.

45. Conwell, *Magnolia Journey*, 48–53, 130–31; letter of Mary Easterly, July 10, 1871, Branner Easterly Papers, Special Collections Library, Duke University; Foster, *Ghosts of the Confederacy*, 29–30, also notes incidents of postwar romance that sprang up between Union soldiers and southern women.

46. "Editor's Easy Chair," *Harper's Monthly* 57 (November 1878): 936; Buck, *Road to Reunion*, 146; the version of Hayne's poem cited here appears in the John Greenleaf Whittier Papers, Special Collections Library, Duke University.

CHAPTER THREE

1. Typescript of clipping from Springfield *Homestead*, August 31, 1889, Greenbrier Archives, White Sulphur Springs, West Virginia. Thanks to Greenbrier archivist Robert Conte for making this clipping and other materials from the Greenbrier Archives available to me. Although no state is indicated for the location of the Springfield *Homestead*, the tone of Bab's article suggests that she is writing to a northern audience.

2. Frederick Law Olmsted, *The Cotton Kingdom: A Traveller's Observations on Cotton and Slavery in the American Slave States*, edited and with an introduction by Arthur M. Schlesinger (New York, 1953; reprint, New York, 1969), 177.

3. Daniel Boorstin, *The Image; or, What Happened to the American Dream* (New York, 1962), 77–117; Daniel Rodgers, *The Work Ethic in Industrial America, 1850–1920* (Chicago, 1974), 105.

4. John Esten Cooke, "The White Sulphur Springs," *Harper's Monthly* 57 (August 1878): 338; M. B. Hillyard, *The New South* (Baltimore, 1887), 45; Charles Barney Cory, *Southern Rambles* (Boston, 1881), 49.

5. Earl Pomeroy, *In Search of the Golden West: The Tourist in Western America* (New York, 1957), 4; Robert LaCour-Cayet quoted in Hugh De Santis, "The Democratization of Travel: The Travel Agent in American History," *Journal of American Culture* 1 (Spring 1978): 6; Anthony Q. Keasbey, *From the Hudson to the St. Johns* (Newark, N.J., 1874), 98; Edward A. Pollard, "The Virginia Tourist," *Lippincott's Magazine* 5 (May 1870): 494; Edward King, *The Great South* (Baton Rouge, 1972), 568.

6. T. J. Jackson Lears, *No Place of Grace: Antimodernism and the Transformation of American Culture, 1880–1920* (New York, 1981); Alan Trachtenberg, *The Incorporation of America: Culture and Society in the Gilded Age* (New York, 1982). Henry D. Shapiro in *Appalachia on Our Mind: The Southern Mountains and Mountaineers in the American Consciousness, 1870–1920* (Chapel Hill, 1978), 3–5, notes a similar change from informative to entertaining in the Appalachian travel literature that appeared in the 1870s.

7. C. Vann Woodward, *Origins of the New South, 1877–1913* (Baton Rouge, 1971), 120–22, discusses the boom in southern railroad building that began in 1879 and the New York domination of this process. William Olcott, *The Greenbrier Heritage* (Greenbrier, W.Va., 1967), 42; Robert S. Conte, "The Celebrated White Sulphur Springs of Greenbrier," *West Virginia History* 42 (Spring–Summer 1981): 213; John Jennings Moorman, *Mineral Springs of North America* (Philadelphia, 1873), 156; Fay Ingalls, *The Valley Road* (Cleveland, 1949), 43; Charles Pilsbury, "The Southern Watering Place," *Potters' American Monthly* (October 1880): 263; "Virginia Summer Resorts," *Harper's Weekly* 29 (October 3, 1885): 647.

8. "The Virginia Springs," *Nation* 25 (September 20, 1877): 179; Ingalls, *The Valley Road*, 43; Conte, "The Celebrated White Sulphur Springs," 213–16; Henry Field, *Bright Skies and Dark Shadows* (New York, 1890), 17; Keasbey, *From the Hudson*, 96; *American Non-Conformist*, August 8, 1889.

9. Harriet Beecher Stowe, *Palmetto Leaves* (Boston, 1873), 37–39; King, *Great South*, 382; "Florida Journal of Charles K. Landis," *Vineland Historical Magazine* 26 (October 1941): 257; Keasbey, *From the Hudson*, 39–43; Hezekiah Butterworth, *A Zig-Zag Journey in the Sunny South* (Boston, 1887), 185.

10. Pomeroy, *In Search of the Golden West*, 16; Sidney Walter Martin, *Florida's Flagler* (Athens, Ga., 1949), 103–31; U.S. Department of the Interior, Census Office, *The Statistics of Wealth and Industry of the United States*, vol. 3 (Wash-

ington, D.C., 1870), table 18, 812–13; U.S. Department of the Interior, Census Office, *Report on Population of the United States at the Eleventh Census: 1890*, vol. 1 (Washington, D.C., 1897), 312.

11. William W. Rogers, *Thomas County, 1865–1900* (Tallahassee, Fla., 1973), 134–41, 331–44.

12. Shapiro, *Appalachia*, 63; Robert Underwood Johnson, *Remembered Yesterdays* (Boston, 1923), 96–97; King, *Great South*, 677; Richmond and Danville Railroad, *The Summer of 1882 Among the Health Resorts of Northeast Georgia, Upper South Carolina, Western North Carolina, and Virginia* (New York, 1882), 16.

13. Prices for some railroad routes and hotel accommodations can be found in Daniel G. Brinton, *A Guidebook of Florida and the South, For Tourists, Invalids, and Emigrants* (Philadelphia and Jacksonville, 1869; reprint, Gainesville, Fla., 1978); Sarah Putnam, Journal, 11:36, Sarah G. Putnam Papers, MHS; "The Second Florida Journal of Charles K. Landis," *Vineland Historical Magazine* 27 (January 1942): 284–85; Noble Lovely Prentis, *Southern Letters* (Topeka, Kans., 1881), 160.

14. Charles Washburn, "The Southern Trip and Camp Life in Florida in 1879 of Three Washburn Brothers," vol. 2, Charles Washburn Papers, AAS; "A Florida Settler of 1877—The Diary of Erastus G. Hill," *Florida Historical Quarterly* 41 (April 1950): 286; Cory, *Southern Rambles*, 139; F. F. A., "Invalid Life in the South," *Lippincott's Magazine* 31 (March 1883): 290; letter of William Lloyd Garrison, Jr., February 20, 1875, Garrison Family Papers, Sophia Smith Collection, Smith College.

15. Mary Dodge, "Virginia in Water Colors," *Lippincott's Magazine* 10 (July 1872): 88; A. Van Cleef, "The Hot Springs of Arkansas," *Harper's Monthly* 56 (January 1878): 203; Cooke, "White Sulphur Springs," 349.

16. "The Virginia Springs," 179.

17. King, *Great South*, 387, 174.

18. Caroline Barrett White Diary, 19:38, Caroline Barrett White Papers, AAS; Albert Webster, "A Jaunt in the South," *Appleton's Journal* 10 (August 30, 1873): 264; Sarah Putnam, Journal, vol. 11, Sarah G. Putnam Papers; Constance Woolson, "Up the Ashley and Cooper," *Harper's Monthly* 52 (December 1875): 22–23.

19. Samuel Proctor, ed., "Leaves from a Travel Diary: A Visit to Augusta and Savannah, 1882," *Georgia Historical Quarterly* 41 (1957): 311; Washburn, "The Southern Trip," Charles Washburn Papers; Chesapeake and Ohio Railway Company, *Virginia Vistas, C&O Route*, [1888?], 3–4.

20. Mrs. Ellen Biddle, *Reminiscences of a Soldier's Wife* (Philadelphia, 1907), 24; Chesapeake and Ohio Railway, *Virginia Vistas*, 4; Lizzie W. Champney, *Three Vassar Girls at Home; A Holiday Trip of Three College Girls Through the South and West* (Boston, 1888), 102; A. Lowry, "Winter Colonies in the South," *Munsey's Magazine* 28 (December 1902): 325–33.

21. Amory Lawrence Journal, Amory A. Lawrence Papers, MHS; Sarah Putnam Journal, vol. 11, Sarah G. Putnam Papers; letter of Edward Atkinson, October 18, 1880, Edward Atkinson Papers, MHS.

22. For more on the cult of the picturesque, see Christopher Hussey, *The*

Picturesque (London, 1967), and Francis Klingender, *Art and the Industrial Revolution* (New York, 1968). Thanks also to Mary Panzer for explaining the changing use of this concept in European and American art.

23. King, *Great South*, 302; Charles Dudley Warner, *Studies in the South and West with Comments on Canada* (New York, 1889), 79; Samuel Clemens [Mark Twain], *Life on the Mississippi* (Boston, 1883; reprint, New York, 1976), 208; Julian Ralph, *Dixie; or Southern Scenes and Sketches* (New York, 1896), 376.

24. King, *Great South*, 275; H. C. Woods, "A Southern Corn-Shucking," *Appleton's Journal* (November 12, 1870): 571; "Richmond, Scenic and Historic," in *Picturesque America; or, the Land We Live In*, ed. William C. Bryant (New York, 1872), 81.

25. Albert Webster, "A Jaunt in the South," *Appleton's Journal* 10 (September 6, 1873): 297; King, *Great South*, 307.

26. Klingender, *Art and the Industrial Revolution*, 85; John Muir, *A Thousand Mile Walk to the Gulf* (Boston and New York, 1916), 51; Rudolf Eickmeyer, *Down South*, with an introduction by Joel Chandler Harris (1900), Division of Photography, National Museum of American History, Smithsonian Institution. For more on Eickmeyer's attachment to the picturesque features of southern life, see Mary Panzer, *In My Studio: Rudolf Eickmeyer, Jr., and the Art of the Camera, 1885–1930* (Yonkers, N.Y., 1986), 56–58.

27. Rodgers, *Work Ethic*, 94–124. Rodgers also notes the frequent connections drawn between women and leisure (see pp. 183–84).

28. *Appleton's Handbook of American Travel, Southern Tour* (New York, 1866), 9; Dodge, "Virginia in Water Colors," 86; "Virginia Summer Resorts," 647.

29. "The Virginia Springs," 178; F. F. A., "Invalid Life in the South," 293–94; "The Virginia Springs," 179; Cooke, "White Sulphur Springs," 357; Dodge, "Virginia in Water Colors," 83; Van Cleef, "Hot Springs of Arkansas," 199; "The Virginia Springs," 179.

30. Pomeroy, *In Search of the Golden West*, 73. My reading of gender in the landscape literature has also been influenced by Annette Kolodny, *The Lay of the Land* (Chapel Hill, 1975). Warner, *Studies in the South*, 40; King, *Great South*, 350; J. Harris Knowles, *From Summer Land to Summer; A Journey from Thomasville, Georgia to New York During April and May, 1899* (New York, 1899), 114–16.

31. King, *Great South*, 380, 85, 28. King's emphasis on the sensuality of the South was influenced by his view of the racial characteristics of the region. Like many white people in the nineteenth century, King saw blacks, especially black women, as more sensual and sexual.

32. Stephen Powers, *Afoot and Alone; a Walk from Sea to Sea by the Southern Route* (Hartford, Conn., 1872), 77; King, *Great South*, 340; Warner, *Studies in the South*, 372–73; John Temple Graves, *The Winter Resorts of Florida, South Georgia, Louisiana, Texas, California, Mexico, and Cuba* (New York, 1883), 13.

33. Marion A. Baker, "The New North," *Cosmopolitan* 2 (September 1886): 55; N. J. Watkins, ed., *The Pine and the Palm Greeting* (Baltimore, 1873), 24.

34. Dodge, "Virginia in Water Colors," 87; King, *Great South*, 670–71, 673–74; John Jennings Moorman, *Virginia White Sulphur Springs* (Baltimore, 1869), 27.

35. Catherine Clinton, *The Plantation Mistress: Woman's World in the Old South* (New York, 1982), 149–50; Ralph, *Dixie*, 169–70; Russell Conwell, *Magnolia Journey: A Union Veteran Revisits the Former Confederate States* (Boston, 1869; reprint, University, Ala., 1974), 128–29; Van Cleef, "Hot Springs of Arkansas," 196; *The Red Sulphur Springs, Monroe County, West Virginia* (Baltimore, 1870), 24.

36. King, *Great South*, 673; clipping from Springfield *Homestead*, August 31, 1889, Greenbrier Archives; New York *World* quoted in Perceval Reniers, *The Springs of Virginia: "Life, Love, and Death at the Waters, 1775–1900"* (Chapel Hill, 1941), 253; Cleveland Amory, *In the Last Resorts* (New York, 1948), 465–66. Influenced by the romantic legacy of these southern resorts, Amory wrote that "the greatest contribution of the Virginia Springs to resort life was by all odds its belles" (p. 455). Reniers, *Springs of Virginia*, 268; Chesapeake and Ohio Railway Company, *Virginia in Black and White* (Washington, D.C., 1893), 25.

37. Letter of Col. James B. Walton to his family, August 27, 1883, Walton-Glenny Family Papers, Historic New Orleans Collection, copy from Greenbrier Archives; Julia Newberry, *Julia Newberry's Diary*, with an introduction by Margaret Ayer Barnes and Janet Ayer Fairbank (New York, 1933), 61.

38. "The Virginia Springs," 178; clipping from Springfield *Homestead*, August 31, 1889, Greenbrier Archives.

39. "A Reminiscence of the White Sulphur Springs," *Harper's Weekly* 32 (October 4, 1888): 576–77; Chicago *Daily Tribune*, November 15, 1895.

40. Graves, *Winter Resorts*.

CHAPTER FOUR

1. Augustus Thomas, *The Print of My Remembrance* (New York, 1922), 3–11, 126.

2. Ibid., 187.

3. For more on the plantation image in nineteenth-century theater, see Francis Pendleton Gaines, *The Southern Plantation: A Study in the Development and Accuracy of a Tradition* (New York, 1924), 95–127, and Paul Buck, *The Road to Reunion* (New York, 1937; reprint, New York, 1959), 241–42. Undated clipping, Robinson Locke Collection of Dramatic Scrapbooks, 39:87–88, and souvenir card, *Alabama* clippings file, both in NYPLPA, Theater Collection.

4. Undated clipping, *Alabama* clippings file, NYPLPA, Theater Collection.

5. Trenton *State Gazette* quoted in Louis C. Gosson, *Post-Bellum Campaigns of the Blue and Gray, 1881–1882* (Trenton, 1882), 181.

6. Biographical background on Edward Atkinson can be obtained from Harold Francis Williamson, *Edward Atkinson: The Biography of an American Liberal, 1827–1905* (Boston, 1934). Also see Edward Atkinson, "Significant Aspects of the

Atlanta Cotton Exposition," *Century Magazine* 23 (February 1882); letter of Edward Atkinson, May 18, 1881, Letterbook #12, and letter of Edward Atkinson, September 16, 1881, Letterbook #12, both in Edward Atkinson Papers, MHS. On Higginson's postwar odyssey, see letter of Thomas W. Higginson to John D. Long, May 14, 1881, MHS, and Thomas W. Higginson, "Some War Scenes Revisited," *Atlantic Monthly* 42 (July 1878): 1–9. On Emerson's visit to Virginia, see Hubert H. Hoeltje, "Emerson in Virginia," *New England Quarterly* 5 (October 1932): 753–68.

7. Grand Army of the Republic, *Decoration Day, New York, May 30, 1882 and Decoration Day, Report of Proceedings, New York, May 30, 1883* (New York, 1883), 94.

8. *National Tribune*, September 24, 1891, quoted in Mary Dearing, *Veterans in Politics* (Baton Rouge, 1952), 409.

9. *National Tribune*, June 23, 1887, June 30, 1887; other accounts of the flag incident can be found in Buck, *Road to Reunion*, 284–86, and Wallace Evans Davies, *Patriotism on Parade: The Story of Veterans' and Hereditary Organizations in America, 1783–1900* (Cambridge, Mass., 1955), 250–60.

10. Lawrence Goodwyn in *The Populist Moment* (New York, 1978) makes frequent reference to the importance of the reunion message in Populist rhetoric, as does Nell Irvin Painter in *Standing at Armageddon: The United States, 1877–1919* (New York, 1987), 100. Col. L. L. Polk, "Sectionalism and the Alliance," in *The Farmers' Alliance History and Agricultural Digest*, ed. Nelson A. Dunning (Washington, D.C., 1891), 251.

11. See, for example, "The Bloody Shirt Again," *National Economist*, November 21, 1891.

12. "What Is Slavery?," *American Non-Conformist*, April 19, 1894; Polk, "Sectionalism and the Alliance," 252; B. H. Clover, "Sectionalism," in *The Farmers' Alliance History and Agricultural Digest*, ed. Nelson A. Dunning (Washington, D.C., 1891), 253; speech of L. L. Polk at Winfield, Kansas, Chautauqua Assembly, July 4, 1890, reprinted in *American Non-Conformist*, July 10, 1890. Polk's appeal to the farmer-veterans of both sections is also discussed in Reid Mitchell, "The Creation of Confederate Loyalties," in *New Perspectives on Race and Slavery in America: Essays in Honor of Kenneth Stampp*, ed. Robert H. Abzug and Stephen E. Maizlish (Lexington, Ky., 1986), 104.

13. Goodwyn, *Populist Moment*, 131–32, 137–38, 186–87; Painter, *Standing at Armageddon*, 101–3; letter from J. F. Tillman in *National Economist*, February 18, 1893.

14. For more on the reunion efforts of labor unions, particularly the Knights of Labor, see Melton A. McLaurin, *The Knights of Labor in the South* (Westport, Conn., 1978).

15. On Coxey's Army, see Painter, *Standing at Armageddon*, 117–19, and Carlos Schwantes, *Coxey's Army: An American Odyssey* (Lincoln, Nebr., 1985).

16. For more on Willard, the WCTU, and the southern tour, see Ruth Bordin, *Woman and Temperance: The Quest for Power and Liberty, 1873–1900* (Philadelphia, Pa., 1981), 76–85.

17. Charleston, S.C., *News and Courier*, March 17, 1881, clipping in Woman's Christian Temperance Union National Headquarters Historical Files, Joint Ohio Historical Society–Michigan Historical Collections, WCTU microfilm edition, roll 32, frame 109, Bentley Historical Library, Ann Arbor, Mich.; Frances E. Willard, "Taking Texas for Temperance," *The Signal*, March 23, 1882, WCTU microfilm, roll 32, frame 45.

18. "Good Sentiments South," *Christian Statesman*, June 9, 1881, WCTU microfilm, roll 32, frames 143–44; Frances E. Willard, "Lead Pencil Letter Number 8," *Our Union*, April 12, 1881, WCTU microfilm, roll 32, frame 131; letter of Mrs. Erwin [last name unknown], February 8, 1882, WCTU microfilm, roll 12.

Of course, it should be pointed out that, in order to secure the commitment of southern white women, the WCTU often waffled on race issues. In general, Willard believed that southern white people would work to bring the antidrinking message to "their" black folks. Furthermore, by the 1890s the organization refused to take a strong position against southern lynchings.

19. The popularity of plantation and Civil War novels, especially after the Reconstruction period, is noted in Gaines, *Southern Plantation*, and in Robert Lively, *Fiction Fights the Civil War: An Unfinished Chapter in the Literary History of the American People* (Chapel Hill, 1957). For more on the theatrical view of reunion, see, in addition to Gaines, Rollin G. Osterweis, *The Myth of the Lost Cause, 1865–1900* (Hamden, Conn., 1973).

20. For more on the antebellum plantation myth, see William Taylor, *Cavalier and Yankee: The Old South and American National Character* (Garden City, N.Y., 1963); on the myth in general, see Gaines, *Southern Plantation*. For more on the northern reception to this myth, see Patrick Gerster and Nicholas Cords, "The Northern Origins of Southern Mythology," in *Myth and the American Experience*, ed. Patrick Gerster and Nicholas Cords (Encino, Calif., 1978), 2:320–34. My assertion that the myth had a larger following among postwar as opposed to prewar northerners stems from my understanding of Eric Foner, *Free Soil, Free Labor, Free Men* (New York, 1970), and his critique of Taylor (pp. 68–69). Paul Gaston, *The New South Creed: A Study in Southern Mythmaking* (New York, 1970), 178–79, notes how New South proponents consciously promoted the old South myth among northerners as a vehicle of reconciliation. On the perpetuation of traditional themes and the creation of a feminine motif in Gilded Age culture, see Robert Roberts, "Gilt, Gingerbread, and Realism: The Public and Its Taste," in *The Gilded Age: A Reappraisal*, ed. H. Wayne Morgan (Syracuse, N.Y., 1963), 169–95, and Alan Trachtenberg, *The Incorporation of America: Culture and Society in the Gilded Age* (New York, 1982), 145–49.

21. Lively, *Fiction Fights the Civil War*, 172.

22. Memorandum of A. Howard Clark, 1886, United States National Museum documents, Box 11, Folder 10, Smithsonian Institution Archives. Thanks to Christine Hoepfner for making this memorandum available to me.

23. John William DeForest, *The Bloody Chasm* (New York, 1881), 27 and passim; undated Philadelphia review, *Alabama* scrapbook, NYPLPA, Theater Collection.

24. Undated clipping, *Held by the Enemy* clippings file, NYPLPA, Theater Collection; Charles Townsend, *The Pride of Virginia* (Chicago, 1901), 11.

25. Charles Dudley Warner, "Their Pilgrimage," *Harper's Monthly* 73 (August 1886): 440.

26. Undated Boston review, *Held by the Enemy* clippings file, NYPLPA, Theater Collection.

27. *Alabama* promptbook, NYPLPA, Theater Collection.

28. Imre Kiralfy, *America* (1893), in "Fairs and Expositions," Box 6, Warshaw Collection, National Museum of American History Archives, Smithsonian Institution. Gaines, *Southern Plantation*, 116, confirms that in Civil War dramas "the heroine is unfailingly the conventional Dixie beauty."

29. Joyce Appleby, "Reconciliation and the Northern Novelist, 1865–1880," *Civil War History* 10 (June 1964): 119–20, refutes Paul Buck's finding that southerners first introduced the themes of conciliation in the 1880s and observes the standard romantic reunion formula in northern novels as early as 1865. John William DeForest, *Miss Ravenal's Conversion From Secession to Loyalty* (New York, 1867; reprint, New York, 1968), 10 and passim.

30. DeForest, *Bloody Chasm*, 205, 145, and passim.

31. Undated review, *The Heart of Maryland* clippings file, NYPLPA, Theater Collection; A. D. Mayo, "The Woman's Movement in the South," *New England Magazine*, n.s. 4 (October 1891): 251.

32. Townsend, *Pride of Virginia*, 10, 16; Charles King, *Kitty's Conquest* (Philadelphia, 1884), 18–19; undated review, *Barbara Frietchie* clippings file, NYPLPA, Theater Collection; Sidney Andrews, *The South Since the War, as Shown by Fourteen Weeks of Travel and Observation in Georgia and the Carolinas* (Boston, 1866), 187.

33. On William Gillette, see Doris Cook, *Sherlock Holmes and Much More* (Hartford, 1970). Undated review, *Secret Service* clippings file, NYPLPA, Theater Collection.

34. Thomas Nelson Page, "Literature in the South Since the War," *Lippincott's Magazine* 48 (December 1891): 752; letter of Thomas Nelson Page, March 31, 1885, Thomas Nelson Page Collection (#8641), Clifton Waller Barrett Library, Manuscripts Division, Special Collections Department, University of Virginia Library.

35. For more on gender and marriage as metaphors in political discourse, see Joan Scott, "Gender: A Useful Category of Historical Analysis," *American Historical Review* 91 (December 1986): 1053–75, and Margaret D. Carroll, "The Erotics of Absolutism: Rubens and the Mystification of Sexual Violence," *Representations* 25 (Winter 1989): 3–30. John T. Trowbridge, *My Own Story* (Boston and New York, 1903), 284.

36. "A Gloomy Outlook," Atlanta *Constitution*, reprinted in *The Woman's Journal*, April 26, 1890; Sheila Rothman, *Woman's Proper Place* (New York, 1978), 46.

37. Thomas Nelson Page, "Old Dominion," *Harper's Monthly* 83 (December 1893): 5; Rebecca Harding Davis, "The Rose of Carolina," *Scribner's Magazine* 8 (October 1874): 724; undated review, *Alabama* clippings file, NYPLPA, Theater Collection.

38. Isabel A. Mallon, "The Colonel and Me," *Ladies' Home Journal* 14 (March 1897): 11; Davis, "Rose of Carolina," 726.

39. Henry James, *The Bostonians* (London, 1977), 238, 290, and passim; James B. Colvert, "Views of Southern Character in Some Northern Novels," *Mississippi Quarterly* 18 (Spring 1965): 59–65.

40. "A Gloomy Outlook"; New York *Herald*, June 12, 1892, clipping found in Anna E. Dickinson Papers, LC.

41. Gaines, *Southern Plantation*, 118, finds that in many Civil War dramas "not infrequently the villain is a young Southern gallant." John DeForest, especially in his earlier novels, *Miss Ravenal's Conversion* (1867) and *Kate Beaumont* (1872), frequently derided the supposed manliness of the South in his critiques of the idle and uncontrolled dispositions of his southern male characters. By the time of his later Civil War writing, *The Bloody Chasm* (1881), DeForest showed less interest in attacking southern manhood. Joe L. Dubbert, *Masculinity in Transition* (Englewood Cliffs, N.J., 1979), 66; Beaumont Fletcher, "Another American Play," *Godey's Magazine* 5 (August 1895): 133.

42. Review, September 29, 1894, *Down in Dixie* clippings file, NYPLPA, Theater Collection; Francis Hopkinson Smith, *Colonel Carter of Cartersville* (New York, 1891); review in *Illustrated American*, April 23, 1892, *Colonel Carter of Cartersville* clippings file, NYPLPA, Theater Collection. Smith was a southerner, but, like Thomas Page, he was acutely aware of his northern literary audience.

43. Fisher oration in Grand Army of the Republic, *Memorial Ceremonies at Monument Cemetery, Philadelphia, Under the Auspices of Post No. 2, Department of Pennsylvania, 1890–1899* (Philadelphia, 1899), 25; interview with Frank Bangs, undated article, *Alabama* clippings file, NYPLPA, Theater Collection. For more on the southern commitment to the lost cause, see Charles R. Wilson, *Baptized in Blood: The Religion of the Lost Cause, 1865–1900* (Athens, Ga., 1980), and, for a contrasting point of view, Gaines Foster, *Ghosts of the Confederacy: Defeat, the Lost Cause, and the Emergence of the New South, 1865–1913* (New York, 1987).

44. Anonymous letter, June 10, 1890, reprinted in Mary Craig Sinclair, *Southern Belle: The Personal Story of a Crusader's Wife* (New York, 1957), 60. Sinclair notes that numerous letters echoed these sentiments. For more on the Wilkinson-Davis affair, see *The Woman's Journal*, April 26, 1890, and the *New York Times*, April 27, 1890. I am especially grateful to Cita Cook for providing me with these references to the Winnie Davis engagement.

CHAPTER FIVE

1. For more on northern "romantic racialism," see George Fredrickson, *The Black Image in the White Mind: The Debate on Afro-American Character and Destiny, 1817–1914* (Middletown, Conn., 1987), 97–129.

2. On the inclusive nationalism of the Reconstruction period, see John Higham,

Strangers in the Land: Patterns of American Nativism, 1860–1925 (New York, 1969), 19–23. *Harper's Weekly*, May 20, 1865, 306.

3. John Hope Franklin, *From Slavery to Freedom: A History of Negro Americans* (New York, 1988), 239–44; Gustavus Pike, *The Jubilee Singers and Their Campaign for Twenty Thousand Dollars* (Boston, 1873), 30.

4. Review of Hampton singers from New York *Weekly Review* quoted in William Austin, *"Susanna," "Jeanie," and "The Old Folks at Home"* (New York, 1975), 289; Cuyler quoted in J. S. T. Marsh, *The Story of the Jubilee Singers; with Their Songs* (New York, 1883), 31.

5. Constance Woolson quoted in Austin, *"Susanna," "Jeanie," and "The Old Folks at Home,"* 290.

6. See, for example, "Slavery Days," words by E. Harrigan and music by Dave Braham, in *Harrigan and Hart's Slavery Days Songster* (New York, 1877); "Since Master Set Us Free," words by Amos D. Arnold and music by E. A. Andre, in M. H. Foley and C. H. Sheffer, *Big Pound Cake Songster* (New York, 1878), 24.

7. J. M. Hager, *The Great Republic. Allegory and Tableaux* (Washington, D.C., 1876), 21–22; "Happy Little Sam," in *The Dockstader's T'Shovel Songster* (New York, 1880).

8. "Down in Alabam," in James A. Bland, *De Golden Wedding Songster* (New York, 1880), 33; "Two Black and Tans," in *Daly Brothers' South Carolina Cloe Songster* (New York, 1878); "Tell de Children Good-bye," words and music by James Bland, in *American Minstrel Songster* (Philadelphia, 1881).

9. Gary Engle, in the introduction to *This Grotesque Essence: Plays from the American Minstrel Stage* (Baton Rouge, 1978), xix, observes that "from the 1840s–1870s, the vast majority of [minstrel] stars were of European immigrant stock." "I Want to See the Old Home," words by Frank Dumont and music by J. E. Stewart, in Foley and Sheffer, *Big Pound Cake*; Jonathan Baxter Harrison, *Certain Dangerous Tendencies in American Life, and Other Essays* (Boston, 1880), 181–86. Harrison's observation is also cited in Herbert Gutman, *Work, Culture, and Society in Industrializing America* (New York, 1977), 45.

10. Robert Toll, *Blacking Up: The Minstrel Show in Nineteenth Century America* (New York, 1974), 162–79; Hager, *Great Republic*, 13.

11. "I Want to See the Old Home"; "My Old Home in Caroline 'For De War," words and music by Roy Leslie, in Foley and Sheffer, *Big Pound Cake*, 58.

12. "We Couldn't Stay Away," words and music by W. H. Delehanty, in *Joe Lang's Old Aunt Jemima Songster* (New York, 1873), 69; "Down in Alabama," in Foley and Sheffer, *Big Pound Cake*, 14.

13. Toll, *Blacking Up*, 200–206; "The Clipper Interviews a Distinguished Amusement Disciple on an Impending and Imposing Enterprise," New York *Clipper*, March 4, 1882, 836 (also quoted in William L. Van Deburg, *Slavery and Race in American Popular Culture* [Madison, Wis., 1984], 114).

14. Untitled review of *Uncle Tom's Cabin*, February 23, 1878, and untitled Boston clipping, December 30, 1929, *Uncle Tom's Cabin* file, HTC.

15. Clipping from the New York *World*, December 29, 1880, and untitled clip-

ping, April 6, 1878, *Uncle Tom's Cabin* file, HTC; program, September 4, 1880, *Uncle Tom's Cabin* scrapbook, NYPLPA, Theater Collection.

16. Reverend John F. Cowan, *A New Invasion of the South* (New York, 1881), 36.

17. J. B. Harrison, "Studies of the South," *Atlantic Monthly* 49 (May 1882): 678; Higham, *Strangers in the Land*, 35–67.

18. Reverend A. D. Mayo, "The Negro American Citizen in the New American Life," in *First Mohonk Conference on the Negro Question Held at Lake Mohonk, Ulster County, New York, June 4, 5, 6, 1890* (New York, 1969), 46; Thomas W. Higginson, "Some War Scenes Revisited," *Atlantic Monthly* 42 (July 1878): 2–3; letter of Edward Atkinson, November 2, 1880, Edward Atkinson Papers, MHS.

19. C. Vann Woodward, *The Strange Career of Jim Crow* (New York, 1966), 31–65; Carl Schurz, *The New South* (New York, 1885), 24–25; Henry B. Field, *Bright Skies and Dark Shadows* (New York, 1890), 152. For most of the 1880s, northern race relations were likewise characterized by a degree of fluidity and a greater degree of tolerance than existed in the 1890s. Nonetheless, there is evidence of growing intolerance in the 1880s as seen in some of the nativist hysteria which was unleashed after 1886 against immigrants and in segregation policies toward southern blacks. On this, see Higham, *Strangers in the Land*, 35–67, and Leslie H. Fishel, "The 1880s: Pivotal Decade for the Black Community," *Hayes Historical Journal* 3 (1980): 85–94.

20. In *Dixie; or Southern Scenes and Sketches* (New York, 1896), northern writer Julian Ralph often notes the "shiftlessness" and absence of a work ethic among southern blacks. Program, Boston production of "Black America," August 11, 1895, Minstrel file, HTC; Francis Pendleton Gaines, *The Southern Plantation: A Study in the Development and Accuracy of a Tradition* (New York, 1924), 107–8.

21. Clipping, Boston *Transcript*, July 1895, and undated clipping in "Black America" scrapbook, NYPLPA, Theater Collection.

22. Van Deburg, *Slavery and Race*, 114; review of *Uncle Tom's Cabin*, in Boston *Advertiser*, August 20, 1888, *Uncle Tom's Cabin* file, HTC.

23. Fredrickson, *Black Image*, 228–55; Richard Hofstadter, *Social Darwinism in American Thought* (Boston, 1955), 172–79.

24. Elliot M. Rudwick and August Meier, "Black Man in the 'White City': Negroes and the Columbian Exposition, 1893," *Phylon* 26 (Winter 1965): 354–61; "Darkies Day at the Fair," *World's Fair Puck*, August 21, 1893, 186–87. Robert W. Rydell, in *All the World's a Fair: Visions of Empire at American International Expositions, 1876–1916* (Chicago, 1984), offers a thorough examination of the racial implications of the world's fair exhibits in both the North and the South.

25. Richard Barry, *Snap Shots on the Midway of the Pan-American Exposition* (Buffalo, N.Y., 1901), 125–26.

26. Ibid.; *Official Catalogue and Guide Book to the Pan-American Exposition* (Buffalo, N.Y., 1901), 40.

27. Joel Chandler Harris, "Plantation Music," *The Critic* 3 (December 15, 1883): 506.

28. Review of *Uncle Remus: His Songs and His Sayings* in *Nation* 31 (December 2, 1880): 398; letter of James Wood Davidson to Joel Chandler Harris, December 14, 1880, in *The Life and Letters of Joel Chandler Harris*, ed. Julia Collier Harris (Boston and New York, 1918), 163. For more on dialect stories, see Van Deburg, *Slavery and Race*, 93–102.

Harris's work has been the subject of extensive controversy, with some critics assaulting his racist presumptions and others viewing him as a more sensitive observer of black culture. See, for example, James A. Miller, "The Other Fellow," a review of R. Bruce Bickley's *Joel Chandler Harris*, in *Nation* 244 (May 9, 1987): 614–17. My intention here is not to question Harris's sincerity but to understand the images that he helped to create.

29. Van Deburg, *Slavery and Race*, 95; Thomas Nelson Page, "Literature in the South Since the War," *Lippincott's Magazine* 48 (December 1891): 749; Walter Hines Page quoted in Julia Harris, *Life and Letters*, 164. In his essay "Writing 'Race' and the Difference It Makes," *Critical Inquiry* 12 (Autumn 1985): 1–20, Henry Louis Gates notes that by assuming African Americans' ignorance of written English, white Americans assured themselves of black people's distance from American culture.

30. Ralph, *Dixie*, 373; J. Harris Knowles, *From Summer Land to Summer; A Journey from Thomasville, Georgia to New York During April and May, 1899* (New York, 1899), 56; Dubuque (Iowa) *Daily Times*, May 29, 1898.

31. For an example of the new historical assessment of slavery, see James Schouler, *History of the United States of America, Under the Constitution* (New York, 1894 and 1899), 2:264; Andrew D. White quoted in *First Mohonk Conference*, 120.

32. Gen. Roeliff Brinkerhoff quoted in *The Negro American: A Documentary History*, ed. Leslie H. Fishel, Jr., and Benjamin Quarles (Glenview, Ill., 1967), 339.

33. Charles Dudley Warner, *Studies in the South and West with Comments on Canada* (New York, 1889), 20; Joshua W. Caldwell, "The South Is American," *Arena* 8 (October 1893): 607–17.

34. Caldwell, "The South Is American," 607–17.

35. Henry D. Shapiro, in *Appalachia on Our Mind: The Southern Mountains and Mountaineers in the American Consciousness, 1870–1920* (Chapel Hill, 1978), 115–16, credits Berea College president William G. Frost for isolating this distinct mountain region and identifying it as "Appalachian America."

36. Jacquelyn Dowd Hall, James Leloudis, Robert Korstad, Mary Murphy, Lu Ann Jones, and Christopher B. Daly, *Like a Family: The Making of a Southern Cotton Mill World* (Chapel Hill, 1987), 9–10; [William] G. Frost, "Our Southern Highlanders," *Independent* 72 (April 4, 1912): 714.

37. James Klotter, "The Black South and White Appalachia," *Journal of American History* 66 (March 1980): 832–49; William M. Brewer, "Moonshining in Georgia," *Cosmopolitan* 23 (June 1897): 132; "The Real Southern Question Again," *World's Work* 4 (May 1902): 2068, 2072.

38. Klotter, "Black South and White Appalachia"; William G. Frost, *University Extension in the Southern Mountains* (New York, 1898), 5.

39. T. J. Jackson Lears, *No Place of Grace: Antimodernism and the Transformation of American Culture, 1880–1920* (New York, 1981), 142–49.

40. Frost, "Our Southern Highlanders," 714; John William DeForest, *A Union Officer in the Reconstruction*, ed. James H. Croushore and David M. Potter (New Haven, 1948), 161; Shapiro, *Appalachia on Our Mind*, 86–97 (includes Hume's quote); Frost, *University Extension*, 8.

41. Mrs. S. M. Davis quoted in Shapiro, *Appalachia*, 97; N. S. Shaler, "The Peculiarities of the South," *North American Review* 151 (October 1890): 483.

42. Frost, *University Extension*, 5.

43. Shaler, "Peculiarities," 484; F. Waldo, "Among the Southern Appalachians," *New England Magazine*, n.s. 24 (May 1901): 246, 243.

44. Shapiro, *Appalachia*, 30; Frank L. Mott, *Golden Multitudes: The Story of Best Sellers in the United States* (New York, 1947), 214. A brief and helpful discussion of John Fox, his career, and *The Little Shepherd of Kingdom Come* can also be found in Jack Temple Kirby, *Media-Made Dixie: The South in the American Imagination* (Athens, Ga., 1986), 39–43.

45. John Fox, Jr., *The Little Shepherd of Kingdom Come* (New York, 1903), 7, 24.

46. Ibid., 69.

47. Ibid., 188–92.

48. Ibid., 208.

49. Kirby, *Media-Made Dixie*, 40; James D. Hart, *The Popular Book* (New York, 1950), 214; Fox, *Little Shepherd*, 100, 171, 181. For more on the new appreciation of southern manhood, see chapter 6.

50. Frost, "Our Southern Highlanders," 711.

51. Background on the life and literary career of Mary Murfree can be obtained from Durwood Dunn, "Mary Noailles Murfree: A Reappraisal," *Appalachian Journal* 6 (Spring 1979): 197–204, and Edd Winfield Parks, "Mary Noailles Murfree," in *Notable American Women: A Biographical Dictionary*, 2 vols. (Cambridge, Mass., 1971), 2:602–3.

52. Undated clipping in Mary Murfree file, Houghton-Mifflin Papers, Houghton Library, Harvard University; Richard W. Gilder, "Nationalizing of Southern Literature," clipping in Box 23, Richard W. Gilder Papers, Rare Books and Manuscripts Division, NYPL; William Baskerville, *Southern Writers. Biographical and Critical Studies. Charles Egbert Craddock* (Nashville, Tenn., 1897), in Murfree file, Houghton-Mifflin Papers.

53. Schouler, *History of the United States of America*, 2:260; Joel Williamson, *The Crucible of Race* (New York, 1984).

54. Field, *Bright Skies*, 184, 170; David Muzzey, *An American History* (Boston, 1911), 621.

55. Williamson, *Crucible of Race*; Edward L. Ayers, *Vengeance and Justice:*

Crime and Punishment in the Nineteenth-Century American South (New York, 1984), 243; "Lynching and Civilization," *New York Times*, January 24, 1898, 6; Thomas Fleming, *Around the "Pan" with Uncle Hank* (New York, 1901), 125.

56. John Hope Franklin observes in *From Slavery to Freedom*, 282, that between 1900 and 1914, 315 lynching victims were accused of rape, compared to 500 accused of homocide. "Southern Lynching of Negroes," clipping from the Washington *Post* [?], September 7, 1897, Rebecca Felton Papers, Hargrett Rare Book and Manuscript Library, University of Georgia; Walter Hines Page, "The Last Hold of the Southern Bully," *Forum* 16 (November 1893): 303.

57. Sarah Barnwell Elliot, "An Incident," *Harper's Monthly* 96 (February 1898): 465, 468. In her unpublished paper, "Ida B. Well's Anti-Lynching Campaign (1892–94) and the Northern Middle Class' 'Masculinity Crisis'" (Presented at the Berkshire Conference of Women Historians, June 1990), Gail Bederman also observes how northern white men saw a model of white manhood in the lynching scenario.

58. Joel Williamson in *The Crucible of Race*, 129, observes that Rebecca Felton "evoked a surprisingly large and sympathetic response from the North" in the 1890s. Williamson also comments on Tillman's popularity with northern audiences (p. 261). On northern concerns regarding immigrant and working-class sexuality, see John D'Emilio and Estelle Freedman, *Intimate Matters: A History of Sexuality in America* (New York, 1988), 183–84, 194–201. Letter of Thomas Collins, November 24, 1898, Rebecca Felton Papers.

59. Letter of Mary Allen, 1898, and letter of Fannie Guilliams, November 18, 1898, Rebecca Felton Papers. I am extremely grateful to Leon Litwack for sharing these references from the Felton Papers with me.

60. Van Deburg, *Slavery and Race*, 78–79; Grand Army of the Republic, *Decoration Day, New York, May 30, 1882 and Decoration Day, Report of Proceedings, New York, May 30, 1883* (New York, 1883), 94.

61. James McPherson, *The Abolitionist Legacy: From Reconstruction to the NAACP* (Princeton, 1975), 132–33; clipping, June 17, 1888, and clipping, Indianapolis *Sentinel*, September 23, 1888, reel 24, Anna E. Dickinson Papers, LC.

62. Douglass's crusade for remembering slavery and the war is recounted in David Blight, "'For Something beyond the Battlefield': Frederick Douglass and the Struggle for the Memory of the Civil War," *Journal of American History* 75 (March 1989): 1156–78; Douglass quoted in ibid., 1161; Kansas *State Ledger*, May 26, 1893.

63. Dunbar's antidialect sentiments are expressed in his letter, November 16, 1892, reel 1, microfilm edition, Paul Laurence Dunbar Papers, Ohio Historical Society, Columbus, Ohio; letter of Will Marion Cook, March 29, 1901, in *The Booker T. Washington Papers*, 9 vols., ed. Louis Harlan and Ray Smock (Urbana, Ill., 1972–82), 6:67. For an interesting interpretation of Dunbar and his contemporaries, see Dickson D. Bruce, Jr., *Black American Writing from the Nadir: The Evolution of a Literary Tradition, 1877–1915* (Baton Rouge, 1989), 56–135.

CHAPTER SIX

1. Robert Wiebe, *The Search for Order, 1877–1920* (New York, 1967), 76–110.

2. Alan Trachtenberg, *The Incorporation of America: Culture and Society in the Gilded Age* (New York, 1982), 179–81; Wallace Evans Davies, *Patriotism on Parade: The Story of Veterans' and Hereditary Organizations in America, 1783–1900* (Cambridge, Mass., 1955), 216–17.

3. For more on the patriotic upsurge of the late nineteenth century, see Merle Curti, *The Roots of American Loyalty* (New York, 1946), 173–99. Grand Army of the Republic, *Journal of the Twenty-Sixth National Encampment* (Albany, N.Y., 1892), 82.

4. Holmes quoted in George Fredrickson, *The Inner Civil War: Northern Intellectuals and the Crisis of the Union* (New York, 1968), 220; Sons of the American Revolution, *Proceedings of the Second Annual Congress . . . Held at Hartford, Connecticut* (New York, 1891), 64.

5. William C. Doane, "Patriotism: Its Defects, Its Dangers, and Its Duties," *North American Review* 166 (March 1898): 320; Reverend Charles L. Kloss, *The New Patriotism. Sermon . . . Delivered at the Public Memorial Service of Ransom Post, No. 131, Department of Missouri, Grand Army of the Republic* (N.p., [1901?]), 5–6.

6. Letter of George William Curtis, June 29, 1891, J. C. Hemphill Papers, Box 8, Special Collections Library, Duke University; Grand Army of the Republic, *Memorial Services of Post No. 2. Department of Pennsylvania* (Philadelphia, 1894), 29.

7. Grand Army of the Republic, *Journal of the Twelfth Annual Session of the Department Encampment. Department of Nebraska* (Schuyler, Nebr., 1888), 91; McMaster quoted in Mary Dearing, *Veterans in Politics* (Baton Rouge, 1952), 483. For more on the GAR's textbook campaign, see Dearing, *Veterans in Politics*, 402–5.

8. Sons of the American Revolution, *Proceedings of the Second Annual Congress*, 64; McDowell quoted in Davies, *Patriotism on Parade*, 277.

9. Jacqueline Goggin, "Politics, Patriotism, and Professionalism: American Women Historians and the Preservation of Southern Culture, 1890–1940" (Unpublished paper, 1989); Mrs. Lucian Cocke quoted in ibid., 5; Mrs. Hugh Hagan, "The Daughters of the American Revolution as Represented in Georgia," *American Monthly Magazine* 1 (September 1892). Although many of the founding members of the DAR were southern and the organization worked to spread its influence in the South, the DAR apparently achieved only moderate success in building up a southern base. This lack of success can, in part, be explained by the much greater influence of rival organizations such as the United Daughters of the Confederacy.

10. Anonymous Diary, 1897, Gates and Moore Family Papers, Rare and Manuscript Collections, University Library, Cornell University; letter of H. Houston, April 6, 1889, Thomas W. Bicknell Papers, AAS.

11. J. Harris Knowles, *From Summer Land to Summer; A Journey from*

Thomasville, Georgia to New York During April and May, 1899 (New York, 1899), 80–81; E. McCracken, "Southern Women and the Reconstruction," *Outlook* 75 (November 21, 1903): 701–2.

12. WRC quoted in Davies, *Patriotism on Parade*, 219.

13. Kloss, *New Patriotism*, 12.

14. Theodore Roosevelt, "What 'Americanism' Means," *Forum* 17 (April 1894): 201; Theodore Roosevelt, "The Monroe Doctrine," reprinted in Theodore Roosevelt, *American Ideals, and Other Essays, Social and Political* (New York, 1897), 241. Thanks to Gail Bederman for calling my attention to the second Roosevelt quote and for making this and other Roosevelt references available to me.

15. For more on the "masculinity" crisis in the late nineteenth century and the search for a more aggressive and active image of manliness, see, for example, John Higham, "The Reorientation of American Culture in the 1890s," in *Writing American History: Essays on Modern Scholarship*, ed. John Higham (Bloomington, Ind., 1970), 73–102; E. Anthony Rotundo, "Body and Soul: Changing Ideals of American Middle-Class Manhood, 1770–1920," *Journal of Social History* 16 (Fall 1983): 23–38; and Carroll Smith-Rosenberg, "The New Woman as Androgyne: Social Disorder and Gender Crisis, 1870–1936," in *Disorderly Conduct: Visions of Gender in Victorian America* (New York, 1985), 245–96. Examining the "anti-modernism" of some disgruntled American intellectuals, T. J. Jackson Lears in *No Place of Grace: Antimodernism and the Transformation of American Culture, 1880–1920* (New York, 1981) also surveys the interest in manly, martial activities on the part of those who rejected the more self-consciously bourgeois ideology of Theodore Roosevelt. George Fredrickson in *The Inner Civil War*, 220–25, explores northern intellectuals' postwar search for virility in the experience of the Civil War. On the masculinity crisis in the South, see Joel Williamson, *The Crucible of Race* (New York, 1984).

16. On the "New Woman," see Smith-Rosenberg, "The New Woman as Androgyne." Sheila Rothman, *Woman's Proper Place* (New York, 1978), 34–35, discusses the "vigorous femininity" model for female college students in the 1880s. Elliot J. Gorn, *The Manly Art* (Ithaca, 1986), 194–247, examines how middle-class men became attracted to notions of working-class virility as epitomized in their fascination with lower-class prizefighting.

17. *Address of Theodore W. Bean of Norristown, Pennsylvania, Delivered at Seven Pines National Cemetery on Memorial Day, May 30, 1888, Under the Auspices of Phil Kearny Post No. 10, GAR of Richmond, Virginia* (Richmond, 1888), 5.

18. Dubuque *Daily Times*, May 31, 1892, May 31, 1894; Theodore Roosevelt, "Brotherhood and the Heroic Virtues" and "Latitude and Longitude Among Reformers," in Theodore Roosevelt, *The Strenuous Life: Essays and Addresses* (New York, 1902), 266, 50.

19. Sons of Veterans, USA, *Journal of the Proceedings of the Sixteenth Annual Encampment* (Reading, Pa., 1897), 148; *Grand Army Record* 8 (December 1898): 91.

20. Godkin quoted in Stuart Charles McConnell, "A Social History of the Grand Army of the Republic, 1867–1900" (Ph.D. dissertation, Johns Hopkins University, 1987), 389; Brander Matthews, "A Decoration Day Revery," *Century Magazine* 40 (May 1890): 103.

21. McConnell, "Social History of the GAR," 389–90; Henry B. Field, *Blood Is Thicker Than Water; a Few Days Among Our Southern Brethren* (New York, 1886), 70; Roosevelt quoted in Abbe Felix Klien, *In the Land of the Strenuous Life* (Chicago, 1905), 328.

22. The background and events connected with the Chicago memorial are recounted in John Cox Underwood, *Report of Proceedings Incidental to the Erection and Dedication of the Confederate Monument* (Chicago, 1896). For specific quotes, see pp. 33, 179, 187.

23. Octave Thanet, "The Farmer in the South," *Scribner's Magazine* 15 (April 1894): 399.

24. Grand Army of the Republic, *Memorial Ceremonies at Monument Cemetery, Philadelphia, Under the Auspices of Post No. 2, Department of Pennsylvania* (Philadelphia, 1890), 24; Henry B. Field, *Bright Skies and Dark Shadows* (New York, 1890), 315; Field, *Blood Is Thicker*, 49; Field, *Bright Skies*, 301; for more on the national cult of Robert E. Lee, including northern acceptance, see Thomas Connelly, *The Marble Man: Robert E. Lee and His Image in American Society* (Baton Rouge, 1977).

25. For a further discussion of northerners and their reactions to southern lynching, see chapter 5; Walter Hines Page, "The Last Hold of the Southern Bully," *Forum* 16 (November 1893): 303.

26. My understanding of the way in which late-nineteenth-century theorists used the concept of "civilization" to highlight specific notions of race and gender is drawn from Gail Bederman, "Ida B. Well's Anti-Lynching Campaign (1892–94) and the Northern Middle Class' 'Masculinity Crisis'" (Paper presented at the Berkshire Conference of Women Historians, June 1990), 3–4.

27. Thanet, "Farmer in the South," 406; "I Am a Southern Gentleman," words by John DeWitt, music by W. H. Bontemps (1907).

28. Lears, *No Place of Grace*, 142–81; "I Am a Southern Gentleman"; N. S. Shaler, "The Peculiarities of the South," *North American Review* 151 (October 1890): 488.

29. Connelly, *Marble Man*, 117; Paul Nagel, "Reconstruction, Adams Style," *Journal of Southern History* 52 (February 1986): 11–13; Fredrickson, *Inner Civil War*, 170–71.

30. Charles Francis Adams, *Lee's Centennial, An Address* (Chicago, 1948), 54, 58, 63–64.

31. Ibid., 44–45; John Higham in "The Reorientation of American Culture" notes how a number of northern intellectuals of the late nineteenth century, including Charles Adams's brother Brooks, dismissed many of Roosevelt's ideas yet incorporated many of the new concepts of masculinity.

32. New York *World*, February 17, 1898; see, for an example of assessments of

southern strength in the Civil War, the article by Col. J. Thomas Scharf in the New York *World*, February 27, 1898; Mrs. Jefferson Davis, "Against a Foreign Foe the Nation Is as One Man," New York *World*, April 3, 1898, 35.

33. McKinley quoted in Gerald Linderman, *The Mirror of War* (Ann Arbor, 1974), 35. Gaines Foster, *Ghosts of the Confederacy: Defeat, the Lost Cause, and the Emergence of the New South, 1865–1913* (New York, 1987), 145–59, ably explores the conciliatory components of the Spanish-American War, mainly from the southern standpoint. Undated flyer; undated Boston review; February 28, 1899, review, *Shenandoah* clippings file, NYPLPA, Theater Collection.

34. "Patriotic Confederate Veterans," *Independent* 52 (July 5, 1900): 1629.

35. George Fredrickson, *The Black Image in the White Mind: The Debate on Afro-American Character and Destiny, 1817–1914* (Middletown, Conn., 1987), 305–11; Michael Rogin, "'The Sword Became a Flashing Vision': D. W. Griffith's *The Birth of a Nation*," *Representations* 9 (Winter 1985), also examines the impact of the Spanish-American War on the racial ideology of southerners like Dixon and Woodrow Wilson, although from a perspective somewhat different from Fredrickson's. Thomas Dixon, *The Leopard's Spots* (Ridgewood, N.J., 1967), 412.

36. "The Race Problem. A Symposium," *Arena* 21 (April 1899): 421; John T. Bramhall, "The Red, Black and Yellow," *Overland Monthly*, n.s. 37 (February 1901): 722–26. Not surprisingly, many African Americans resisted the racially oriented reunion message that emerged during the Spanish-American War. For an analysis of their response to the war, see Willard B. Gatewood, Jr., *Black Americans and the White Man's Burden, 1898–1903* (Urbana, Ill., 1975), esp. 180–221, 300–319.

37. G. Edward White, *The Eastern Establishment and the Western Experience* (New Haven, 1968), 154–55; Roosevelt quoted in ibid., 161.

38. Roosevelt, "Monroe Doctrine," 241; New York *World*, February 9, 11, 1898; Linderman, *Mirror of War*, 131; *New York Times*, April 28, 1898.

39. "A Lee Incident," New York *World*, April 1, 1898; Dubuque *Daily Times*, May 29, 1898; "The Re-United States," words by Q. E. Browning, music by C. H. Dummer (1898); "The Blue and Gray Together," words and music by C. H. Addison (1898).

40. Preface to *The Leopard's Spots*, enclosed with letter, Thomas Dixon to Wallace H. Cathcart, October 29, 1901, Thomas Dixon Papers, Special Collections Department, Robert W. Woodruff Library, Emory University. Dixon, *The Leopard's Spots*, 443, 440.

41. Dixon, *The Leopard's Spots*, 86; Thomas Dixon, *The Clansman: An Historical Romance of the Ku-Klux Klan* (Lexington, Ky., 1970), 98, 149.

42. Thomas Nelson Page, *Red Rock* (New York, 1909); B. W. Wells, "Southern Literature of the Year," *Forum* 29 (June 1900): 501.

43. Roosevelt quoted in Trachtenberg, *Incorporation of America*, 13; for more on this late-nineteenth-century image of the West, see ibid., 11–37.

44. Ibid., 11–17; Frederick Jackson Turner, "The Significance of the Frontier in American History," in *Frontier and Section: Selected Essays of Frederick Jack-*

son Turner, with an introduction by Ray Allen Billington (Englewood Cliffs, N.J., 1961), 37–62. Turner's thesis should be placed in the context of new concerns for balance and "objectivity" in the historical profession which were arising at the time. On this, see Peter Novick, *That Noble Dream: The "Objectivity Question" and the American Historical Profession* (Cambridge, 1988), 63–80.

45. Review of *The Virginian* in *Nation* 75 (October 23, 1902): 331.

46. Darwin Payne, *Owen Wister* (Dallas, Tex., 1985), 3–27; Ben M. Vorpahl, *My Dear Wister: The Frederic Remington–Owen Wister Letters* (Palo Alto, Calif., 1972), 5.

47. Payne, *Owen Wister*, 29–45; "Rededication and Preface" in Owen Wister, *The Virginian: A Horseman of the Plains* (New York, 1979). For more on the ideological affinities between Wister and Roosevelt, see White, *Eastern Establishment*.

48. Payne, *Owen Wister*, 77–90; Wister quoted in Vorpahl, *My Dear Wister*, 20; Owen Wister, "The Evolution of the Cowpuncher," *Harper's New Monthly Magazine* 91 (September 1895): 610.

49. Fanny Kemble Wister, ed., *Owen Wister Out West: His Journals and Letters* (Chicago, 1958), 246; Wister, "The Evolution of the Cowpuncher," 608.

50. Although he does not discuss southerners who became cowboys, Daniel Sutherland in *The Confederate Carpetbaggers* (Baton Rouge, 1988), 17, refers to one Louisianan who saw swarms of southerners in San Francisco. Vorpahl, *My Dear Wister*, 54, 291–93; Frederic Remington, "A Sergeant of Orphan Troop," *Harper's Monthly* 95 (August 1897): 327–36.

51. Owen Wister, "Em'ly," *Harper's Monthly* 87 (November 1893): 941–48.

52. Wister, *The Virginian*, 8. My view of male hegemony in *The Virginian* is derived largely from Lee Clark Mitchell, "'When You Call Me That . . . ': Tall Talk and Male Hegemony in *The Virginian*," *Publication of the Modern Language Association* 102 (January 1987): 66–77.

53. Wister quoted in Julian Mason, "A Symposium: Owen Wister and the South," *Southern Humanities Review* 6 (Winter 1972): 25; Mitchell, "'When You Call Me That . . . ,'" 70–72; Wister, *The Virginian*, 91, 281.

54. Wister, *The Virginian*, 272–73; for more on northern views of southern lynching, see chapter 5.

55. James Schouler, *History of the United States of America, Under the Constitution*, vol. 6 (New York, 1899), 319–20. In a letter to Frederick Turner, Schouler confessed that "one cannot in truth picture both North and South . . . as equally right in their cause" (Novick, *That Noble Dream*, 84).

56. Owen Wister, *Lady Baltimore* (Ridgewood, N.J., 1968), 78, 157.

SELECT BIBLIOGRAPHY

PRIMARY SOURCES

Archives and Manuscript Collections

Ann Arbor, Michigan
  Bentley Historical Library
    Buchanan Family Papers
  William L. Clements Library, University of Michigan
    American Travel Collection
Athens, Georgia
  Hargrett Rare Book and Manuscript Library, University of Georgia
    Rebecca Felton Papers
Atlanta, Georgia
  Special Collections Department, Robert W. Woodruff Library, Emory University
    Thomas Dixon Papers
Boston, Massachusetts
  Boston Public Library
    William Lloyd Garrison Papers
    Thomas W. Higginson Papers
  Massachusetts Historical Society
    Charles Francis Adams II Papers
    Edward Atkinson Papers
    William Lloyd Garrison Papers
    Edward Kinsley Papers
    Amory A. Lawrence Papers
    Charles Lawrence Peirson Papers
    Sarah G. Putnam Papers
Cambridge, Massachusetts
  Harvard Theater Collection, Harvard University
    Miscellaneous Theater Files
  Houghton Library, Harvard University
    Thomas B. Aldrich Papers
    William C. Clapp Papers
    E. L. Godkin Papers

Henry Lee Higginson Papers
Thomas W. Higginson Papers
Houghton-Mifflin Papers
William Dean Howells Papers
Miscellaneous Papers
Charles Eliot Norton Papers
Walter Hines Page Papers
Carlisle, Pennsylvania
Dickinson College Library
Robert Bridges Papers
Chapel Hill, North Carolina
Southern Historical Collection, University of North Carolina at Chapel Hill
John Luther Bridgers Papers
John Fox Papers
Maurice Family Papers
Mary Murfree Papers
Margaret Preston Papers
George Wesley Race Diary
Slack Family Papers
Albion W. Tourgee Papers
Charlottesville, Virginia
Manuscripts Division, Special Collections Department, Clifton Waller Barrett
Library, University of Virginia Library
Richard Harding Davis Collection (#6109)
Thomas Nelson Page Collection (#8641)
Durham, North Carolina
Special Collections Library, Duke University
Thomas Dixon Papers
Branner Easterly Papers
Joel Chandler Harris Papers
Paul Hamilton Hayne Papers
William Hayne Papers
James C. Hemphill Papers
Munford-Ellis Family Papers
John Greenleaf Whittier Papers
Ithaca, New York
Rare and Manuscript Collections, University Library, Cornell University
Gates and Moore Family Papers
Madison, Wisconsin
State Historical Society of Wisconsin
Gideon Allen Papers
New Orleans, Louisiana
Howard-Tilton Memorial Library, Tulane University
George W. Cable Papers

New York, New York
  New York Public Library for the Performing Arts
    Miscellaneous Files from the Music Collection
    Miscellaneous Files from the Theater Collection
  Rare Books and Manuscripts Division, New York Public Library, Astor,
    Lenox, and Tilden Foundations
    Edward Atkinson Papers
    Baldwin-McDowell Papers
    Andrew Carnegie Papers
    Century Papers
    William C. Church Papers
    Walter Fleming Papers
    Richard W. Gilder Papers
    Horace Greeley Papers
    Levi Hayden Diary
    Robert U. Johnson Papers
    MacMillan Papers
    John Walcott Phelps Papers
    Unknown Soldier Diary
Northampton, Massachusetts
  Sophia Smith Collection, Smith College
    Garrison Family Papers
Salem, Massachusetts
  James Duncan Phillips Library, Peabody and Essex Museum
    Waters Family Papers
San Marino, California
  Huntington Library
    Anonymous Diary (1868)
Washington, D.C.
  Library of Congress
    James D. and David R. Barbee Papers
    Mary Ann Bickerdyke Papers
    Breckinridge Family Papers
    Broadsides Collection
    George W. Cable Papers
    Anna E. Dickinson Papers
    Thomas Dixon Papers
    Paul Laurence Dunbar Papers
    Mary E. Freeman Papers
    E. N. Gilpin Papers
    Grand Army of the Republic Papers
    Harrison Family Papers
    Harper's Magazine Papers
    Josiah Gilbert Holland Papers

Jedediah Hotchkiss Papers
James Knox Papers
John Alexander Logan Papers
Edward Morley Papers
Robert Ogden Papers
Abram Parmenter Diary
Edmund Poole Papers
Sons of the American Revolution Records
Benjamin Ticknor Papers
U.S. Sanitary Commission Scrapbook
Henry Watterson Papers
Owen Wister Papers
National Museum of American History Archives Center, Smithsonian Institution
Warshaw Collection
Sam DeVincent Collection of Illustrated American Sheet Music
Smithsonian Institution Archives
Exposition Records of the Smithsonian Institution and United States National Museum
White Sulphur Springs, West Virginia
Greenbrier Archives
Miscellaneous Papers
Worcester, Massachusetts
American Antiquarian Society
Thomas W. Bicknell Papers
Abigail K. Foster Papers
Charles Washburn Papers
Caroline Barret White Papers

Memoirs, Letters, and Diaries

Abbott, Martin, ed. "A New Englander in the South, 1865." *New England Quarterly* 32 (September 1959): 388–93.

Adams, Henry. *The Education of Henry Adams.* Boston, 1918.

Ames, Mary. *From a New England Woman's Diary in Dixie in 1865.* Norwood, Mass., 1906.

Benham, George C. *A Year of Wreck; a True Story by a Victim.* New York, 1880.

Biddle, Mrs. Ellen. *Reminiscences of a Soldier's Wife.* Philadelphia, 1907.

Bikle, Lucy L. C. *George W. Cable: His Life and Letters.* New York, 1928.

Boney, F. N., ed. *A Union Soldier in the Land of the Vanquished: The Diary of Sergeant Mathew Woodruff, June–December, 1865.* University, Ala., 1969.

Botume, Elizabeth Hyde. *First Days Amongst the Contrabands.* Boston, 1898. Reprint. New York, 1968.

DeForest, John William. *A Union Officer in the Reconstruction.* Edited by James H. Croushore and David M. Potter. New Haven, 1948.

"George W. Julian's Journal—The Assassination of Lincoln." *Indiana Magazine of History* 2 (1915): 324–37.

Gilder, Rosamond, ed. *Letters of Richard Watson Gilder.* Boston, 1916.

Greeley, Horace. *Recollections of a Busy Life.* New York, 1968.

Helen Griffith, ed. *Dauntless in Mississippi: The Life of Sarah Dickey, 1838–1904.* South Hadley, Mass., 1966.

Hamilton, Holman, and Gayle Thornbrough, eds. *Indianapolis in the 'Gay Nineties': High School Diaries of Claude G. Bowers.* Indianapolis, 1964.

Harlan, Louis, and Ray Smock, eds. *The Booker T. Washington Papers.* 9 vols. Urbana, Ill., 1972–82.

Harris, Julia Collier, ed. *The Life and Letters of Joel Chandler Harris.* Boston and New York, 1918.

Higginson, Mary Thatcher, ed. *Letters and Journals of Thomas Wentworth Higginson, 1846–1906.* New York, 1921.

Higginson, Thomas. *Cheerful Yesterdays.* Boston, 1900.

Holland, Rupert S., ed. *Letters and Diary of Laura M. Towne, Written from the Sea Islands of South Carolina, 1862–1884.* New York, 1969.

Hubbell, Jay B. "Some New Letters of Constance Fenimore Woolson." *New England Quarterly* 14 (December 1941): 715–35.

Hughes, Sarah Forbes, ed. *Letters and Recollections of John Murray Forbes.* 2 vols. Boston and New York, 1899.

Ingalls, Fay. *The Valley Road.* Cleveland, 1949.

Jaquette, Henrietta S., ed. *South after Gettysburg: Letters of Cornelia Hancock, 1863–1865.* Philadelphia, 1937.

Johnson, Robert Underwood. *Remembered Yesterdays.* Boston, 1923.

Leigh, Frances Butler. *Ten Years on a Georgia Plantation Since the War.* New York, 1969.

Lynch, Charles H. *The Civil War Diary, 1862–1865, of Charles H. Lynch, 18th Connecticut Volunteers.* Hartford, 1915.

Marchione, William. "Go South, Young Man! Reconstruction Letters of a Massachusetts Yankee." *South Carolina Historical Magazine* 80 (January 1979): 18–35.

"A Memory: Lincoln's Body Comes to Albany." *New York History* 46 (1965): 187–88.

Mohr, James C., ed. *The Cormany Diaries: A Northern Family in the Civil War.* Pittsburgh, 1982.

Mooney, Chase C., ed. "A Union Chaplain's Diary." *Proceedings of the New Jersey Historical Society* 75 (January 1957): 1–17.

Moore, John H., ed. "The Last Officer—April, 1865." *South Carolina Historical Magazine* 67 (January 1966): 1–14.

Morton, Richard, ed. "Life in Virginia by a 'Yankee Teacher,' Margaret Newbold Thorpe." *Virginia Magazine of History and Biography* 64 (April 1956): 180–207.

Mugleston, William F., ed. "The Freedmen's Bureau and Reconstruction in Virginia." *Virginia Magazine of History and Biography* 86 (January 1978): 45–102.

Nevins, Allan, and Milton H. Thomas, eds. *The Diary of George Templeton Strong.* 4 vols. New York, 1952.

Newberry, Julia. *Julia Newberry's Diary.* Introduction by Margaret Ayer Barnes and Janet Ayer Fairbank. New York, 1933.

Pearson, Elizabeth Ware, ed. *Letters from Port Royal, 1862–1868.* Boston, 1906.

Perry, Bliss. *Life and Letters of Henry Lee Higginson.* New York, 1921.

Richards, Caroline Cowles. *Village Life in America, 1852–1872, Including the Period of the American Civil War as Told in the Diary of a School-Girl.* Introduction by Margaret E. Sangster. New York, 1913.

Stearns, Charles. *The Black Man of the South, and the Rebels.* New York, 1872.

Sylvis, James C., ed. *The Life, Speeches, Labors, and Essays of William H. Sylvis.* Philadelphia, 1872.

Trowbridge, John T. *My Own Story.* Boston and New York, 1903.

Vorpahl, Ben M. *My Dear Wister: The Frederic Remington–Owen Wister Letters.* Palo Alto, Calif., 1972.

Wainwright, Nicholas B., ed. *A Philadelphia Perspective: The Diary of Sidney George Fisher Covering the Years 1834–1871.* Philadelphia, 1967.

Wister, Fanny Kemble, ed. *Owen Wister Out West: His Journals and Letters.* Chicago, 1958.

Wittenmyer, Annie. *Under the Guns: A Woman's Reminiscences of the Civil War.* Boston, 1895.

Travel and Tourist Accounts and Promotional Pamphlets

Allen, James Lane. *The Bluegrass Region of Kentucky and other Kentucky Articles.* New York, 1892.

Andrews, Sidney. *The South Since the War, as Shown by Fourteen Weeks of Travel and Observation in Georgia and the Carolinas.* Boston, 1866.

Appleton's Handbook of American Travel, Southern Tour. New York, 1866.

Barry, Richard. *Snap Shots on the Midway of the Pan-American Exposition.* Buffalo, N.Y., 1901.

Beadle, John H. *The Undeveloped West; or, Five Years in the Territories.* Philadelphia, 1873.

Beecher, Eunice White. *Letters from Florida.* New York, 1879.

Beecher, Henry Ward. *A Circuit of the Continent: Account of a Tour Through the West and South.* New York, 1884.

Bishop, Nathaniel H. *Four Months in a Sneak-Box. A Boat Voyage of 2600 Miles Down the Ohio and Mississippi Rivers.* Boston and New York, 1879.

Brinton, Daniel G. *A Guidebook of Florida and the South, For Tourists, In-*

valids, and Emigrants. Philadelphia and Jacksonville, 1869. Reprint. Gainesville, Fla., 1978.

Bryant, William C., ed. *Picturesque America; or, the Land We Live In.* New York, 1872.

Butterworth, Hezekiah. *A Zig-Zag Journey in the Sunny South.* Boston, 1887.

Champney, Lizzie W. *Three Vassar Girls at Home; A Holiday Trip of Three College Girls Through the South and West.* Boston, 1888.

Chesapeake and Ohio Railway Company. *Virginia in Black and White.* Washington, D.C., 1893.

———. *Virginia Vistas, C&O Route.* [1888?].

Clemens, Samuel [Mark Twain]. *Life on the Mississippi.* Boston, 1883. Reprint. New York, 1976.

Conwell, Russell. *Magnolia Journey: A Union Veteran Revisits the Former Confederate States.* Boston, 1869. Reprint. University, Ala., 1974.

Cory, Charles Barney. *Southern Rambles.* Boston, 1881.

Cowan, Reverend John F. *A New Invasion of the South.* New York, 1881.

Cutter, Charles. *Cutter's Guide to the Hot Springs of Arkansas.* St. Louis, Mo., 1893.

Dearborn, Dr. R. F. *Saratoga, and How to See It.* Albany, N.Y., 1873.

Dennett, John R. *The South as It Is, 1865–66.* New York, 1965. Reprint. Athens, Ga., 1986.

Dodge, Mary Abigail [Gail Hamilton]. *Wool-Gathering.* Boston, 1867.

Emery, Miss E. B. *Letters from the South, on the Social, Intellectual, and Moral Conditions of the Colored People.* Boston, 1880.

Field, Henry B. *Blood Is Thicker Than Water; a Few Days Among Our Southern Brethren.* New York, 1886.

———. *Bright Skies and Dark Shadows.* New York, 1890.

Fleming, Thomas. *Around the "Pan" with Uncle Hank.* New York, 1901.

"Florida Journal of Charles K. Landis." *Vineland Historical Magazine* 26 (October 1941): 255–60.

"A Florida Settler of 1877—The Diary of Erastus G. Hill." *Florida Historical Quarterly* 41 (April 1950): 271–95.

Ford, E. A. *A Handbook of the South.* Chicago, 1890.

French, Justus C. *The Trip of the Steamer Oceanus to Fort Sumter and Charleston, South Carolina. . . .* Brooklyn, 1865.

Gatchell, Edwin A. *The Standard Guide to Asheville and Western North Carolina.* Asheville, N.C., 1887.

Goddard, Frederick Bartlett. *Where to Emigrate and Why. . . .* Philadelphia, 1869.

Gosson, Louis C. *Post-Bellum Campaigns of the Blue and Gray, 1881–1882.* Trenton, N.J., 1882.

Graves, John Temple. *The Winter Resorts of Florida, South Georgia, Louisiana, Texas, California, Mexico, and Cuba.* New York, 1883.

Greeley, Horace. *Mr. Greeley's Letters from Texas and the Lower Mississippi.* New York, 1871.

Green, James. *The Dream of "Ellen N."; An Illustrated Descriptive and Historical Narrative of Southern Travels.* Cincinnati, 1886.

Hamsun, Knut. *The Cultural Life of Modern America.* Cambridge, Mass., 1969.

Harrison, Z. *Description of the Cincinnati Southern Railway from Cincinnati to Chattanooga.* Cincinnati, 1878.

Hillyard, M. B. *The New South.* Baltimore, 1887.

Keasbey, Anthony Q. *From the Hudson to the St. Johns.* Newark, N.J., 1874.

Kelley, William D. *The Old South and the New.* New York, 1888.

King, Edward. *The Great South.* Baton Rouge, 1972.

Knowles, J. Harris. *From Summer Land to Summer; A Journey from Thomasville, Georgia to New York During April and May, 1899.* New York, 1899.

Loring, Frederick W., and C. F. Atkinson. *Cotton Culture and the South Considered with Reference to Emigration.* Boston, 1869.

MacCorkle, William A. *The White Sulphur Springs.* New York, 1916.

Mahaffey, Joseph H., ed. "Carl Schurz's Letters from the South." *Georgia Historical Quarterly* 35 (September 1951): 222–57.

Moorman, John Jennings. *Mineral Springs of North America.* Philadelphia, 1873.

———. *Virginia White Sulphur Springs.* Baltimore, 1869.

Muir, John. *A Thousand Mile Walk to the Gulf.* Boston and New York, 1916.

Nordhoff, Charles. *The Cotton States in the Spring and Summer of 1875.* New York, 1876.

Official Catalogue and Guide Book to the Pan-American Exposition. Buffalo, N.Y., 1901.

Olmsted, Frederick Law. *The Cotton Kingdom: A Traveller's Observations on Cotton and Slavery in the American Slave States.* Edited and with an Introduction by Arthur M. Schlesinger. New York, 1953. Reprint. New York, 1969.

Pike, J.S. *The Prostrate State.* New York and Evanston, 1968.

Powers, Stephen. *Afoot and Alone; a Walk from Sea to Sea by the Southern Route.* Hartford, Conn., 1872.

Prentis, Noble Lovely. *Southern Letters.* Topeka, Kans., 1881.

Presbrey, Frank. *The Empire of the South: An Exposition of the Present Resources and Development of the South, 1899.* Washington, D.C., 1898.

———. *The Land of the Sky—Western North Carolina.* [1900?].

Proctor, Samuel, ed. "Leaves from a Travel Diary: A Visit to Augusta and Savannah, 1882." *Georgia Historical Quarterly* 41 (1957): 309–15.

Ralph, Julian. *Dixie; or Southern Scenes and Sketches.* New York, 1896.

The Red Sulphur Springs, Monroe County, West Virginia. Baltimore, 1870.

Reid, Whitelaw. *After the War: A Southern Tour.* Cincinnati and New York, 1866.

Richmond and Danville Railroad. *The Summer of 1882 Among the Health Resorts of Northeast Georgia, Upper South Carolina, Western North Carolina, and Virginia.* New York, 1882.

Sargeant, Angelina M. *Notes of Travel and Mementoes of Friendship*. Rochester, N.Y., 1894.

The Scenic Attractions and Summer Resorts Along the Railways of the Virginia, Tennessee and Georgia Air Line. New York, 1883.

"Second Florida Journal of Charles K. Landis." *Vineland Historical Magazine* 27 (January 1942): 277–85.

Stowe, Harriet Beecher. *Palmetto Leaves*. Boston, 1873.

Trowbridge, John T. *The Desolate South*. Hartford, Conn., 1866.

Warner, Charles Dudley. *Studies in the South and West with Comments on Canada*. New York, 1889.

Watkins, N. J., ed. *The Pine and the Palm Greeting*. Baltimore, 1873.

"A Woman Abolitionist Views the South in 1875." *Georgia Historical Quarterly* (December 1948): 241–51.

Addresses, Official Proceedings, and Memorial Day Books

Adams, Charles Francis. *Lee at Appomattox and Other Papers*. Freeport, N.Y., 1970.

———. *Lee's Centennial, An Address*. Chicago, 1948.

Address by Col. Edward Jay Allen to McPherson Post No. 117, Grand Army of the Republic at Homewood Cemetery, Pittsburgh on Memorial Day, 1901. Pittsburgh, 1901.

An Address by Norwood Penrose Hallowell. Boston, 1896.

Address delivered by Hon. Moses E. Clapp at the Memorial Exercises Held at Gettysburg, Pa., on May 30, 1914. Washington, D.C., 1914.

Address of Edward Atkinson of Boston, Mass. Given in Atlanta, Georgia in October, 1880, for the Promotion of an International Cotton Exhibition. Boston, 1880.

Address of Theodore W. Bean of Norristown, Pennsylvania, Delivered at Seven Pines National Cemetery on Memorial Day, May 30, 1888, Under the Auspices of Phil Kearny Post No. 10, GAR of Richmond, Virginia. Richmond, 1888.

Dumont, N., ed. *What Northern Men Say of the South*. Charlotte, N.C., 1879.

Faehtz, Ernest. *National Memorial Day*. Washington, D.C., 1870.

Fatout, Paul, ed. *Mark Twain Speaking*. Iowa City, 1976.

Grady, Henry W. *The New South and other Addresses*. New York, 1904.

Grand Army of the Republic. *Decoration Day, New York, May 30, 1882 and Decoration Day, Report of Proceedings, New York, May 30, 1883*. New York, 1883.

———. *Journal of the Nineteenth Annual Session of the National Encampment of 1885 of the Grand Army of the Republic*. Toledo, 1885.

———. *Journal of the Thirtieth National Encampment*. Indianapolis, 1896.

———. *Journal of the Twelfth Annual Session of the Department Encampment. Department of Nebraska*. Schuyler, Nebr., 1888.

————. *Journal of the Twenty-Fifth National Encampment.* Rutland, Vt., 1891.

————. *Journal of the Twenty-Second Annual Encampment of the Department of Vermont.* Brattleboro, Vt., 1889.

————. *Journal of the Twenty-Second Annual Session of the National Encampment.* Minneapolis, 1888.

————. *Journal of the Twenty-Sixth National Encampment.* Albany, N.Y., 1892.

————. *Memorial Ceremonies at Monument Cemetery, Philadelphia, Under the Auspices of Post No. 2, Department of Pennsylvania.* Philadelphia, 1870–99.

————. *Memorial Ceremonies at the National Cemetery, Arlington, Virginia, Under the Auspices of the Grand Army of the Republic.* Washington, D.C., 1868.

————. *Memorial Services of Commemoration Day, Held in Canton, May 29, 1880, Under the Auspices of Revere Encampment, Post 94, Grand Army of the Republic.* Boston, 1880.

————. *Memorial Services of Post No. 2. Department of Pennsylvania.* Philadelphia, 1890–99.

————. *Memorial Ceremonies of Post No. 2, Grand Army of the Republic, Philadelphia, Department of Pennsylvania, 1880–1889.* Philadelphia, 1889.

————. *Proceedings of the Sixth Annual Encampment. Department of North Dakota.* Grand Forks, N.D., 1895.

Holmes, Oliver Wendell. *Speeches.* Boston, 1896.

Kloss, Reverend Charles L. *The New Patriotism. Sermon . . . Delivered at the Public Memorial Service of Ransom Post, No. 131, Department of Missouri, Grand Army of the Republic.* N.p., [1901?].

Mackay, Constance D. *Memorial Day Pageant.* New York, 1916.

Memorial Day Address by Franklin G. Fessenden before Edwin E. Day Post, Grand Army of the Republic, Greenfield, Mass. Greenfield, Mass., 1915.

Memorial Day Programme. Quincy, Calif., 1895.

Robertson, Charles A. *Oration.* Albany, N.Y., 1875.

Roosevelt, Theodore. *The Strenuous Life: Essays and Addresses.* New York, 1902.

Saunders, Frederick, ed. *Our National Centennial Jubilee . . . on the Fourth of July, 1876, in the Several States of the Union.* New York, 1877.

Schauffler, Robert H. *Memorial Day: Its Celebration, Spirit and Significance as Related in Prose and Verse.* New York, 1911.

Shedd, J. A. *Practical Memorial Day Exercises.* Lebanon, Ohio, 1892.

Sons of Veterans, USA. *Journal of Proceedings of Annual Encampments.* 1885–98.

Sumner, Charles A. *Memorial Day Oration.* San Francisco, 1888.

Underwood, John Cox. *Report of Proceedings Incidental to the Erection and Dedication of the Confederate Monument.* Chicago, 1896.

The West Point Centennial Historic Oration by Major Henry C. Dane. New York, 1878.

Women's Relief Corps. *Journals of the National Convention.* 1883–98.

Novels and Short Story Collections

Adams, Henry. *Democracy.* New York, 1961.

Adams, William T. [Oliver Optic]. *Fighting Joe.* New York, 1865.

———. *An Undivided Union.* New York, 1899.

Beecher, Henry Ward. *Norwood: Or, Village Life in New England.* New York, 1868.

Brady, Cyrus Townsend. *A Little Traitor to the South.* New York, 1904.

———. *The Southerners.* New York, 1906.

Churchill, Winston. *The Crisis.* New York, 1900.

Clemens, Samuel [Mark Twain]. *The Adventures of Huckleberry Finn.* Berkeley, Calif., 1985.

———. *Pudd'nhead Wilson.* New York, 1972.

Clemens, Samuel [Mark Twain], and Charles Dudley Warner. *The Gilded Age.* New York, 1873.

DeForest, John W. *The Bloody Chasm.* New York, 1881.

———. *Kate Beaumont.* Boston, 1872.

———. *Miss Ravenal's Conversion From Secession to Loyalty.* New York, 1867. Reprint. New York, 1968.

Dixon, Thomas. *The Clansman: An Historical Romance of the Ku-Klux Klan.* Lexington, Ky., 1970.

———. *The Leopard's Spots.* Ridgewood, N.J., 1967.

Fox, John, Jr. *The Kentuckians; a Knight of the Cumberland.* New York, 1910.

———. *The Little Shepherd of Kingdom Come.* New York, 1903.

Harris, Joel Chandler. *Mingo.* Boston, 1884.

———. *Uncle Remus: His Songs and Sayings.* New York, 1921.

Holley, Marietta. *Samantha Among the Colored Folks.* New York, 1898.

Holmes, Mary Jane. *Rose Mather.* New York, 1868.

James, Henry. *The Bostonians.* London, 1977.

Johnston, Annie Fellows. *The Little Colonel.* Boston, 1896.

King, Charles. *The General's Double.* Philadelphia, 1898.

———. *Kitty's Conquest.* Philadelphia, 1884.

———. *A War-Time Wooing.* New York, 1888.

Murfree, Mary. *In the Tennessee Mountains.* Knoxville, Tenn., 1970.

Page, Thomas Nelson. *Red Rock.* New York, 1909.

Read, Opie. *The Jucklins.* Chicago, 1896.

———. *A Kentucky Colonel.* Chicago, 1889.

Roe, E. P. *Miss Lou.* New York, 1888.

Smith, Francis Hopkinson. *Colonel Carter of Cartersville.* New York, 1891.

Spencer, Bella. *Tried and True or Love and Loyalty.* Springfield, Mass., 1866.

Stockton, Frank. *The Late Mrs. Null.* New York, 1886.

Tourgee, Albion. *A Fool's Errand.* New York, 1879.

Wister, Owen. *Lady Baltimore.* Ridgewood, N.J., 1968.

———. *The Virginian: A Horseman of the Plains.* New York, 1979.

Woolson, Constance Fenimore. *For the Major and Selected Short Stories.* New Haven, 1967.

Contemporary Commentaries and Histories

Beecher, Catharine, and Harriet B. Stowe. *The American Woman's Home.* New York, 1869.

Blackwell, Henry B. *What the South Can Do.* 1867.

Cable, George Washington. *The Negro Question.* New York, 1888.

———. *The Silent South.* New York, 1885.

Dunne, Finley Peter. *Dissertations by Mr. Dooley.* New York, 1906.

Dunning, Nelson A., ed. *Farmers' Alliance History and Agricultural Digest.* Washington, D.C., 1891.

Eggleston, Edward. *A Household History of the United States and Its People.* New York, 1889.

Frost, William G. *University Extension in the Southern Mountains.* New York, 1898.

Goodrich, Charles. *History of the United States of America.* New York, 1880.

Goodrich, Samuel Griswold. *A Pictorial History of the United States, with Notices of Other Portions of America, North and South.* Philadelphia, 1867.

Harrison, Jonathan Baxter. *Certain Dangerous Tendencies in American Life, and Other Essays.* Boston, 1880.

Harvey, William H. ["Coin"]. *The Patriots of America.* Chicago, 1895.

Klien, Abbe Felix. *In the Land of the Strenuous Life.* Chicago, 1905.

Lease, Mary Elizabeth. *The Problem of Civilization Solved.* Chicago, 1895.

McGuffey's Sixth Eclectic Reader, 1879 Edition. New York, 1963.

McMaster, John B. *A School History of the United States.* New York, 1897.

Marsh, J. S. T. *The Story of the Jubilee Singers; with Their Songs.* New York, 1883.

Montgomery, David H. *The Student's American History.* Boston, 1897.

Morris, Charles. *A Primary History of the United States.* Philadelphia, 1899.

Muzzey, David. *An American History.* Boston, 1911.

Nye, Edgar Wilson. *Bill Nye's History of the United States.* Philadelphia, 1894.

Page, Thomas Nelson. *The Negro: The Southerner's Problem.* New York, 1904.

Pike, Gustavus. *The Jubilee Singers and Their Campaign for Twenty Thousand Dollars.* Boston, 1873.

Schouler, James. *History of the United States of America, Under the Constitution.* Vols. 2, 5, 6, 7. New York, 1894 and 1899.

Schurz, Carl. *The New South.* New York, 1885.

Steele, Joel D. and Esther B. *A Brief History of the United States for Schools*. New York, 1871.
Stowe, Harriet Beecher. *Men of Our Times; Or, Leading Patriots of the Day*. Hartford, Conn., 1868.
Thomas, William Hannibal. *The American Negro*. New York, 1901.
Willard, Emma. *Abridged History of the United States, or Republic of America*. New York, 1869.

Minstrel Songsters, Handbooks, and Scripts

American Minstrel Songster. Philadelphia, 1881.
Bland, James A. *De Golden Wedding Songster*. New York, 1880.
Burgess, Cool. *I'll Be Gay Songster*. New York, [1880?].
Daly Brothers' South Carolina Cloe Songster. New York, 1878.
The Dockstader's T'Shovel Songster. New York, 1880.
Dumont, Frank. *The Witmark Amateur Minstrel Guide and Burnt Cork Encyclopedia*. Chicago, 1899.
Engle, Gary D., ed. *This Grotesque Essence: Plays from the American Minstrel Stage*. Baton Rouge, 1978.
Foley, M. H., and C. H. Sheffer. *Big Pound Cake Songster*. New York, 1878.
Hager, J. M. *The Great Republic. Allegory and Tableaux*. Washington, D.C., 1876.
Harrigan and Hart's Slavery Days Songster. New York, 1877.
Jay Rial's Ideal Uncle Tom's Cabin Song Book. New York, 1883.
Joe Lang's Old Aunt Jemima Songster. New York, 1873.
Newcomb, Bobby. *A Guide to the Minstrel Stage*. New York, [188?].
Pelham, Nettie H. *The Belles of Blackville*. New York, 1897.
Power, Thomas. *The Virginia Veteran*. Boston, 1874.
Roorbach, Orville Augustus, ed. *Minstrel Gags and End Men's Hand-book*. New York, 1875.
The Songs of Paul Dresser. New York, 1927.
Townsend, Charles. *The Dark Tragedian*. Chicago, 1898.
———. *Negro Minstrels with End Men's Jokes, Gags, Speeches, Etc*. Chicago, 1891.
———. *The Pride of Virginia*. Chicago, 1901.
Vautrot, George S. *Black Vs. White, or the Nigger and Yankee*. Clyde, Ohio, 1880.
White, Charles. *Oh, Hush! Or, the Virginny Cupids!* New York, 1873.
———. *Old Dad's Cabin*. Clyde, Ohio, [189?].

Articles

Adkins, Milton. "The Mountains and Mountaineers of Craddock's Fiction." *Magazine of American History* 24 (October 1890).

Aldrich, Thomas Bailey. "My Cousin the Colonel." *Harper's Monthly* 84 (December 1891).

Allen, James Lane. "Kentucky." *Harper's Monthly* 74 (August 1889).

———. "Kentucky Fairs." *Harper's Monthly* 74 (September 1889).

———. "Mrs. Stowe's 'Uncle Tom' at Home in Kentucky." *Century* 34 (October 1887).

Atkinson, Edward. "Significant Aspects of the Atlanta Cotton Exposition." *Century Magazine* 23 (February 1882).

Baker, Marion A. "The New North." *Cosmopolitan* 2 (September 1886).

Ballou, William. "In the Tennessee Bluegrass." *Frank Leslie's Popular Monthly* 24 (April 1890).

Bonner, Sherwood. "Dialect Tales." *Harper's Weekly* 27 (August 11, 1883).

———. "The Revolution in the Life of Mr. Balingall." *Harper's Monthly* 59 (October 1879).

Boyd, William K. "Southern History in American Universities." *South Atlantic Quarterly* 1 (July 1902).

Bradford, J. S. "'Crackers' of the South." *Lippincott's Magazine* 6 (November 1870).

Brewer, William M. "Moonshining in Georgia." *Cosmopolitan* 23 (June 1897).

Brown, J. M. "Songs of the Slave." *Lippincott's Magazine* 4 (December 1868).

Brown, William P. "A Peculiar People." *Overland Monthly* 12 (November 1888).

Caldwell, Joshua W. "The South Is American." *Arena* 8 (October 1893).

Chandler, W. E. "Our Southern Masters." *Forum* 5 (July 1888).

Clark, Thomas H. "Frederick Law Olmsted on the South, 1889." *South Atlantic Quarterly* 3 (1904).

Coleman, Charles W. "The Recent Movement in Southern Literature." *Harper's Monthly* 74 (May 1887).

Cooke, John Esten. "The White Sulphur Springs." *Harper's Monthly* 57 (August 1878).

Cope, Henry F. "Two Thousand Miles of Playground." *World To-day* 15 (October 1908).

Curry, J. L. M. "The South, Her Condition and Needs." *Galaxy* 23 (April 1877).

"Darkies Day at the Fair." *World's Fair Puck* (August 21, 1893).

Davis, J. Frank. "Tom Shows." *Scribner's* 77 (April 1925).

Davis, Rebecca Harding. "Here and There in the South." *Harper's Monthly* 75 (July–August 1887).

———. "The Rose of Carolina." *Scribner's Magazine* 8 (October 1874).

DeForest, J. "The Great American Novel." *Nation* 6 (January 9, 1868).

Dickson, H. "Gentlemen of the South." *Everybody's Magazine* 23 (August 1910).

Doane, William C. "Patriotism: Its Defects, Its Dangers, and Its Duties." *North American Review* 166 (March 1898).

Dodge, Julia. "An Island of the Sea." *Scribner's* 14 (September 1877).

Dodge, Mary. "Virginia in Water Colors." *Lippincott's Magazine* 10 (July 1872).

Dunne, Finley P. "Mr. Dooley on the Midway." *Cosmopolitan* 31 (1901).

Dutcher, A. P. "A Lecture on the Temperaments." *Medical and Surgical Reporter* 15 (December 1, 1866).

Eggleston, George Cary. "A Rebel's Recollections." *Atlantic Monthly* 33 and 34 (June–November 1874).

Elliot, Sarah Barnwell. "An Incident." *Harper's Monthly* 96 (February 1898).

F. F. A., "Invalid Life in the South." *Lippincott's Magazine* 31 (March 1883).

"Fair-minded South." *Nation* 83 (July 5, 1906).

"Free Speech at the South." *Independent* 55 (January 15, 1903).

Freeman, H. E., and E. G. Cummings. "Dismal Swamp and How to Go There." *Chautauquan* 33 (August 1901).

French, A. "Farmer in the South." *Illustrated Scribner's Monthly* 15 (April 1894).

Frost, William G. "Our Contemporary Ancestors in the Southern Mountains." *Atlantic Monthly* 83 (March 1899).

———. "Our Southern Highlanders." *Independent* 72 (April 4, 1912).

Galsworthy, John. "That Old Time Place." *Scribner's* 52 (August 1912).

Godkin, E. L. "The Influence of Homocide on Southern Progress." *Nation* 35 (October 26, 1882).

———. "Lessons of the Campaign." *Nation* 15 (October 17, 1872).

———. "The Rationale of Southern Homocide." *Nation* 35 (December 7, 1882).

———. "Southern Homocide." *Nation* 46 (February 16, 1888).

———. "The White Side of the Southern Question." *Nation* 31 (August 19, 1880).

Grady, Henry. "In Plain Black and White." *Century* 29 (April 1885).

Hamilton, S. A. "The New Race Question in the South." *Arena* 27 (April 1902).

Harney, W. W. "The Southern Planter." *Lippincott's Magazine* 11 (January 1873).

Harris, Joel Chandler. "Plantation Music." *The Critic* 3 (December 15, 1883).

Harris, Mrs. L. H. "The Southern White Woman." *Independent* 52 (February 15, 1900).

Harrison, Burton. "The Capture of Jefferson Davis." *Century* 27 (November 1883).

Harrison, Mrs. Burton. "A Daughter of the South." *Cosmopolitan* 12 (December 1891).

Harrison, J. B. "Studies of the South." *Atlantic Monthly* 49–51 (January 1882–January 1883).

Higginson, Thomas W. "Negro Spirituals." *Atlantic Monthly* 19 (June 1867).

———. "Some War Scenes Revisited." *Atlantic Monthly* 42 (July 1878).

Jewett, Sarah Orne. "Decoration Day." *Harper's Monthly* 85 (June 1892).

Johnston, J. Stoddard. "Romance and Tragedy of Kentucky Feuds." *Cosmopolitan* 27 (September 1899).

Kirke, Edmund. "The Southern Gateway of the Alleghanies." *Harper's Monthly* 74 (April 1887).

Levermore, C. H. "Impressions of a Yankee Visitor in the South." *New England Magazine* 3 (November 1890).

"Life of a Georgia Cracker." *Current Literature* 27 (January 1900).

Link, S.A. "Pioneers of Literature in the South." *New England Magazine* 10 (March 1894).

"Literature in the South." *The Critic* 10 (June 25, 1887).

Lowry, A. "Winter Colonies in the South." *Munsey's Magazine* 28 (December 1902).

McCracken, E. "Southern Women and the Reconstruction." *Outlook* 75 (November 21, 1903).

Marble, Earl. "Origins of Memorial Day." *New England Magazine* 32 (June 1905).

Marchmont. "Southern Society." *Lippincott's Magazine* 6 (August 1870).

Matthews, Brander. "Rise and Fall of Negro Minstrelsy." *Scribner's* 57 (June 1915).

Mayo, A. D. "The Third Estate in the South." *New England Magazine* 3 (November 1890).

———. "The Woman's Movement in the South." *New England Magazine*, n.s. 4 (October 1891).

Mell, Annie White. "Obstacles to DAR Work in the South." *American Monthly Magazine* 11 (October 1897).

Meriwether, Lee. "Mountain Life in Tennessee." *Cosmopolitan* 4 (February 1888).

Mooney, James. "Folk-lore of the Carolina Mountains." *Journal of American Folk-lore* 2 (April–June 1889).

"The New South." *Harper's Weekly* 48 (April 23, 1904).

"North and South Fifty Years After Appomattox." *Literary Digest* 50 (May 1, 1915).

"The North in the South." *Nineteenth Century* 1 (June 1869).

"Northern Men and Women." *Independent* 55 (March 12, 1903).

Owens, William. "Folk-lore of the Southern Negroes." *Lippincott's Magazine* 20 (December 1877).

Page, Thomas Nelson. "Literature in the South Since the War." *Lippincott's Magazine* 48 (December 1891).

———. "The Old Dominion." *Harper's Monthly* 83 (December 1893).

Page, Walter Hines. "A Journey Through the Southern States." *World's Work* 14 (June 1907).

———. "The Last Hold of the Southern Bully." *Forum* 16 (November 1893).

———. "Rebuilding of Old Commonwealths." *Atlantic Monthly* 89 (May 1902).

———. "Study of an Old Southern Borough." *Atlantic Monthly* 47 (May 1881).

"Patriotic Confederate Veterans." *Independent* 52 (July 5, 1900).

Peck, William F. "Glimpses of the South." *Cosmopolitan* 2 (January 1887).

Pilsbury, Charles. "The Southern Watering Place." *Potters' American Monthly* (October 1880).

Poe, Clarence. "The Rebound of the Upland South." *World's Work* 9 (June 1907).

Pollard, Edward A. "The Real Condition of the South." *Lippincott's Magazine* 6 (December 1870).

———. "The Romance of the Negro." *Galaxy* 12 (October 1871).

———. "The Virginia Tourist." *Lippincott's Magazine* 5 (May, June, and August 1870).

"Poor White Trash." *Eclectic Magazine* 36 (July 1882).

Porter, J. Hampden. "Notes on the Folk-lore of the Mountain Whites of the Alleghenies." *Journal of American Folk-lore* 7 (April–June 1894).

Putnam, E. J. "Lady of the Slave States." *Atlantic Monthly* 106 (October 1910).

Pyle, Howard. "Chincoteague." *Scribner's* 13 (April 1877).

"The Race Problem. A Symposium." *Arena* 21 (April 1899).

"The Real Southern Man." *Independent* 56 (January 28, 1904).

"The Real Southern Question Again." *World's Work* 4 (May 1902).

"A Remedy for Southern Provincialism." *The American* 10 (June 27, 1885).

Remington, Frederic. "A Sergeant of Orphan Troop." *Harper's Monthly* 95 (August 1897).

"A Reminiscence of the White Sulphur Springs." *Harper's Weekly* 32 (October 4, 1888).

Rice, Elizabeth. "A Yankee Teacher in the South: An Experience in the Early Days of Reconstruction." *Century* 62 (May 1901).

Seabrook, E. A. "The Poor Whites of the South," *Galaxy* 4 (October 1867).

Schindler, Rabbi Solomon. "What Is Nationalism?" *New England Magazine* 7 (September 1892).

Shaler, N. S. "The Peculiarities of the South." *North American Review* 151 (October 1890).

"Soldiers' Memorial Services." *Century* 38 (May 1889).

"South at the World's Fair." *Scientific American* (supplement) 58 (August 6, 1904).

"Southern Man." *Independent* 56 (January 21, 1904).

"Southern Women." *Godey's Magazine* 131 (October 1895).

Spofford, Harriet Prescott. "A Guardian Angel." *Harper's Monthly* 94 (May 1897).

Stowe, Harriet Beecher. "Letter from a Verandah." *Christian Union* 12 (December 8, 1875).

———. "The Noble Army of Martyrs." *Atlantic Monthly* 16 (August 1865).

Tillett, W. F. "Southern Womanhood as Affected by the War." *Century* 43 (November 1891).

Tourgee, A. W. "The South as a Field for Fiction." *Forum* 6 (December 1888).

Trowbridge, John T. "A Carpet-bagger in Pennsylvania." *Atlantic Monthly* 23 (April 1869).

Van Cleef, A. "The Hot Springs of Arkansas." *Harper's Monthly* 56 (January 1878).

Vance, Lee. "King Cotton and His Subjects." *Godey's Magazine* 131 (October 1895).

Vandervort, Leon. "National Playground in the South." *Outing* 42 (September 1903).

"The Virginia Springs." *Nation* 25 (September 20, 1877).

"Virginia Summer Resorts." *Harper's Weekly* 29 (October 3, 1885).

Waldo, F. "Among the Southern Appalachians." *New England Magazine*, n.s. 24 (May 1901).

Warner, Charles Dudley. "Their Pilgrimage." *Harper's Monthly* 73 (August 1886).

Webster, Albert. "From Charleston to Savannah." *Appleton's Journal* 10 (June 28, 1873).

———. "A Jaunt in the South." *Appleton's Journal* 10 (August 30, September 6, September 13, 1873).

———. "Southern Home Politics." *Atlantic Monthly* 36 (October 1875).

Wells, B. W. "Southern Literature of the Year." *Forum* 29 (June 1900).

"What Is Patriotism?" *Grand Army Record* 9 (September 1894).

"Where Shall I Spend the Winter?" *Harper's Weekly* 49 (January 7, 1905).

Wister, Owen. "Em'ly." *Harper's Monthly* 87 (November 1893).

———. "The Evolution of the Cowpuncher." *Harper's New Monthly Magazine* 91 (September 1895).

Woolson, Constance F. "The French Broad." *Harper's Monthly* 50 (April 1875).

———. "Up the Ashley and Cooper." *Harper's Monthly* 52 (December 1875).

SECONDARY SOURCES

Aaron, Daniel. *The Unwritten War: American Writers and the Civil War.* New York, 1973.

Anderson, Benedict. *Imagined Communities: Reflections on the Origin and Spread of Nationalism.* London, 1983.

Appleby, Joyce. "Reconciliation and the Northern Novelist, 1865–1880." *Civil War History* 10 (June 1964).

Austin, William. *"Susanna," "Jeanie," and "The Old Folks at Home."* New York, 1975.

Baker, Paula. *The Moral Frameworks of Public Life: Gender, Politics, and the State in Rural New York.* New York, 1991.

Ballard, Michael B. "Yankee Editors on Jefferson Davis." *Journal of Mississippi History* 43 (November 1981).

Barbee, David R. "The Capture of Jefferson Davis." *Tyler's Quarterly Historical and Genealogical Magazine* 29 (July 1947).

Blight, David. "'For Something beyond the Battlefield': Frederick Douglass and the Struggle for the Memory of the Civil War." *Journal of American History* 75 (March 1989).

Boorstin, Daniel. *The Image; or, What Happened to the American Dream.* New York, 1962.

Boskin, Joseph. *Sambo: The Rise and Demise of an American Jester.* New York, 1986.

Braden, Waldo W. *Oratory in the New South.* Baton Rouge, 1979.

Bradley, Chester. "Was Jefferson Davis Disguised as a Woman When Captured?" *Journal of Mississippi History* 36 (August 1974).

Buck, Paul. *The Road to Reunion.* New York, 1937. Reprint. New York, 1959.

Campbell, Edward, D.C. *The Celluloid South: Hollywood and the Southern Myth.* Knoxville, Tenn., 1981.

Cecil, L. Moffitt. "William Dean Howells and the South." *Mississippi Quarterly* 20 (Winter 1966–67).

Clawson, Mary Ann. *Constructing Brotherhood: Class, Gender, and Fraternalism.* Princeton, N.J., 1989.

Colvert, James B. "Views of Southern Character in Some Northern Novels." *Mississippi Quarterly* 18 (Spring 1965).

Connelly, Thomas. *The Marble Man: Robert E. Lee and His Image in American Society.* Baton Rouge, 1977.

Cooper, John M., Jr. *Walter Hines Page: The Southerner as American.* Chapel Hill, 1977.

Couvares, Francis G. *The Remaking of Pittsburgh: Class and Culture in an Industrializing City, 1877–1919.* Albany, N.Y., 1984.

Current, Richard N. *Northernizing the South.* Athens, Ga., 1983.

Curti, Merle. *The Roots of American Loyalty.* New York, 1946.

Davies, Wallace Evans. *Patriotism on Parade: The Story of Veterans' and Hereditary Organizations in America, 1783–1900.* Cambridge, Mass., 1955.

Davis, Stephen. "'A Matter of Sensational Interest': The Century 'Battles and Leaders' Series." *Civil War History* 27 (December 1981).

Dearing, Mary. *Veterans in Politics.* Baton Rouge, 1952.

Dimick, Howard T. "The Capture of Jefferson Davis." *Journal of Mississippi History* 9 (October 1947).

Donald, David. "A Generation of Defeat." In *From the Old South to the New: Essays on the Transitional South,* edited by Walter J. Fraser, Jr., and Winfred B. Moore, Jr., pp. 3–20. Westport, Conn., 1981.

Douglas, Mary. *Natural Symbols: Explorations in Cosmology.* London, 1973.

Douglass, Ann. "The Literature of Impoverishment: The Women Local Colorists in America, 1865–1914." *Women's Studies* 1 (1972).

DuBois, Ellen. *Feminism and Suffrage.* Ithaca, 1978.

Ellingsworth, Huber. "The Confederate Invasion of Boston." *Southern Speech Journal* 35 (Fall 1969).

Felstiner, Mary Lowenthal. "Family Metaphors: The Language of an Independence Revolution." *Comparative Studies in Society and History* 25 (1983).

Fishel, Leslie H. "The 1880s: Pivotal Decade for the Black Community." *Hayes Historical Journal* 3 (1980).

Fishwick, Marshall William. *Springlore in Virginia.* Bowling Green, Ohio, 1978.

Flusche, Michael A. "The Private Plantation: Versions of the Old South Myth, 1880–1914." Ph.D. dissertation, Johns Hopkins University, 1973.

Foner, Eric. *Free Soil, Free Labor, Free Men.* New York, 1970.

———. *Politics and Ideology in the Age of the Civil War.* New York, 1980.

——. *Reconstruction: America's Unfinished Revolution, 1863–1877.* New York, 1988.

Foner, Philip. "Black Participation in the Centennial of 1876." *Phylon* (December 1978).

Forgie, George. *Patricide in the House Divided: A Psychological Interpretation of Lincoln and His Age.* New York, 1979.

Foster, Gaines. *Ghosts of the Confederacy: Defeat, the Lost Cause, and the Emergence of the New South, 1865–1913.* New York, 1987.

Foster, John T., and Sarah W. Foster. "John Sanford Swaim: A Life at the Beginning of Modern Florida." *Methodist History* 26 (July 1988).

Fox-Genovese, Elizabeth. "Scarlett O'Hara: The Southern Lady as New Woman." *American Quarterly* 33 (Fall 1981).

——. *Within the Plantation Household: Black and White Women of the Old South.* Chapel Hill, 1988.

Franklin, John Hope. *From Slavery to Freedom: A History of Negro Americans.* New York, 1988.

Fredrickson, George. *The Black Image in the White Mind: The Debate on Afro-American Character and Destiny, 1817–1914.* Middletown, Conn., 1987.

——. *The Inner Civil War: Northern Intellectuals and the Crisis of the Union.* New York, 1968.

Friedman, George S. "Reconstruction and Redemption in Selected American Novels, 1878–1915." Ph.D. dissertation, Duke University, 1972.

Gaines, Francis Pendleton. *The Southern Plantation: A Study in the Development and Accuracy of a Tradition.* New York, 1924.

Gara, Larry. "A Glorious Time: The 1874 Abolitionist Reunion in Chicago." *Journal of the Illinois State Historical Society* 65 (Autumn 1972).

Gaston, Paul M. *The New South Creed: A Study in Southern Mythmaking.* New York, 1970.

Gatewood, Willard B., Jr. *Black Americans and the White Man's Burden, 1898–1903.* Urbana, Ill., 1975.

Gerster, Patrick, and Nicholas Cords. "The Northern Origins of Southern Mythology." In *Myth and the American Experience,* 2 vols., edited by Patrick Gerster and Nicholas Cords, 2:320–34. Encino, Calif., 1978.

Gillette, William. *Retreat from Reconstruction, 1869–1879.* Baton Rouge, 1979.

Gorn, Elliot J. *The Manly Art.* Ithaca, 1986.

Gossett, Thomas. *Uncle Tom's Cabin and American Culture.* Dallas, 1985.

Hahn, Steven. *The Roots of Southern Populism.* New York, 1983.

Hall, Jacquelyn Dowd, James Leloudis, Robert Korstad, Mary Murphy, Lu Ann Jones, and Christopher Daly. *Like a Family: The Making of a Southern Cotton Mill World.* Chapel Hill, 1987.

Halttunen, Karen. *Confidence Men and Painted Women: A Study of Middle-Class Culture in America, 1830–1870.* New Haven, 1982.

Handlin, Oscar. "The Civil War as Symbol and as Actuality." *Massachusetts Review* 3 (Fall 1961).

Harlan, Louis. "The Southern Education Board and the Race Issue in Public Education." *Journal of Southern History* 23 (May 1957).

Harris, Neil. *Humbug: The Art of P. T. Barnum.* Chicago, 1973.

Harris, Trudier. *From Mammies to Militants: Domestics in Black American Literature.* Philadelphia, 1982.

Hart, James D. *The Popular Book.* New York, 1950.

Harwell, Richard B. "Gone with Miss Ravenal's Courage; or Bugles Blow So Red: A Note on the Civil War Novel." *New England Quarterly* 35 (June 1962).

Hess, Earl. *Liberty, Virtue and Progress: Northerners and Their War for the Union.* New York, 1988.

Hibben, Paxton. *Henry Ward Beecher: An American Portrait.* New York, 1927.

Higham, John. "The Reorientation of American Culture in the 1890s." In *Writing American History: Essays on Modern Scholarship*, edited by John Higham, pp. 73–102. Bloomington, Ind., 1970.

———. *Strangers in the Land: Patterns of American Nativism, 1860–1925.* New York, 1969.

Hirshson, Stanley. *Farewell to the Bloody Shirt: Northern Republicans and the Southern Negro, 1877–1893.* Chicago, 1968.

Hoeltje, Hubert H. "Emerson in Virginia." *New England Quarterly* 5 (October 1932).

Hoffert, Sylvia D. "Yankee Schoolmarms and the Domestication of the South." *Southern Studies* 24 (Summer 1985).

Holmes, Amy E. "'Such is the Price we Pay': American Widows and the Civil War Pension System." In *Toward a Social History of the Civil War*, edited by Maris Vinovskis, pp. 171–95. Cambridge, 1990.

Hubbell, Jay B. *The South in American Literature, 1607–1900.* Durham, N.C., 1954.

Jimerson, Randall C. *The Private Civil War: Popular Thought during the Sectional Conflict.* Baton Rouge, 1988.

Jones, Jacqueline. *Soldiers of Light and Love: Northern Teachers and Georgia Blacks, 1865–1873.* Chapel Hill, 1980.

Kirby, Jack Temple. *Media-Made Dixie: The South in the American Imagination.* Athens, Ga., 1986.

Klotter, James. "The Black South and White Appalachia." *Journal of American History* 66 (March 1980).

Kolodny, Annette. *The Lay of the Land.* Chapel Hill, 1975.

Kreyling, Michael. "Nationalizing the Southern Hero." *Mississippi Quarterly* 34 (Fall 1981).

Lawrence, Henry. "Southern Spas: Source of the American Resort Tradition." *Landscape* 27 (1983).

Lears, T. J. Jackson. *No Place of Grace: Antimodernism and the Transformation of American Culture, 1880–1920.* New York, 1981.

Lebsock, Suzanne D. "Radical Reconstruction and the Property Rights of Southern Women." *Journal of Southern History* 42 (May 1977).

Linderman, Gerald. *Embattled Courage: The Experience of Combat in the Civil War.* New York, 1987.

———. *The Mirror of War.* Ann Arbor, 1974.

Lively, Robert. *Fiction Fights the Civil War: An Unfinished Chapter in the Literary History of the American People.* Chapel Hill, 1957.

Lonn, Ella. "Reconciliation Between the North and the South." *Journal of Southern History* 13 (February 1947).

McConnell, Stuart Charles. "A Social History of the Grand Army of the Republic, 1867–1900." Ph.D. dissertation, Johns Hopkins University, 1987.

McDonald, Archie. "Travel Notes of Reconstruction Days." *Louisiana Studies* 8 (Fall 1969).

McIlwaine, Shields. *The Southern Poor White from Lubberland to Tobacco Road.* New York, 1970.

McLaurin, Melton A. *The Knights of Labor in the South.* Westport, Conn., 1978.

McLoughlin, William G. *The Meaning of Henry Ward Beecher.* New York, 1970.

McPherson, James. *The Abolitionist Legacy: From Reconstruction to the NAACP.* Princeton, 1975.

McWhiney, Grady. "Jefferson Davis—the Unforgiven." *Journal of Mississippi History* 42 (May 1980).

Marszalek, John. "Celebrity in Dixie: Sherman Tours the South, 1879." *Georgia Historical Quarterly* (Fall 1982).

Martin, Sidney Walter. *Florida's Flagler.* Athens, Ga., 1949.

Mason, Julian. "A Symposium: Owen Wister and the South." *Southern Humanities Review* 6 (Winter 1972).

Matison, Sumner. "The Labor Movement and the Negro during Reconstruction." *Journal of Negro History* 33 (October 1948).

Mitchell, Reid. "The Creation of Confederate Loyalties." In *New Perspectives on Race and Slavery in America: Essays in Honor of Kenneth Stampp,* edited by Robert H. Abzug and Stephen E. Maizlish, pp. 93–108. Lexington, Ky., 1986.

Mixon, Kenneth. "The New South Movement in Imaginative Literature, 1865–1910." Ph.D. dissertation, University of North Carolina, 1974.

Montgomery, David. *Beyond Equality: Labor and the Radical Republicans, 1862–1872.* New York, 1967.

Moore, Rayburn. "Southern Writers and Northern Literary Magazines, 1865–1890." Ph.D. dissertation, Duke University, 1956.

Mott, Frank L. *Golden Multitudes: The Story of Best Sellers in the United States.* New York, 1947.

Muldowny, John. "Jeff Davis: The Postwar Years." *Mississippi Quarterly* 23 (Winter 1969–70).

Nagel, Paul. "Reconstruction, Adams Style." *Journal of Southern History* 52 (February 1986).

Neely, Mark E., Harold Holzer, and Gabor S. Borritt. *The Confederate Image.* Chapel Hill, 1987.

Norton, Anne. *Alternative Americas: A Reading of Antebellum Political Culture*. Chicago, 1986.

Novak, Barbara. *Nature and Culture: American Landscape Painting, 1825–1875*. New York, 1980.

Novick, Peter. *That Noble Dream: The "Objectivity Question" and the American Historical Profession*. Cambridge, 1988.

Nye, Russel B. *The Unembarrassed Muse: The Popular Arts in America*. New York, 1970.

Ogden, Florence. "The Blue and the Gray: The Story of Decoration Day." *DAR Magazine* (May 1968).

Olcott, William. *The Greenbrier Heritage*. Greenbrier, W.Va., 1967.

Osterweis, Rollin G. *The Myth of the Lost Cause, 1865–1900*. Hamden, Conn., 1973.

Ownby, Ted. *Subduing Satan: Religion, Recreation, and Manhood in the Rural South, 1865–1920*. Chapel Hill, 1990.

Painter, Nell Irvin. *Standing at Armageddon: The United States, 1877–1919*. New York, 1987.

Paludan, Phillip. *"A People's Contest": The Union and Civil War, 1861–1865*. New York, 1988.

Panzer, Mary. *In My Studio: Rudolf Eickmeyer, Jr., and the Art of the Camera, 1885–1930*. Yonkers, N.Y., 1986.

Papashvily, Helen Waite. *All the Happy Endings: A Study of the Domestic Novel in America, the Women Who Wrote It, the Women Who Read It, in the Nineteenth Century*. New York, 1956.

Pettit, Arthur G. *Mark Twain and the South*. Lexington, Ky., 1974.

Pomeroy, Earl. *In Search of the Golden West: The Tourist in Western America*. New York, 1957.

Powell, Lawrence. *New Masters: Northern Planters during the Civil War and Reconstruction*. New Haven, 1980.

Pressley, Thomas J. *Americans Interpret Their Civil War*. Princeton, 1954.

Quill, J. Michael. *Prelude to the Radicals: The North and Reconstruction during 1865*. Washington, D.C., 1980.

Rable, George C. "Bourbonism, Reconstruction and the Persistence of Southern Distinctiveness." *Civil War History* 29 (June 1983).

Reed, John Shelton. *Southern Folk, Plain and Fancy: Native White Social Types*. Athens, Ga., 1986.

Reniers, Perceval. *The Springs of Virginia: "Life, Love, and Death at the Waters, 1775–1900."* Chapel Hill, 1941.

Rodgers, Daniel. *The Work Ethic in Industrial America, 1850–1920*. Chicago, 1974.

Rogers, William W. *Thomas County, 1865–1900*. Tallahassee, Fla., 1973.

Rogin, Michael. "'The Sword Became a Flashing Vision': D. W. Griffith's *The Birth of a Nation*." *Representations* 9 (Winter 1985).

Rose, Willie Lee. "Race and Region in American Historical Fiction." In *Region,*

Race and Reconstruction: Essays in Honor of C. Vann Woodward, edited by
J. Morgan Kousser and James M. McPherson, pp. 113–39. New York, 1982.

————. *Rehearsal for Reconstruction: The Port Royal Experiment.* New York,
1964.

Rosenzweig, Roy. *Eight Hours for What We Will.* Cambridge, 1985.

Rotundo, E. Anthony. "Body and Soul: Changing Ideals of American Middle-
Class Manhood, 1770–1920." *Journal of Social History* 16 (Fall 1983).

Rowe, Anne. *The Enchanted Country: Northern Writers in the South, 1865–
1910.* Baton Rouge, 1978.

Rubin, Louis D., Jr. "Southern Local Color and the Black Man." *Southern Review* 6 (October 1970).

Rudwick, Elliot M., and August Meier. "Black Man in the 'White City': Negroes
and the Columbian Exposition, 1893." *Phylon* 26 (Winter 1965).

Rydell, Robert W. *All the World's a Fair: Visions of Empire at American International Expositions, 1876–1916.* Chicago, 1984.

Scott, Anne Firor. *The Southern Lady: From Pedestal to Politics, 1830–1930.*
Chicago, 1970.

Scott, Joan. "Gender: A Useful Category of Historical Analysis." *American Historical Review* 91 (December 1986).

Seidel, Kathryn Lee. *The Southern Belle in the American Novel.* Tampa, Fla.,
1985.

Sellers, Charles, ed. *The Southerner as American.* Chapel Hill, 1960.

Shapiro, Henry D. *Appalachia on Our Mind: The Southern Mountains and
Mountaineers in the American Consciousness, 1870–1920.* Chapel Hill, 1978.

Small, Sandra. "The Yankee Schoolmarm in Freedmen's Schools: An Analysis of
Attitudes." *Journal of Southern History* 45 (August 1979).

Smith, John David. *An Old Creed for the New South: Proslavery Ideology and
Historiography, 1865–1918.* Westport, Conn., 1985.

Smith-Rosenberg, Carroll. *Disorderly Conduct: Visions of Gender in Victorian
America.* New York, 1985.

Somkin, Fred. *Unquiet Eagle: Memory and Desire in the Idea of American
Freedom, 1815–1860.* Ithaca, N.Y., 1967.

Sproat, John. *"The Best Men": Liberal Reformers in the Gilded Age.* Chicago,
1968.

Stark, Cruce. "Brothers at/in War: One Phase of the Post–Civil War Reconciliation." *Canadian Review of American Studies* 6 (Fall 1975).

Sterne, Richard. *Political, Social and Literary Criticism in the New York Nation, 1865–1881: A Study in Change of Mood.* New York, 1987.

Stover, John. "The Ruined Railroads of the Confederacy." *Georgia Historical
Quarterly* 42 (December 1958).

Sutherland, Daniel. *The Confederate Carpetbaggers.* Baton Rouge, 1988.

Swint, Henry Lee. *The Northern Teacher in the South, 1862–71.* New York, 1941.

Taylor, William. *Cavalier and Yankee: The Old South and American National
Character.* Garden City, N.Y., 1963.

Tindall, George B. "Mythology: A New Frontier in Southern History." In *The Idea of the South*, edited by Frank E. Vandiver, pp. 1–15. Chicago, 1964.

Tipton, Robert. "The Fisk Jubilee Singers." *Tennessee Historical Quarterly* 29 (Spring 1970).

Toll, Robert. *Blacking Up: The Minstrel Show in Nineteenth Century America.* New York, 1974.

———. *On with the Show: The First Century of Show Business in America.* New York, 1976.

Trachtenberg, Alan. *The Incorporation of America: Culture and Society in the Gilded Age.* New York, 1982.

Van Deburg, William L. *Slavery and Race in American Popular Culture.* Madison, Wis., 1984.

Van Tassel, David. "The American Historical Association and the South, 1884–1913." *Journal of Southern History* 23 (November 1957).

Weiner, Jonathan. "Coming to Terms with Capitalism: The Postwar Thought of George Fitzhugh." *Virginia Magazine of History and Biography* 87 (Fall 1979).

Whisnant, David E. *All That Is Native and Fine: The Politics of Culture in an American Region.* Chapel Hill, 1983.

White, Deborah Gray. *Ar'n't I a Woman?: Female Slaves in the Plantation South.* New York, 1985.

White, G. Edward. *The Eastern Establishment and the Western Experience.* New Haven, 1968.

Williamson, Harold Francis. *Edward Atkinson: The Biography of an American Liberal, 1827–1905.* Boston, 1934.

Williamson, Joel. *The Crucible of Race.* New York, 1984.

Wilson, Charles R. *Baptized in Blood: The Religion of the Lost Cause, 1865–1920.* Athens, Ga., 1980.

Woodward, C. Vann. *American Counterpoint: Slavery and Racism in the North-South Dialogue.* Boston, 1971.

———. "The Anti-Slavery Myth." *American Scholar* 31 (Spring 1962).

———. *The Burden of Southern History.* Baton Rouge, 1968.

———. *Origins of the New South, 1877–1913.* Baton Rouge, 1971.

Wyatt-Brown, Bertram. *Southern Honor: Ethics and Behavior in the Old South.* New York, 1982.

———. *Yankee Saints and Southern Sinners.* Baton Rouge, 1985.

Wynes, Charles. "Fanny Kemble's South Revisited: South as Seen Through the Eyes of Her Daughter." *Louisiana Studies* 12 (Fall 1973).

Zelinsky, Wilbur. *Nation into State: The Shifting Symbolic Foundations of American Nationalism.* Chapel Hill, 1988.

Zinn, Howard. *The Southern Mystique.* New York, 1959.

Index

Printed in the United States
209718BV00004B/43/A